TWAYNE'S WORLD AUTHORS SERIES
A Survey of the World's Literature

GERMANY

Ulrich Weisstein, Indiana University, Bloomington

EDITOR

Johann Georg Hamann

TWAS 527

Johann Georg Hamann

JOHANN GEORG HAMANN

By JAMES C. O'FLAHERTY

Wake Forest University

TWAYNE PUBLISHERS

A DIVISION OF G. K. HALL & CO., BOSTON

Published in 1979 by Twayne Publishers,
A Division of G. K. Hall & Co.
All Rights Reserved

Printed on permanent/durable acid-free paper and bound
in the United States of America

First Printing

Library of Congress Cataloging in Publication Data

O'Flaherty, James C
Johann Georg Hamann.

(Twayne's world authors series ; TWAS 527)
Bibliography: p. 185–92
Includes index.
1. Hamann, Johann Georg, 1730–1788.
B2993.028   193   78-20785
ISBN 0-8057-6371-6

For Lucy

Contents

About the Author

James C. O'Flaherty, born in Richmond, Virginia, received his undergraduate training at the College of William and Mary and Georgetown College, with a B.A. from the latter. He received an M.A. degree in German from the University of Kentucky and a Ph.D. degree from the University of Chicago in historical theology. In 1935 and 1936 he attended the University of Heidelberg, Germany, hearing lectures on philosophy and theology. Currently he is professor of German at Wake Forest University, where he has taught since 1947, chairing the Department of German from 1961 to 1969. For some years he has also lectured on European literature in translation. In 1958 he was the recipient of an American Philosophical Society grant for research in Germany, and in 1960–61 was a Fulbright research scholar at the University of Heidelberg. His publications include: *Unity and Language: A Study in the Philosophy of Hamann* (Chapel Hill, 1952; rpt. New York, 1966); *Hamann's Socratic Memorabilia: A Translation and Commentary* (Baltimore, 1967); *Raabe's Else von der Tanne: A Translation and Commentary* (co-author; University, Alabama); *Studies in Nietzsche and the Classical Tradition* (senior editor and contributor; Chapel Hill, 1976). In 1953–55 and 1961–63 he edited *The Hamann Newsletter*. He has written a number of journal articles which, in addition to those on Hamann, deal with German cultural history, and paedogogical subjects.

Preface

Johann Georg Hamann, known as the "Magus of the North," is one of the most influential, yet enigmatic, figures in the history of German thought. An obscure Prussian bureaucrat of the eighteenth century, living in a remote corner of Germany, he nevertheless has been known to generations of students of German literature as "the father of the Storm and Stress and the progenitor of the Romantic movement" (Unger). Through the mediation of Johann Gottfried Herder, the young Goethe was so greatly influenced by Hamann in the marvelously creative pre-Weimar years that he once confessed to the Swiss writer Johann Kaspar Lavater that Hamann was the author from whom he had learned most. Many years later Goethe was to confirm the importance of Hamann for his own development in the fascinating literary portrait of the Magus which he sketches in *Dichtung und Wahrheit*. During his Italian journey he prophesied that some day Hamann would become a "codex" for Germany as Giambattista Vico had for Italy.

The nature and extent of the Hamannian influence on the development of German Idealism and Romanticism is in dispute, but there can be no dispute about his impact on individuals such as Herder, Theodor Hippel, Friedrich Heinrich Jacobi, Jean Paul, Kierkegaard, and, in our own day, Ernst Jünger. His impact on Søren Kierkegaard was such that, upon his first encounter with Hamann's writings, he hailed him as "Emperor!"; and it is through the Danish philosopher that Hamann became a major source of Christian existentialism. On the other hand, the dialectical philosophy of Hegel owes much, despite all differences, to the stimulus which Hamann's philosophy provided. Quite apart from the question of his influence, Hamann's significance also lies, to a great extent, in his reckoning with such figures as Moses Mendelssohn, Lessing, Kant, and the "philosopher king," Frederick the Great. Moreover, a thinker who is credited with a "Copernican revolution" in the philosophy of language (Schweppenhäuser), anticipating the thought of Sapir, Whorf, and Lévi-Strauss (George Steiner), who relates sexuality to cognition in an illuminating way, and who, along with Herder, "begins in the literary arena that passionate interest in everything Oriental which came into full bloom in Romantic literature" (Unger), deserves wider attention than he has hitherto received.

Despite Hamann's importance in the history of German literature and philosophy, his writings were the last of the classics of the eighteenth century to appear in a critical-historical edition, even though no less a person than Goethe expressed the wish to edit them or at least to promote an edition. Two reasons seem to account for this neglect: first, the notorious difficulty of Hamann's prose, and, secondly, his strongly religious orientation. Small wonder that the great editors of the nineteenth century, who were generally positivistic in orientation, found it easy to avoid the task. Nevertheless, there did appear in the second decade of the century an edition of the works, including selected letters, by Friedrich Roth, which, though by no means complete, filled a great need and still has its uses. It was this edition to which Hegel devoted the longest review he ever wrote, and which had to suffice for serious students of Hamann for well over a century.

Josef Nadler's (disputed, but indispensable) edition of the works (1949–57) and the Ziesemer-Henkel edition of the letters (1955–75) have at long last made the entire corpus of the Hamannian writings available. It is true that great progress in the interpretation of Hamann was made before the general availability of the complete works, especially by scholars like Rudolf Unger, Erwin Metzke, and Fritz Blanke. But it is obvious that, with the appearance of the complete critical editions, supplemented by Nadler's biography (1949), Hamann scholarship has entered a new phase in which much more light may be shed on his thought.

Until the middle years of this century Hamann was very little known in the English-speaking world. Since that time, several monographs, an anthology, and a number of journal articles dealing with him have appeared. Only one of his major works, however, has been translated into English in its entirety (*Socratic Memorabilia*). The present volume is intended as an introduction to Hamann's life and work for those who have little or no previous acquaintance with that author, but it is hoped that others will also find it helpful.

A word should be said about my procedure in dealing with Hamann's works. Although most of the important writings have been dealt with under one heading or another, two have been accorded almost a full chapter each. In the case of the Socratic essay (Chapter 3) it was deemed best to offer a paraphrase, for here Hamann is his own best interpreter; in the case of the essay on aesthetics (Chapter 4) a systematic analysis was obviously called for. It was an idiosyncrasy of Hamann's to emphasize words and phrases in an often seemingly capricious way. I deemed it best not to retain such emphasis in translation. Unless otherwise indicated, all translations are my own.

Chronology

1730 Johann Georg Hamann born August 27, in Königsberg, East Prussia.

1746 Matriculates at University of Königsberg, first as student of theology, later of law.

1749 Collaborates with Johann Christoph Berens(1729–92), Johann Gotthelf Lindner (1729–76), and others on *Daphne*, a weekly periodical for women.

1752 Leaves university without degree in November. Becomes private tutor of the son of Baroness Budberg in Livonia, later tutor of the sons of Count von Witten in Courland. Frequent sojourns in Riga. Reads widely in philosophy and political economy.

1756 Translates Plumard de Dangeuil's treatise on political economy, publishes *Beylage zu Dangeuil*. Enters into contract with Berens's firm in Riga. Leaves for Königsberg on account of his mother's illness. Death of mother, July 16. Leaves Königsberg for protracted trip to England as agent of the Berens family October 1. Meets Johann Georg Sulzer, Karl Ramler, and Moses Mendelssohn in Berlin.

1757 Arrives in London April 18. Delivers message in person at Russian embassy, later in writing, but is rebuffed. In despair, decides to remain in London in the hope of earning money by lute-playing. Falls into dissolute company.

1758 March 13 to 31 reads Bible and writes "Tagebuch eines Christen" and "Gedanken über meinen Lebenslauf." Undergoes conversion experience by end of March. Leaves London June 27, arrives in Riga July 27.

1759 Returns to Königsberg in January. Remains in the home of his father, unemployed, reading voraciously, especially Luther. Johann Christoph Berens (1729–92) and Immanuel Kant meet with Hamann in July for purpose of neutralizing the effects of his conversion. Kant suggests translation of articles from French *Encyclopédie*, and proposes collaboration on physics textbook for children. *Sokratische Denkwürdigkeiten*.

1760 *Vermischte Anmerkungen über die Wortfügung in der fran-*

zösischen Sprache. Die Magi aus Morgenlande, zu Bethlehem. Versuch über eine akademische Frage. Intensive Greek, Hebrew studies. Begins to learn Arabic.

1761 *Beylage zum zehnten Theile der Briefe die Neuste Literatur betreffend. Lettre néologique et provinciale sur l'inoculation du bon sens. Französisches Project. Wolken. Ein Nachspiel Sokratischer Denkwürdigkeiten.* Completes reading of Koran in Arabic.

1762 Declines offer by Nicolai to collaborate on *Literaturbriefe. Essais à la Mosaique. Kreuzzüge des Philologen. Leser und Kunstrichter. Schriftsteller und Kunstrichter.*

1763 *Fünf Hirtenbriefe das Schuldrama betreffend.* In February begins "marriage of conscience" ("Gewissensehe") with Anna Regina Schumacher (1736–89). Becomes copyist in municipal administration of Königsberg, transferring three weeks later to Department of War and Crown Lands as chancery clerk and copyist. Dubbed "Magus of the North" by Friedrich Karl von Moser. Von Moser mediates offer of job tutoring the son of the Princess of Hesse.

1764 Father suffers stroke. Hamann quits his job to help in his care. Herder becomes his pupil in English and Italian. Edits *Königsbergsche Gelehrte und Politische Zeitungen.* Journeys to Darmstadt to see von Moser about employment, but misses him.

1765 Secretary to *Hofrat* Christoph Anton Tottien, accompanying him to Warsaw and Mitau.

1766 Father dies in September.

1767 Returns to Königsberg in January. Clerk and translator with General Excise and Customs Administration under French tax collectors. Salary: 25 thaler monthly.

1768 Establishes household with Anna Regina Schumacher.

1769 Johann Michael, son, born September 27.

1772 Elisabeth Regina, daughter, born April 12. *Beylage zun Denkwürdigkeiten des seligen Sokrates. Zwo Recensionen nebst einer Beylage, betreffend den Ursprung der Sprache. Des Ritters von Rosencreuz letzte Willensmeynung über den göttlichen und menschlichen Ursprung der Sprache.* "Philologische Einfälle und Zweifel über eine akademische Preisschrift" and "Au Solomon de Prusse" written, but not published.

1773 *Neue Apologie des Buchstabens h. Lettre perdue d'un sauvage du nord à un financier de Pe-kim.*

1774 Translates essays of Bolingbroke, James Hervey, Thomas Hunter. *Über die neueste Auslegung der ältesten Urkunde des menschlichen Geschlechts.* Magdalena Katharina, daughter, born December 2.

1775 *Hierophantische Briefe. Versuch einer Sibylle über die Ehe.*

1776 Plans to sell library, but is saved with Herder's aid. Gives up editorship of *Königsbergsche Gelehrte und Politische Zeitungen* permanently. *Zweifel und Einfälle über eine vermischte Nachricht der allgemeinen deutschen Bibliothek.*

1777 Becomes *Packhofverwalter*, February 13. Salary: 300 thaler yearly, plus 100 thaler perquisites ("Fooigelder"). "Schürze von Feigenblättern" sketched, but not published.

1778 Death of brother, Johann Christoph, August 25, after fifteen-year decline. Birth of Marianne Sophie, daughter, November 18.

1779 *Konxompax. Fragmente einer apokryphischen Sibylle über apokalyptische Mysterien.*

1780 Hume's *Dialogues concerning Natural Religion* translated, but not published. *Zwey Scherflein zur neusten deutschen Literatur.* Renews intensive reading of Luther.

1781 Reads Voltaire's complete works. "Kritik der reinen Vernunft" (review) written, but not published.

1782 Income reduced from 460 to 300 thaler due to loss of "Fooigelder."

1784 Franz Kaspar Buchholtz (1756–1812) donates 4,000 thaler for the education of Hamann's children. "Metakritik über den Purismum der reinen Vernunft" written, but not published. *Golgatha und Scheblimini!*

1785 Suffers light stroke, December 7.

1786 *Entkleidung und Verklärung. Ein Fliegender Brief an Niemand, den Kundbaren.*

1787 Petitions tax administration for leave, but discharged with pension of 200 thaler. Departs June 21 for Münster at invitation of Amalia Princess von Gallitzin. Visits alternately Jacobi and Buchholtz.

1788 Dies June 21 in Münster. Buried in Münster in the garden of Princess Gallitzin. His remains are transferred in 1851 to the Überwasserfriedhof (Catholic).

CHAPTER 1

Magus of the North

JOHANN Georg Hamann was born August 27, 1730, in Königsberg, East Prussia, the elder son of Johann Christoph Hamann, a barber-surgeon who also supervised the public bathing establishment of the old part of the city, and who enjoyed great popularity among its citizens.[1] Hamann's paternal grandfather had been a village pastor in Lusatia, and his maternal grandmother a pastor's daughter from the same region. The father's older brother, also named Johann Georg (1697–1733), was a writer and editor of no mean ability, who lived first in Leipzig and subsequently in Hamburg. He was the author of a sequel to the Baroque novel *The Asiatic Banise*, and compiled a *Poetic Lexicon*, which was reprinted as late as 1765; he also composed hymns and texts for musical compositions, some of the latter being set to music by Georg Philipp Telemann. Hamann's mother, Maria Magdalena, née Nuppenau, was born and reared in Lübeck, and was therefore, like the father, a newcomer to Königsberg. Although in ill health for many years, she survived until Johann Georg was in his twenty-sixth year. Johann Christoph, the second son, was born two years after Johann Georg, and these two sons completed the family circle. The Hamann household was characterized by the spirit of genuine religion (albeit in mild Pietistic form) and a sense of contentment, despite its modest means and the ill health of the mother. Johann Georg was at no time alienated from his parents, rather the opposite. Particularly deep and enduring was his affection and respect for his father, and an early publication attests to his feeling for his mother.[2] The modest home was an unusually hospitable one, and the circle of friends was large. As a result, the young Johann Georg was early apprenticed to the art of friendship, so much cultivated in the eighteenth century, and which was to play such an important part in his later life. If one were to criticize the domestic atmosphere it would have

17

to be on the grounds that the children were given too much rather than too little freedom.

Hamann's elementary and secondary education was quite desultory. At first he was tutored at home by university students, acquiring thereby bits of Greek, French, and Italian, as well as some instruction in music, dancing, and painting. Apparently this kind of instruction continued as a supplement to more formal schooling later. In any case, the youthful Hamann attended two "hedge schools," neither of which was pedagogically sound. Concerning the instruction in the second one he wrote: "I could translate a Roman author into German without understanding either the language or the author's meaning" (II, 14). Hamann always felt that the unsystematic nature of his early schooling had robbed him of any sense of order or desire for it (II, 13–14). Later he attended the Kneiphof-Gymnasium, where Pietistic influence prevailed, but in one of its less oppressive forms. Under a great disadvantage at first, he gradually improved until, in his last year, he stood at the head of his class. In addition to the prescribed studies, he dabbled in philosophy, mathematics, theology, and Hebrew. "My brain," he wrote of this period," became a fair-booth full of brand new wares. I brought this conglomeration with me to the university where it really belonged, and where I was matriculated as a student March 30, 1746" (II, 19).

Though originally matriculated at the University of Königsberg as a student of theology, Hamann subsequently transferred to the faculty of law. Reflecting on this period later, under the influence of his religious conversion, he wrote:

> While I was wandering about in the vestibules of the sciences, I lost the calling which I had thought I had for divinity. I found an obstacle in my tongue [a tendency to stammer], in my weak memory, and I found many hypocritical obstacles in my manner of thought, in the corrupt morals of the clergy . . . . What spoiled my taste for theology and all serious sciences was an inclination which had developed in me toward antiquities, criticism— then to so-called belles lettres, poetry, novels, philology, the French writers and their gift of creative writing, of painting with words, of vivid description, of pleasing the imagination and so forth . . . (II, 20–21).

Thus the transference from the theological faculty was merely a matter of appearance since he had no more interest in the "serious science" of law than in divinity:

My folly [he continues] caused me to see a kind of magnanimity and nobility in not studying for a profession but according to inclination, for amusement and out of love for the sciences themselves, believing that it was better to be a martyr than a day-laborer and a hireling of the muses (II, 21).

It is true that the University of Königsberg did not at that time provide an opportunity for the study of literature and philology, either ancient or modern. Leipzig at least had a Gottsched and a Gellert, who for all their faults were living proof of a more humanistic atmosphere than that which prevailed at Königsberg, where orthodox Lutheranism and Pietism determined the theological climate, and Wolffian rationalism the philosophical.

Two of Hamann's professors stand out as having made a lasting impression on him. The first, Martin Knutzen (1713–51), who lectured on mathematics and philosophy, was the most eminent member of the faculty at that time. Knutzen sought to combine the rationalism of Wolff with Pietistic Christianity. Harry Sievers[3] calls attention to the likely influence of ideas derived from Knutzen's book, *Philosophical Proof of the Truth of the Christian Religion*,[4] on Hamann at the time of his conversion. Knutzen's teaching that physical influences originating in the body may influence the mind—thus a deviation from the strictly Leibnizian-Wolffian position on preestablished harmony—also appealed to the young Hamann. But it was Karl Heinrich Rappolt (1702–53) for whom Hamann developed a warm affection. Rappolt was professor of physics and a member of the Berlin Academy. He wrote about such diverse things as amber, prehistoric discoveries, and waterspouts (NB, 36). Although Rappolt was an outspoken opponent of Pietism, his sense of humor, his dedication to Latin humanism, and his interest in poetry made him most attractive to the young Johann Georg. Even after his conversion he spoke of Rappolt as a "Christian philosopher" (II, 19). But despite these and other influences, Hamann profited little from his formal studies at the university. His main energies were absorbed by what we would today call extracurricular activities.

Of such activities the principal one was his collaboration on a weekly periodical for women, *Daphne*, published for slightly over a year. The publication was patterned after the English *Tatler* and *Spectator*, and was also influenced by German writers such as

Friedrich von Hagedorn and Christian Fürchtegott Gellert. Contributions to *Daphne* were published under pseudonyms, but those which clearly stem from Hamann sound the more serious ethical and religious notes of the publication. But they also "breathe the spirit of the psychological and progressive literature of France as they appeared at the time when it was preparing the European revolution" (NB, 43). During this period Hamann also took instruction in lute-playing, which was to remain a favorite pastime for a number of years. During his university days he made lasting friends, men like Johann Christoph Berens (1729–92), who was destined to play an important role in his life, Johann Gotthelf Lindner (1729–76), and Samuel Gotthelf Hennings (1725–87). These friendships are simply the earliest of those which would become so important for the cultural history of Germany. Certainly Hamann had an unusual capacity for friendship. Goethe, who never met him, illuminates this characteristic well: "He [Hamann] seems to me to have been very perceptive about the circumstances of life and of friendship and to have sensed quite correctly the relations of other people to one another and to himself."[5]

At the age of twenty-two, Hamann left the university, without a degree, to become *Hofmeister* or private tutor on various estates of the minor nobility in the Baltic area. He was peremptorily discharged from his first position after he attempted to inform the mother of his young charge of the truth about her spoiled son. His second position was far happier, and as a result he remained on excellent terms with the family. During these years he was frequently in the nearby city of Riga, in the home of his friend Berens. In the summer of 1756 Hamann gave up his tutorial post to become associated with the Berens's family firm, which was engaged in the wholesale trade in Riga.

Although Hamann had always been a conscientious tutor—perhaps overly so—with a genuine interest in pedagogical theory and practice, he spent much of his time while in the Baltic provinces pursuing his favorite studies. He read widely in both ancient and modern philosophy, particularly Descartes. But it was his friend Berens who stimulated him to the main literary production of these years: an essay on political economy. The work was a supplement to a translation from the French of Plumard de Dangeuil, *Anmerkungen über die Vortheile und Nachtheile von Frankreich und Grossbritannien in Ansehung des Handels und der übrigen Quellen*

von der Macht der Staaten, 1756 (On the Advantages and Disadvan-
tages of France and Great Britain with Regard to Commerce and
Other Sources of State Power).[6] Hamann's essay is important on two
scores: first, as a document reflecting the outlook and aspirations of
the German middle class at the time, and, secondly, as expressing
the practical ideals of the Enlightenment against which the author
was to inveigh, subsequent to his religious conversion, for the rest of
his life. In the essay he combines humanistic with mercantilistic
ideals, and sees the merchant replacing the warrior-hero as the
nobleman of the future. For trade and commerce, he argues, promote peace, liberty, civic virtue, and create a nobility based on
achievement rather than birth. Though he later repudiated the
work, the idealism which he espoused in it foreshadows his later
devotion to the life of the spirit. It is significant also that he acidu-
lously criticizes the Prussian bureaucracy as harmful to the public
welfare and dehumanizing to the individual long before his personal
involvement with it (IV, 229). Further, when one remembers to
what extent the military was glorified in Prussia (even Lessing
joined in the chorus in sketching the character of his fictional Major
von Tellheim!), it is all the more striking that the young Hamann
looked to the merchant as his ideal.

By the summer of 1756 Hamann had entered into a contract with
the Berens firm, the terms of which we do not know, but which did
involve his undertaking a rather mysterious journey to London.
Whether the purpose of the trip was primarily commercial or
whether it was quasi-diplomatic, as Josef Nadler thinks, cannot be
determined (NB, 73–74). Certainly it was partially intended as a
Bildungsreise or educational experience for the raw recruit to the
vocation of merchant. In any case, by the end of June he had left for
Königsberg, having received news of the approaching death of his
mother, which occurred in mid-July. He remained in Königsberg
until the first of October, when he boarded the mail-coach for Berlin. There he was to see old friends and make new acquaintances,
among them young leaders of the Enlightenment such as Moses
Mendelssohn, J. G. Sulzer, and K. W. Ramler. From Berlin he
proceeded to Lübeck, where he tarried, visiting relatives of his
mother. Following a prolonged interruption of the journey, this
time in Amsterdam, he arrived in London on April 18, 1757.

After a few days in that city, Hamann undertook to carry out his
mission. His statements concerning what actually happened are

quite brief and cryptic. It is obvious that he visited the Russian embassy and delivered some sort of message. "There was astonishment," he reports, "at the importance of my affair, even more at the choice of the person to whom it was entrusted" (II, 34). After recovering from their astonishment, members of the diplomatic staff began to smile, then "to give their frank opinion of those who had sent me, the reasons for which I had come, and indicated that they felt sorry for me" (II, 34–35). As the result of such a reception, Hamann was understandably "upset" and "exasperated" (II, 35). He thereupon followed the only course open to him, and wrote a memorandum ("Memorial") to the Russian ambassador.[7] In an apparently benign reply the ambassador indicated that Hamann's mission was hopeless (II, 35).

What is the meaning of this curious episode? Nadler's conjecture that we have here a matter involving both commerce and politics ("handelspolitisch") is reasonable: since the Berens family expected Frederick II to lose East Prussia in the Seven Years' War, which was then impending, they hoped to secure a sort of Hanseatic independence for the Baltic ports. Consequently Hamann could have been sent to England with a special assignment in the matter. If indeed he had such a mission, it was foredoomed to failure by the political and military events which had taken place since the plan was hatched. For in the meantime England had abandoned Russia, had concluded a treaty with Prussia, and was now supporting her newly acquired ally in the war which had broken out months before.

As a result of the failure of his undertaking, Hamann was "near despair" and sought to lose himself in dissipation (II, 35). He remained in London, however, and as his funds began to vanish he thought of earning money from his lute-playing. In this endeavor he became involved with an Englishman, who, he discovered later, was supported by a rich friend for immoral purposes. Hamann's guilt or innocence in this affair has been much discussed in recent years. It is very unlikely, however, that he himself had a homosexual experience, as has been maintained.[8] In any event it is clear that his situation was now desperate: his original mission had failed; he had spent months in London, accomplishing nothing; his health was beginning to suffer from the irregular life he had been leading; and finally he had fallen into dissolute company. Obviously the time was ripe for a change.

Early in February 1758 Hamann rented a room in a decent and

friendly household. He thereupon closeted himself with his books, and subsisted on a meager diet—which fortunately resulted in an improvement in his health. In his deep distress he turned to the Bible, immersing himself in it. It was in the following weeks of studying the Scriptures, of meditation, and of painful soul-searching that he underwent a religious experience which was to change his life permanently, and, indirectly, to have a considerable impact on the cultural life of eighteenth-century Germany. As he read the Bible, Hamann was seized with the awareness that he was not simply reading the history of Israel, but the record of his own life (II, 40). It was the story of Cain and Abel, however, which appeared to illuminate his situation in a special way:

I could no longer conceal it from my God that I was the fratricide, the fratricide of his only begotten Son. The Spirit of God continued to reveal to me more and more the mystery of divine love and the blessing of faith in our gracious and only Savior in spite of my great weakness, in spite of the long resistance which I had until then offered to his testimony and his compassion. . . . I feel now, thank God, my heart calmer than ever before in my life (II, 41).

He felt that God has asked for his heart, and responded: "Here it is, Lord. You have desired it, however blind, hard, adamant, perverse, and unrepentant it was. Cleanse it, create it anew, and let it become the workshop of your good Spirit. . . . It is a Leviathan which you alone can tame" (II, 42–43). Thus by the end of March 1758 the radical change had taken place. Hamann summed up his experience with the expression that God had poured him "from one vessel into another" (II, 42). Nadler's statement that "with this experience of Hamann's in London there was born the intellectual Germany of his century" is an exaggeration. Yet there is more than a grain of truth in it (NB, 76).

While Hamann's conversion manifests many typical Pietistic traits, there are significant differences. For instance, although he used the Pietistic metaphor "inner desert" (innere Wüste) for the condition of his soul prior to the conversion, he understood it as the primordial chaos. Such chaos corresponds to the condition of the world before the creation. His inner renewal was understood accordingly as a second creation or, in relation to his individual existence, as a rebirth.[9] His conversion had therefore the effect of restoring the original relation to God, thus essentially overcoming the effects of the Fall, which had resulted in "infinite mis-relations of man to God" (III, 312). Moreover, worldliness appeared in a new light. Unlike the Pietist who tends to withdraw from the world, and to draw a line between the sacred and profane, between the pure and the impure, Hamann turned even more openly toward the things of the world than before, seeing them in the steady light of his new view of the entire creation. It is important for an understanding of his later thought to recognize that the chaos which he had experienced both within himself and in the external world now came into focus *in a new sense of order, biblically derived.* Further, it was a conception of world-order directly at odds with that of the Newtonians. This fact becomes quite clear in the important letter of July 27, 1759, which Hamann wrote to Kant in reply to the latter's solicitation of Hamann's collaboration on a physics textbook for children (1, 377–78). Thus Hamann's conversion was not simply a matter of resolving the intellectual doubts which stood in the way of his faith by somehow squaring them with the prevailing rationalism. Rather it was a matter of recognizing the creational order which God had intended from the beginning, and which in fact informs everything at the deepest level, no matter how many rational superstructures may be reared upon it. From the vantage point of his newly gained perspective Hamann would see the relation of reason and experience or reason and faith, in a new light, and his subsequent writings are largely an attempt to lay bare the true nature of that relation. In addition to the moral implications of his conversion, then, the intellectual ones were very great.

In the weeks immediately following his conversion Hamann showed a remarkable burst of creative energy, writing more copiously than at any other time in his life. In a period of about two months he produced *Biblische Betrachtungen* (Biblical Reflections), *Betrachtungen zu Kirchenliedern* (Reflections on Hymns of the Church), *Brocken* (Fragments Left Over), *Gebet* (Prayer), and *Betrachtungen über Newtons Abhandlung von den Weissagungen* (Reflections on Newton's Treatise on Prophecy). These five works he also referred to collectively as the *Tagebuch eines Christen* (Diary of a Christian). The important *Gedanken über meinen Lebenslauf* (Thoughts concerning My Life) is also a product of this period. *Biblical Reflections*, unavailable in its entirety until Nadler's edition of 1949,[10] is actually a commentary on the entire Bible, book by book, and, while intensely personal, contains in germinal form some of his most important thoughts. He records that he was inspired to the undertaking by a reading of James Hervey's reflections on Edward Young's *Night Thoughts* (I, 8).

Hamann returned to Riga sometime late in July 1758. That he was well received by the Berens family may be explained by the fact that they understood why his main mission had failed. It was obvious that the whole political situation in Europe had changed in the more than two years since the Berens family had hatched its mysterious plan. Moreover, if the trip had also been conceived of as *Bildungsreise* or an educational journey, they could be satisfied—that is, until they learned, as they soon did, what had happened to their young charge. Johann Christoph Berens was naturally disgusted at the turn of events, and we shall subsequently note his efforts to nullify Hamann's conversion. By March of the following year Hamann had returned to Königsberg, taking up residence with his father, where he remained for the next four years without taking a job. This period was, nevertheless, one of great intellectual activity—reading, writing, and fruitful conversation and correspondence with friends and acquaintances. Like his Greek mentor, he too was leading a "Socratic" existence, dedicated to the pursuit of truth, at least for a time. After the Peace of Hubertusburg and the consequent end to the Russian occupation of Königsberg, Hamann found it expedient to seek a government post, however distasteful it might be. In July 1763 he became a copyist in the municipal administration of Königsberg, a post he held only three weeks. Thereafter he transferred to the Department of War and Crown Lands, thus becoming a civil servant of the Prussian state; at this post he worked as chancery clerk and copyist until January 1764. On the twenty-fifth of that month his father suffered a stroke, and Hamann gave up his job in order to help in caring for him. It was in these months also that there developed a close friendship between Hamann and the young Johann Gottfried Herder, who became his pupil in Italian and English.

By the summer of that year it was urgent for Hamann to seek employment again, and this time he was to seek it outside Prussia. Consequently in June he made a journey to Darmstadt to see Friedrich Karl von Moser (1723–98), the Hessian statesman and writer on political subjects. It was von Moser who had first applied the epithet "Magus of the North" to Hamann as one who had "seen the star," i.e., the Star of Bethlehem.[11] Von Moser had in the previous year offered him a post as private tutor in a princely family, and Hamann was now ready to explore the possibility of such a position. Unfortunately von Moser was not in Darmstadt at the time, and therefore the trip was, from the practical standpoint, a failure. Nevertheless, Hamann, always ready to travel, enlarged his itinerary, which included Lübeck, Frankfurt, Strassburg, Basel, Berlin, and other cities; on the journey he not only visited relatives but renewed old acquaintances and made new ones. In the summer of 1765 he became secretary to a lawyer, one Christoph Anton Tottien, in Mitau, spending the fall of that year and part of the following winter with his employer in Warsaw. A fortunate result of his residence in Mitau was the proximity to Herder, who by then was employed at the cathedral school in Riga. Hamann's restless wanderings during this period strike one as quite strange until it is realized that they represented a flight from sexual temptation at home, on the one hand, and from a threatening political situation on the other. I shall discuss below the first point, regarding his "marriage of conscience" ("Gewissensehe"). As for the second point, the recovery of East Prussia by Frederick II at the end of the Seven Years' War cannot have been good news for Hamann (cf. Chapter 9).

In January 1767, Hamann returned to Königsberg, which was to remain his home until his death. With the assistance of Kant he obtained the job of clerk and translator with the General Excise and Customs Administration. This particular bureau was literally an importation from France. Frederick II, whose coffers had been severely depleted by the Sevens Years' War and who had to cope with an international financial crisis, imported from France about two hundred specialists in tax-collecting. These "specialists" supervised about eighteen hundred native German tax officials, among whom Hamann occupied a minor post. As a result of such high-handed measures as detaining and searching citizens on the streets and invading the privacy of their homes, searching for taxable wares, these Frenchmen soon made the system anathema even to those who were most loyal to the king. After ten years of drudgery as clerk and translator, Hamann secured the position of Superintendent of the Customs Warehouse (Packhofverwalter), with a somewhat larger income and less arduous duties. He remained in this position until 1787, when he petitioned the king for a leave, and, as a result of the petition, was summarily retired on a small pension.

Certainly the strangest aspect of Hamann's life was his so-called marriage of conscience. Sometime in 1763 he entered into a liaison with an uneducated peasant girl, Anna Regina Schumacher (1736–89), who had been employed in the Hamann household to help Johann Georg take care of his invalided father. A son and three daughters were born to this union, which, despite its unconventionality, turned out to be a stable and happy one. This is all the more surprising when one bears in mind the great intellectual and social gulf between the partners as well as the straitened financial circumstances which always prevailed in the household. It is difficult to fathom why Hamann did not legitimize his relationship with Anna Regina. Perhaps it was his earlier love for Katharina Berens, the sister of Johann Christoph, whom he had wooed in Riga and would have married but for the opposition of the Berens family. Katharina had been divinely destined for him, he believed,[12] and it is entirely possible that he always felt inwardly wedded to her. Be that as it may, the union with Anna Regina was a felicitous one for him, and he knew how to appreciate his "hamadryad," his way of alluding to her rustic origin and elemental attractiveness (II, 354). Criticisms of the liaison there were, but they grew less and less vigorous with the passage of time. The irony here is that this "marriage of conscience," which violated the usual bourgeois norms, was essentially bourgeois in character, for Hamann was evidently quite faithful to Anna Regina, and always concerned with the rearing of his children. When one considers further that the home was a friendly haven to Johann Christoph, Hamann's brother, during his long mental decline until his death in 1778, one is further persuaded of its inner soundness.

Hamann was destined to spend the last year of his life far from Königsberg, and in the most unusual circumstances. Ever since the publication of the *Socratic Memorabilia (Sokratische Denkwürdigkeiten)* in 1759 he had been admired, and at first almost canonized, by Pietists and other religiously inclined individuals (though he had at times shocked and dismayed them by the coarseness and grotesquery of some of his writings). Among his staunch admirers, however, was the Princess Amalia von Gallitzin (1748–1806), who had withdrawn from the circles of nobility to devote herself to the rearing of her children and to self-perfection through philosophy and religion. Separated from her husband, she had settled in Westphalia, and had become a leading figure of the so-called "Münster Circle," a group originally gathered around Franz Friedrich von Fürstenberg, the first statesman of the episcopal principal-

ity of Münster, whose school reform was much admired throughout
the Germanies. Having read the *Socratic Memorabilia* and other
writings of Hamann's, the Princess Gallitzin was deeply impressed,
and resolved to lure him somehow into the Münster Circle. As a
result she invited him to visit her, a trip which was in fact made
possible through the generosity of another admirer of Hamann's,
Franz Kaspar Buchholtz (1756–1812), a young Westphalian aristo-
crat, who had, several years earlier, donated a considerable amount
of money for the education of Hamann's children.

In spite of rapidly declining health Hamann made the long, arduous trip by stagecoach from one end of Germany to the other from
June 21 to July 16, 1787. His twenty-year-old son, Johann Michael,
and his physician and longtime friend, Gottlob Immanuel Lindner,
accompanied him. Father and son were alternately guests of Buchholtz, of Friedrich Heinrich Jacobi in Düsseldorf, and of the Princess Gallitzin. In Münster Hamann associated with Fürstenberg,
Franz Hemsterhuis, the Dutch philosopher who preceded Hamann
as the mentor of the princess, with Johann Michael Sailer, and with
other figures of the Münster Circle. The Münster sojourn is not only
important for an understanding of Hamann's life and thought, but
also for the impact it made on the princess, whose influence in
certain religious and philosophical circles was felt in Germany for
several decades. Until her encounter with Hamann she had clung to
the notion that the only proper goal for a Christian was religious and
ethical self-perfection. After referring to the series of spiritual coun-
selors to whom she had listened, she writes:

Finally there came Hamann and showed me the heaven of true humility
and submission—a child-like attitude toward God . . . . All my other
friends, including Fürstenberg, had previously regarded my strong urge
toward perfection as the most amiable thing, indeed as something fine
about me, which was to be admired. . . . But Hamann saw in it pride and
told me so. . . . It seemed to me that an only crutch was being snatched
from me as from a cripple, but I loved and honored him too profoundly not
to receive his declaration into my soul (NB, 453–54).

During his year in Münster Hamann was frequently ill and
confined to bed. The shock to his friends was, therefore, not too
great, when at the age of fifty-eight he died on June 21, 1788, in the
presence of Johann Michael Hamann, the Princess Gallitzin, Franz
Friedrich von Fürstenberg, and his two physicians. He was buried
shortly thereafter in the garden of the townhouse of the Princess

Gallitzin.[13] The Latin inscription on his tombstone, from Corinthians 1:23, 25, refers to the paradox of revelation: "Unto the Jews a stumblingblock, and unto the Greeks foolishness . . . because the foolishness of God is wiser than men, and the weakness of God is stronger than men."

Apart from the *Diary of a Christian* and *Thoughts concerning My Life*, both composed in 1758, Hamann's literary activity may be, somewhat arbitrarily, divided into three periods. Writings of the first period (1759–63) generally treat aesthetic and literary subjects; those of the second period (1772–76), language and religious mysteries; and those of the third period (1778–79), chiefly philosophy and theology. It is important to note that after the London conversion experience almost all of Hamann's writings are "occasional," that is, they arose in response to external stimuli, usually the publications of his philosophical or theological adversaries. Hamann is a very polemical writer. Yet his most influential ideas are positive rather than negative, as we shall see in the pages that follow. The most important publications of the first period are: *Sokratische Denkwürdigkeiten für die lange Weile des Publicums zusammengetragen von einem Liebhaber der langen Weile*, 1759 (Socratic Memorabilia. Compiled for the Boredom of the Public by a Lover of Boredom), the work which he considered the beginning of his "authorship"; *Wolken. Ein Nachspiel Sokratischer Denkwürdigkeiten*, 1761 (Clouds: A Sequel to the Socratic Memorabilia), designed as an answer to critics of the preceding work; *Kreuzzüge des Philologen*, 1762 (Crusades of the Philologist), a compilation of more than a dozen works, some negligible, others among the most important he ever wrote, and with which we shall deal subsequently, e.g., *Aesthetica in nuce* (Aesthetics in a Nutshell); *Kleeblatt Hellenistischer Briefe* (Clover-Leaf of Hellenistic Letters); *Die Magi aus Morgenlande, zu Bethlehem* (The Wise-Men from the East at Bethlehem); *Versuch über eine akademische Frage* (Essay on an Academic Question); *Chimärische Einfälle* (Chimerical Ideas); and *Vermischte Anmerkungen über die Wortfügung in der französischen Sprache* (Miscellaneous Notes on Word Order in the French Language). With the exception of the first two works, all the inclusions in the *Crusades of the Philologist* were reprints. In this earliest period he also published the important French-language essays against Frederick II, which were reprinted in the *Crusades* under the collective title *Essais à la Mosaique* (A Mosaic of Essays; see Chapter 9 for discussion). Further works of the first period were: *Leser und*

Kunstrichter, 1762 (Readers and Critics) and *Fünf Hirtenbriefe das Schuldrama betreffend*, 1763 (Five Pastoral Letters on the School-Drama). The last-named work, though occasioned by the author's defense of a questionable drama written by his friend Johann Gotthelf Lindner, goes far beyond that and presents some of Hamann's most important ideas on aesthetics.[14] It was this first period of his literary activity that became so influential for the Storm and Stress. Some of the writings are also remarkable for their bold criticism of the Prussian state and its monarch.

Noteworthy in the second period are: *Des Ritters von Rosencreuz letzte Willensmeynung über den göttlichen und menschlichen Ursprung der Sprache*, 1772 (The Last Will and Testament of the Knight of the Rose-Cross concerning the Divine and Human Origin of Language), dealing with Herder's prize-winning treatise on language, and following two reviews of the same. In the *Beylage zun Denkwürdigkeiten des seligen Sokrates*, 1773 (Supplement to the Memorabilia of the Canonized Socrates), he attacks a recent work by Johann August Eberhard in which Socrates is presented in a thoroughly rationalistic light. Against Kant's criticism of Herder's *Oldest Document of the Human Race* Hamann polemicizes in the work *Über die neueste Auslegung der ältesten Urkunde des menschlichen Geschlechts*, 1774 (On the Newest Interpretation of the Oldest Document of the Human Race). As we shall see, he develops his most telling attacks against the historical method of the Deists as well as their misunderstanding of the mystery religions in *Hierophantische Briefe*, 1775 (Hierophantic Letters). To this period belong also two works most important for understanding Hamann's view of sexuality: *Versuch einer Sibylle über die Ehe*, 1775 (Essay of a Sibyl on Marriage), and *Schürze von Feigenblättern* (Aprons of Fig-Leaves) written in 1777, but not published during his lifetime. Nadler refers to the latter work as the "key" to Hamann's thought in this area (NB, 243). The second period of the "authorship" concludes with *Zweifel und Einfälle über eine vermischte Nachricht der allgemeinen deutschen Bibliothek*, 1776 (Doubts and Ideas about a Miscellaneous Report of the "Allgemeine Deutsche Bibliothek"). Not published during Hamann's lifetime but of great significance are the twin essays *Philologische Einfälle und Zweifel über eine akademische Preisschrift* (Philological Ideas and Doubts about an Academic Prize-Essay) and *Au Salomon de Prusse* (To the Solomon of Prussia), both composed in 1772.

The third and last period opens with *Konxompax. Fragmente einer apokryphischen Sibylle über apokalyptische Mysterien*, 1779 (Fragments of an Apocryphal Sibyl on Apocalyptic Mysteries). In this work Hamann sees the ancient mystery religions as forerunners of genuine Christianity, not mere anticipations of a rationalistic system such as Deism; but he also sees them as sharing with the Enlightenment the idea that man can ascend to God through his own efforts. The work is concerned primarily with the ideas of Johann August Starck and to a lesser extent with those of Lessing. It is in this last period that Hamann subjects Kant's critical philosophy to penetrating critical scrutiny in a review of the *Critique of Pure Reason* and in his essay *Metakritik über den Purismum der Vernunft*, 1781 (Metacritique of the Purism of Reason). Nevertheless neither work was published during Hamann's lifetime, largely out of his feeling of friendship and sense of gratitude for his sometime benefactor. These writings, however, have in recent years become the focus of considerable attention since they criticize Kant's philosophy in terms of its neglect of the fundamental role which language plays in all cognition. In *Zwey Scherflein zur neusten Deutschen Literatur*, 1780 (Two Small Contributions to the Most Recent German Literature), Hamann deplores Klopstock's defection to the rank of the orthographic reformers, and once again stresses natural language[15] as the matrix of reason and religion. *Golgatha und Scheblimini! Von einem Prediger in der Wüsten*, 1784 (Golgotha and Scheblimini! By a Voice Crying in the Wilderness) was occasioned by a hostile review of the previous work. The title refers to the crucifixion of Christ ("Golgatha") and His elevation ("Scheblimini") to God's right hand. "Scheblimini" is a transcription of the Hebrew: "Sit thou at my right hand" (Psalm 110:1). Hamann adapted its use from Luther (HE, VII, 19–23). (See Chapter 10 for a discussion of the work.) The unfinished *Entkleidung und Verklärung. Ein Fliegender Brief an Niemand, den Kundbaren*, 1786 (Divestiture and Transfiguration: A Flying Letter to Nobody, the Notorious), exists in two versions, and is important in that it is Hamann's attempt to survey his entire "authorship" and to offer a justification of it. The so-called *Das letzte Blatt* (Final Page), written a month before his death in Münster, is a remarkably concentrated expression of his profoundest beliefs.

Scarcely less important than Hamann's formal writings are his numerous letters. They are of inestimable value in understanding the published works, for Hamann was given to discussing them considerably with his correspondents. His correspondence with Herder and Jacobi is a veritable gold mine for the student of the cultural history of Germany, as are certain individual letters such as the one to Kant of July 27, 1759, in which the gulf between the thought of the two men is strikingly illustrated. In addition to his formal writings and his copious correspondence, Hamann was active as a journalist and translator. We have already noted his collaboration on the moralistic weekly *Daphne* in his student days. But from 1764 to 1776 he edited the *Konigsbergsche Gelehrte und Politische Zeitungen*. Among his translations were: Ferdinando Warner, *A Full and Plain Account of the Gout* (1770), translated for a friend; a volume of essays by Henry St. John Bolingbroke, James Hervey, and Thomas Hunter on the subject of history. By far the most important translation, however, was that of David Hume's *Dialogues concerning Natural Religion* (1780), a rendering praised by Kant but which Hamann never published,[16] inasmuch as a rival version had already appeared. For many years Hume had been both ally and adversary for Hamann in his continuing campaign against Deism and the Enlightenment. We shall have occasion to note his great influence on the conception underlying Hamann's Socratic essay.

Thanks to a catalogue published in 1776 we know the titles of the books in Hamann's private collection. His close friend Johann Gotthelf Lindner had died in that year, leaving the request that Hamann should sell his considerable library at auction on behalf of his estate. Since Hamann was now the father of three children, and desperately trying to eke out an existence on a meager salary, he decided to sell his own library along with Lindner's, and as a result published a catalogue of both collections, indicating the ownership of each volume. Fortunately Hamann was saved from this painful sacrifice by the timely generosity of Herder, and as a result Hamann's library remained intact. The happy result of this minor crisis was, however, that a complete record of the books in Hamann's library has been preserved.[17] According to the catalogue the collection contained 1,356 books in the fields of classical literature, theology, philology, history, philosophy, politics, poetry, prose fiction, and miscellanea. A local Königsberg historian described the collection, shortly after Hamann's death, as "a very respectable library, rich in works on philology and criticism" (NB, 269).

At a time when the art of friendship was particularly cultivated in the literary circles of Germany, Hamann manifested a singular capacity for making and holding friends. It will be well at this point to note those relationships which were particularly important from the literary and philosophical standpoint, for in such a way we gain a special understanding of his position and influence. We have already spoken of his friendship with Herder and Jacobi. Within the environs of Königsberg it was his relationship with Theodor Gottlieb Hippel, author of the well-known *Lebensläufe nach aufsteigender Linie* and the now-timely *Über die bürgerliche Verbesserung der Weiber* as well as mayor of Königsberg, which was one of the most pleasant and satisfactory of Hamann's life. Nadler says of this association: "Hamann's significance for Hippel was, from the intellectual standpoint, infinitely great" (NB, 314). An especially warm friendship obtained between Hamann and Christian Jakob Kraus, who became professor of practical philosophy and of economics at the university of Königsberg, and who was, next to Kant, the most brilliant docent there., Although much younger than Hamann, Kraus was probably closer to him in his later life than anyone except Herder.

As Hamann's reputation grew, the stream of visitors to his home from the far corners of Germany increased. Among them were men like Johann Heinrich Merck of Darmstadt, the critic and mentor of the young Goethe, who came in 1773; Friedrich Karl von Moser (1773), Christoph Kaufmann, protégé of Lavater and ardent apostle of the Storm and Stress (1777); Moses Mendelssohn (1777); Viktor Plessing, the young man who had become the occasion of Goethe's Harz journey and his poem on the subject (1780); Johann Friedrich Reichardt, musician and director of the Royal Symphony Orchestra in Berlin (1782); Johann Christian Schmohl, Reichardt's cousin and author of a forbidden book on America and democracy (1782); Friedrich Leopold Count von Stolberg (1785); and numerous others. It was doubtless often embarrassing for Hamann and Anna Regina to receive distinguished, and sometimes noble, guests in their modest and crowded home; but it was always done with the ease and grace of genuine hospitality. Perhaps nothing underscores the remarkable cultural influence of this subaltern Prussian bureaucrat than the homage implied in these visits.

CHAPTER 2

The Whole Man

IN *Dichtung und Wahrheit* Goethe characterizes the thought of Johann Georg Hamann as follows: "All that a man undertakes to perform, whether by deed, by word, or otherwise, must proceed from all his powers united; everything isolated is worthless!"[1] This well-known summation of Hamann's philosophy may be taken as a felicitous one, provided its limitations are recognized. For it would be a serious error to conclude from such a formulation that Hamann's idea of the whole man can be understood apart from his theological presuppositions. It is true that the idea of "das Ganze" or wholeness lies at the center of his thought, but such wholeness may be achieved only in response to the Logos, the divine revelation. By no means is man capable of harmonizing the often disparate and contradictory elements of his nature out of his own resources. God's speech to man is never directed merely to intellect (as the contemporary Deists would have it) or to feeling alone (as the contemporary Pietists would have it) but to both at the same time. Having achieved wholeness through his response to the divine initiative, man is able to act, as far as that is humanly possible, "with all his powers united." Viewed from this angle, Goethe has inverted Hamann's principle, for the latter's theocentrism requires that God, not man, be understood as the source of harmony. This does not mean that Hamann was a determinist, and that, as a consequence he held that man has no real power to act. But it does mean that his response to the divine initiative in all areas of life is decisive. It is the image of God in man, not entirely obliterated by the Fall, which enables him to choose the response which he will make to the divine Logos.

Once it is clearly understood that the Hamannian idea of wholeness results from man's creatureliness, not from any humanistic idea—which presupposes man's autonomy—one may proceed to

34

treat the concept as central to his thought. Only then will one understand his particular conception of "das Ganze," to which he attests frequently in such statements as: "My mind seems to comprehend nothing so well as the whole" (3, 103); "rather nothing than half";[2] "to do nothing or everything; the mediocre is my antipathy" (1, 202); "the character of each part depends after all on the whole."[3] Although such positive statements concerning wholeness occur fairly frequently in the Magus's writings, it is the negative statements which render his conception of the integrated human being most vivid. For in them he attacks the disintegrating, atomizing effect of reason on the human mind most drastically. "The philosophers," he writes in *Philological Ideas and Doubts* (1772), "have always given truth a bill of divorcement by separating that which nature has joined and vice versa" (III, 40). Using even more stringent language, he describes such a separation as a "violent, unjustified, willful separation of that which nature has joined together."[4] In these strictures he inveighs not only against the divisive effects of excessive ratiocination on the individual human being but also on the concerns of society. He goes so far as to liken this propensity of reason to "nitric acid of the greatest potency" (IV, 414).

Hamann's penetration of the most hidden and frightening recesses of his own nature, which he vividly termed the "descent into Hell of self-knowledge" (II, 164), led him to a keen awareness of the painful opposites within his own nature, and, further, his observations of life in general convinced him that what was true of himself was also true of others. Nevertheless, it is equally certain that God did not intend that man should be torn apart by the contradictions of his nature, but that he should be an integrated human being. Although the creational unity of man was disrupted by the Fall, he was not abandoned to the hopeless internal strife of his native powers. The only hope of reconciling the warring aspects of human nature, however, is through faith in the One in whom all opposites coincide.

If the rationalists were right, and, if there were no need for faith in order to gain genuine knowledge of God, man, and nature, then "the love of wonder, which is deeply ingrained in our nature and the sinew of all poetic and historical powers" (III, 385), as well as the Scriptural revelation itself, must be discarded. After his conversion experience in London such a conclusion was for Hamann unthinkable, and therefore he conceived it to be his principal task to attack the forces of his age which were hostile to religious faith at the very center of their power, namely, in their theory of knowledge. Comparing himself to Socrates, he set out, as he wrote to Immanuel Kant in his famous letter of July 27, 1759, "to disturb others in their faith," which paradoxically meant to disturb them in their faith in reason (1, 377).

To be a whole man, i.e., to be concerned with life in its concrete fullness, means for Hamann *to know* in a certain way. For he was far more concerned with the question of right knowledge than that of right action. This position is not to be confused with the rationalistic principle that right knowledge will lead to right action, for the Magus's conception of knowledge always requires belief or faith, and this in itself constitutes, whether consciously or not, an act of obedience to the divine Will. The basis of religion, he writes in reply to his rationalistic critics, lies in "our whole existence and outside the sphere of our cognitive powers, which taken together comprise the most fortuitous and abstract mode of our existence" (III, 191). Here he is referring to the Enlighteners' conception of cognition, which rigidly excludes that which cannot be subjected to rational analysis. But a conception of "our cognitive powers" which opens the door to faith and the so-called irrational aspects of human nature, that is, to "our whole existence," is necessary for the apprehension of truth. Hamann's first important work, the *Socratic Memorabilia*, is essentially an extended explication of this point of view, for the Socrates there portrayed overcame his ignorance not by means of abstract reasoning but through "sensibility" (Empfindung) and "faith." Most of Hamann's followers (with the notable exception of Kierkegaard) undoubtedly misunderstood him on this vital point. Yet Hamann must be judged in terms of his own thought rather than in terms of its misinterpretation by others, however stimulating and fruitful such distortions may have turned out to be in the course of German cultural history. It is interesting to observe that Hamann shares with the protagonist of Goethe's *Ur-faust* the emphasis on knowledge, but unlike that seeker after truth he does not abandon revelation in its pursuit.

If right knowledge alone can make man whole, what are its essential conditions? First, it is helpful to consider them under the heading of their subjective and objective aspects. (Despite the fact that Hamann does not make such a distinction, it *is* implicit in his thought.) The subjective conditions of knowledge are twofold: faith or belief, on the one hand, and *Geschlecht* or sexuality on the other. The objective condition is, however, unitary, involving language or the Logos (5, 177). Let us first consider the subjective aspects of cognition.

Although Hamann's understanding of faith is derived from biblical revelation, he was very much concerned to buttress his theory with the arguments of those philosophers who admit belief or faith as an integral part of the cognitive process. Chief among these was the Scottish philosopher David Hume. Long before Kant was awakened from his "dogmatic slumber," as he put it, Hamann had appropriated in his own way the Humean skepticism. Thus he wrote to F. H. Jacobi many years after the publication of the *Socratic Memorabilia:* "I was steeped in Hume when I wrote the Socr. Mem., and the following passage of my little book has reference to that: 'Our own existence and the existence of all things outside of us must be believed, and can be determined in no other way," (G, 506). To be sure, he deplored Hume's limitation of belief to the sphere of habitual actions and everyday occurrences: "The Attic philosopher Hume finds faith necessary, if he desires to eat an egg and drink a glass of water. . . . If he finds faith necessary for eating and drinking, why does he deny his own principle when judging higher things than sensual eating and drinking?" (1, 379).

Nevertheless, Hamann continued throughout his life to appeal to Hume as his philosophical ally: "Hume is always my man," he wrote to Herder in 1781, "because he has at least ennobled the principle of faith and included it in his system. Our compatriot [Kant] is always rehashing his blustering about causality while ignoring that principle. That doesn't seem honest to me" (4, 294). For Hamann faith is indivisible, that is, he makes no distinction between sacred and profane or between religious and secular faith. Accordingly, the same kind of faith is required to establish one's own existence or the existence of an object of ordinary experience such as an "egg" or a "glass of water" as that which is required to establish the existence of "higher things than physical eating and drinking." Faith in God is more sublime than faith in the existence of one's self or any physical object, simply because God is more sublime than any human being or any physical object. Therefore, Hamann can say unequivocally that faith belongs to the "natural conditions of our cognitive powers and to the basic instincts of our soul" (III, 190). It should be borne in mind, however, that Hamann's understanding of faith arose in response to the Logos, and not from philosophical speculation. "God's Word and God's work," he wrote in the same period when he was intensely occupied with the philosophy of Hume, "is that alone upon which I rest, that which I believe" (1, 307).

While for Hamann faith lies at the basis of all knowledge, this does not mean that reason plays no part in his philosophy. Quite the contrary. So firm was his belief in the essential role of reason that he could say: "Faith has need of reason just as much as reason needs faith. Philosophy is composed of idealism and realism just as our nature is composed of body and soul" (G, 504). But it is important to bear in mind that he conceived of the legitimate use of reason as restricted to its intuitive function. Subsequently we shall investigate the precise nature of the Hamannian conception of intuitive knowledge or "anschauende Erkäntniß" (Chapter 5). In the present context, however, it is illuminating to observe that intuitive knowledge involves that mode of reasoning which is compatible with faith, in direct contrast to that mode which is incompatible with faith, namely, abstract or discursive reasoning. The abstract reason of the Enlighteners, which we may term "denkende Vernunft,"[5] inevitably results in a "violent divestiture of real objects so that they become naked concepts and merely conceivable signs, pure appearances and phenomena" (III, 385). "Academic reason," he wrote to Jacobi in 1787, "is divided into idealism and realism. Correct and genuine reason knows nothing of this imagined difference, which is not grounded in the nature of the matter itself, and which contradicts the unity which forms the basis of all our concepts or at least should form it" (G, 504).

One of the most distinctive—and certainly one of the most difficult—aspects of Hamann's philosophy has to do with the subject of *Geschlecht* or sexuality. Recent Hamann research has faced the fact that sexuality does play a central role in the Magus's thought, and that the attempt to sweep under the carpet, as it were, the ubiquitous references to human sexuality which appear in his writings is obviously doomed to failure. Earlier scholars had either ignored such references as best they could or, as in the case of Rudolf Unger,[6] simply ascribed them to a natural tendency in Hamann toward the crude, the scurrilous, and the obscene, or at best to the fact that, having grown up in the home of a barber-surgeon and *Bader*, his sensibilities on this score were not the conventional ones. The more recent investigations of scholars such as Josef Nadler,[7]

H. A. Salmony,[8] and Martin Seils[9] have demonstrated beyond any doubt, however, that *Geschlecht* does indeed occupy a central place in Hamann's philosophy, but the whole subject has by no means been clarified. Yet there are certain principles which are clear enough, and which throw a considerable amount of light on the subject.

Hamann's basic principle here is the notion that abstraction is the castration of thought. For instance, in the *Aesthetica in nuce* he indicts the rationalists thus:

You desire to rule over nature, and bind yourselves hand and foot by means of Stoicism in order to be able to sing in a falsetto voice, like a castrato, more movingly of the diamond-hard chains of fate (II, 208; cf. ibid., 97, 293).

If abstraction is the castration of knowledge, it follows that all veridical knowledge must contain an erotic component. That this is indeed the case in Hamann's epistemology is by no means an inference. For he states quite directly and positively that sexuality is an essential condition of genuine knowledge: "Do not undertake to delve into the metaphysics of the fine arts," he admonishes those who aspire to creativity, "without being initiated into the orgies and Eleusinian mysteries. The senses are, however, Ceres, and Bacchus the passions;—old foster-parents of beautiful nature" (II, 201). Further, "my coarse imagination has never been able to conceive of a creative spirit without genitalia" (2, 415), and "the *pudenda* of our nature are so intimately related to the chambers of our heart and brain that a rendering strictly abstract of such a natural bond is impossible" (5, 167).

The subjective conditions of knowledge thus far considered, faith and sexuality, however closely intertwined they may be in Hamann's thought, do pose difficult theoretical problems when taken together as essential conditions of cognition. Hamann never claimed, of course, to be a systematic thinker. "System is by its very nature a hindrance to truth," he wrote to his friend Jacobi (G, 228). Therefore, it would be folly to attempt to impose it in this case. But it is important to recognize that for Hamann *Glaube* and *Geschlecht* are coordinate powers of the human psyche, and that taken together they represent the inescapable subjective conditions of veridical knowledge. In fact he goes so far as to identify faith and love on occasion: "Love itself often embraces the concept of faith and is nothing but an active faith, the breath, or the life and the garment of faith" (I, 245). Thus, a jurisdictional dispute between these two capacities need not, in Hamann's conception, arise at all.

One further observation regarding the Hamannian view of sexuality should be made, namely that *Geschlecht*, like faith, is indivisible. Accordingly, the quality of love is determined by the object toward which it is directed. This facet of Hamann's thought is well illustrated by a passage in the *Socratic Memorabilia* where the love which the legendary Pygmalion manifests for the sculpture of a woman which he has created is compared with the feeling of Peter the Great for a statue of Richelieu which the young Czar saw on his visit to Paris.[10] Pygmalion's love for the image of a beautiful woman is more human and more marvelous in its consequences than the feeling of the youthful sovereign for the image of the French statesman, but both men were so irresistibly drawn to the objects of their admiration as to embrace them in love. It is quite clear that in each case it is the *object* of affection which determines the quality of the subjective feelings. This is the reason why one should not speak of sublimation (in its Freudian sense) in connection with Hamann's thought, for in the latter's view there is no process taking place in the human psyche which determines the nature and direction of eros. In other words, there is in Hamann's view no dualism of earthly and spiritual love. As Walter Leibrecht has well said, "It is characteristic that Hamann never tries to distinguish between *eros* and *agape*. Just as he believes that all creation derives solely from the love of God, so all man's behavior, if it is to be genuine and creative, must spring from love and passion."[11]

Sexual metaphors and allusions occur, of course, in abundance in the writings of many other authors. Hamann's case appears unique, however, not only because of the superabundance of them in his writings, but because his allusions stem from an epistemological principle. Hamann was fond of referring to himself as "Spermologe" (III, 45; cf. 137), a word whose double meaning he exploits: the first is that applied to the Apostle Paul in Acts 17:18, translated by Luther as "Lotterbube" (rascal), and in the Authorized Version of the English Bible as "babbler"; the second meaning, however, clearly denotes one who speaks of *Geschlecht*. The following expressions are typical of the metaphors and similes which abound in his writings: language is referred to as the "womb of language, which is the DEIPARA [mother of God] of our reason" (3, 239); in order to be sincerely patriotic one must love "the mother-tongue and mother church," which are equated with "the shameful parts" (parties honteuses) of his country (III, 231). In a drastic (and scarcely fair-minded) analogy he compares the Kantian critical philosophy to the lewd old hag Baubo's attempt to divert by means of an obscene gesture the forlorn goddess Demeter, who was grieving for her lost daughter. Not only does he compare the Kantian philosophy with "the form-play of an old Baubo with herself," but also, by way of varying the analogy, with "a new immaculate virgin, who however may be no mother of God" (3, 287).

Hamann was perfectly aware that his frequent references to sexuality would cause others to say of him, as was said of Jesus in another context and with another meaning: "He has an unclean spirit" (Mark 3:30). But he saw his position as simply human—midway between the extremes of virginal purity and lubricity, on the one hand, and of Pietistic posturing and decadence on the other. The fact is that Hamann's notion of the relation of sexuality to knowledge is principally biblical in origin. One need only recall that the verb "to know" is frequently used in Scripture to denote the sexual act. This strain of his thought was further reinforced by the emphasis on sexuality in the non-Christian traditions of the West, as his frequent allusions to the relevant myths, rites, and symbols of the classical heritage attest. Undoubtedly his own personal experiences and observations also play an important part in this connection. But it was, above all, the authority of Scripture which emboldened him to speak as he did of a forbidden subject.

It should be recognized that Hamann's notion of *Geschlecht* is unlike that of a Freud or a Havelock Ellis in that he does not view sexuality within a naturalistic context but within that of transcendence. As a result of the Fall, sexuality is evidence of the brokenness of human nature. This involves a paradox, for in order to attain to wholeness man must not deny the "pudenda" of his nature. For to do so would mean further estrangement from God. One may say that for Hamann such estrangement constitutes a second falling away from the divine order of things. For then one seeks to replace faith with reason, and denies that side of his nature which he supposes to be base or "impure," and begins to talk of a reason and a morality which is "pure."

It is quite erroneous to consider Hamann as espousing a subjective philosophy, as some critics and historians of philosophy are accustomed to do. What saves him from such putative subjectivism is his insistence upon language as the *sine qua non* of all thought.[12] An individual word is an objective event in time (as in the case of the spoken word) or in space (as in the case of the written word). Further, a historically developed vernacular is an objective cultural fact of the utmost importance, containing, as it does, much of the history of the people who speak it. "In the language of each people," he wrote to G. I. Lindner in 1759, "we find their history" (1, 393). While it is correct to say that Hamann stands in the empirical tradition of Francis Bacon, John Locke, and Hume, the important qualification must be added that for him experience is always crystalized in language. There exists, of course, an inner correlate of the objective facts of language, "the invisible essence of our soul" which is conjoined with the outer correlate by an "incomprehensible bond" (1, 393), which he describes, invoking religious terminology, as a "sacrament" (III, 289). But whatever the nature of the inner correlate, it is the evidence of the objective facts of language to which Hamann appeals, and from which he draws inferences as to the nature of mind and of reality. "I concern myself with the letter and with what is visible and material," he wrote to Herder in 1768, "like the hand of a clock—but what is behind the face of the clock is the skill of the master . . ." (2, 416).

The roots of Hamann's belief in the primacy of language are, however, not philosophical but theological. In his view, God is above all a speaking God, indeed an Author: "God reveals Himself; the Creator of the World is a Writer . . ." (I, 9; cf. 5). It is always God's Word which evokes our rational powers in the first place. Hamann employs a sexual metaphor in this connection, stating that our reason must be "impregnated" (geschwängert) by the "seed of the divine Word" (Saamen des göttlichen Worts, I, 52). Therefore, those who would render reason autonomous must fail in their endeavor.

In summary we may say that Hamann offers no conception of "the whole man," if by that phrase is meant the conscious shaping of one's life in terms of an aesthetic, psychological, ethical, or religious ideal. Such unity as man possesses is mysterious in its origins, and derives from a source which lies outside of himself. Only through the individual's positive response to the Logos can man's collective powers of faith, passion, and reason be brought into harmony. Otherwise they fall all too easily into strife with one another. For

Hamann, God is the One in whom all opposites coincide, and it is this principle of the *coincidentia oppositorum* which, embodied in the Logos and manifested above all in the "form of a servant," in which Christ appeared (Knechtsgestalt Christi), succeeds in reconciling the opposites within the human psyche. Only when such a reconciliation has taken place may one speak as a whole human being, in acceptance of, and in no way ashamed of, his full humanity: "Homo sum," Hamann wrote to a friend late in his life, "the basis of all other relationships" (5, 169).

It is important to recognize that for Hamann man never achieves complete wholeness or absolute integrity in this life. He repudiated unequivocally all forms of perfectionism, whether religious or secular: "Here on this earth," he wrote to Jacobi in 1785, "there is no possibility of a metamorphosis or transfiguration into the divine nature, but only the old message of rebirth" (G, 51). Thus, Hamann's theonomous conception of wholeness is quite different from the mature Goethe's conception of the individual's autonomous power to shape his life in accordance with his own ideals, resulting in what Walter Pater has aptly termed "a kind of passionate coldness."[13] Hamann's idea that the passions are "weapons of manhood" could, if the theological presuppositions were ignored, readily become a signal for the unbridled expression of emotion. This is, to be sure, what happened in the case of those adherents of the *Sturm und Drang* who looked to Hamann as their mentor. All too eagerly embracing his ideas on the role of the passions, they misunderstood or ignored the equally important role which religious faith and "anschauende Erkäntniβ" play in his thought.

CHAPTER 3

Socratic Existence

HAMANN launched his career as a writer in 1759 with the essay entitled *Socratic Memorabilia*. It is the most personal of his formal writings simply because in it he identifies to a great extent with the protagonist. In adopting the Socratic mask—he calls the work "mimic" on this account—he was also taking metaschematic advantage of a cult which had grown up in many and diverse circles in his day around the father of Western philosophy. Not only did such theological antipodes as Count Zinzendorf on the religious Right and Johann Christian Edelmann on the religious Left venerate Socrates, but a philosopher-king like Frederick II of Prussia and a philosopher-wit like Voltaire could mutually acknowledge seeing Socrates embodied in the other. Or again, figures as diverse as Johann Christoph Gottsched and Goethe, or Mendelssohn and Jacobi, saw in Socrates an embodiment of their own world-views.[1]

Upon Hamann's return from London, Christoph Berens undertook to show his protégé the error of his new ways and, in effect, to reconvert him to the tenets of the Enlightenment after his conversion to evangelical Christianity. It was Berens's strategy to enlist the young university professor Immanuel Kant as an ally in his singular enterprise. Hence, the meeting of the three in a rural tavern near Königsberg and the subsequent visit of Berens and Kant at Hamann's home (1, 381). As a practical suggestion, Kant proposed to Hamann that he should translate articles from the French *Encyclopédie*. Three factors in this encounter are worthy of note: first, the genuine, if somewhat misguided friendship for Hamann exhibited by Berens; second, the respect evidenced by Kant's cooperation in the endeavor and, third, the challenge posed by the invitation to Hamann to spend his time translating, thus disseminating, the ideas of that fountainhead of rationalism and opposition to Christianity, the *Encyclopédie*.

In order to comprehend the full impact of these developments on the young Hamann, however, one must see the composition of the Socratic essay against the objective background of his recent philosophical and religious studies. We have previously noted the strong influence of Hume's skeptical philosophy on the conceptual framework of the treatise (see pp. 37–38). Hamann had also recently been studying, though to a lesser extent, another British philosopher, Francis Bacon. If Hume and Bacon were his philosophical mentors at the time, his concomitant studies in the Greek New Testament provided the countervailing force to the skeptical aspect of their philosophies; indeed they appealed to him especially as an effective propaedeutic to religious faith (1, 356, 393).

There is, however, another and quite rewarding angle from which to approach the matter. In a letter of July 16 (20), 1759, to his friend, J. G. Lindner, Hamann reveals most clearly why his reply to Berens and Kant would inevitably take the literary form which it did. For Hamann, like the Spanish dramatist Calderón, compares the ordinary waking state of man to a dream. Unlike Calderón, however, he does not simply select and emphasize those aspects of the dream state which are seen, upon reflection, to be even more descriptive of waking reality. Rather, taking issue with Klopstock, who had maintained that to be awake means to be "conscious of oneself," Hamann avers that such a state is in fact "the true sleep of the soul." Only when one is "conscious of God, thinks and feels Him" and "recognizes the omnipresence of God in and around himself," is he truly awake: "A man, therefore, who lives in God is to a natural man as a person awake is to one snoring in a deep sleep—to a dreamer—to a sleepwalker" (1, 369).

In this passage, Hamann eloquently turns the tables on his rationalistic adversaries, for in their eyes *he* was the visionary, the dreamer (Schwärmer). By describing the man of reason as "snoring in a deep sleep," as "a dreamer," and "a sleepwalker," he is reversing the usual order of things. The dreamer is so engrossed in his dream—which takes on a kind of life of its own—that it is absolutely impossible for him, so long as he is in the trancelike state, to come to terms with the circumambient reality, because he fails to recognize its ultimate source, which is God. The sleepwalker may seem ever so confident in his actions, but he will inevitably collide with reality if he persists in his somnambulism. Even God himself could not persuade a dreamer that he was asleep as long as he remained in that state: He too would have first to speak the "word of power": "Awake, O thou who sleepest" (1, 369–70).

Therefore the attempt to argue with Kant and Berens or with the rationalists in general on their own terms would, in Hamann's eyes, have been tantamount to engaging in a conversation with a sleepwalker, in which case only a " confusion of ideas" would result, for the waking person and the sleepwalker would be talking past each other (1, 369–70). Therefore an indirect approach was required. The "dreamer" must not be addressed in such a way as to strengthen his conviction that his state of mind corresponded to reality. He must first be stabbed awake. The means of accomplishing this were consequently not rational argument but irony and analogy interspersed with humor. "I have written," he states at the beginning of the Socratic essay," about Socrates in a Socratic manner. Analogy constituted the soul of his reasoning, and he gave it irony for a body" (II, 61). Further, Socrates "preferred a mocking and humorous exhibition to a serious investigation," and even when he engaged in "logical deductions" he did so "according to sensation and analogy" (II, 76).

The *Socratic Memorabilia* exhibits three levels of meaning. First, it is a representation, both in form and content, of the historical Socrates as Hamann understood him; second, it is a typological interpretation of the Greek philosopher as a forerunner of Christ; and, third, it functions as a mask for Hamann vis-à-vis the "modern Athenians," the eighteenth-century Enlighteners. It is in this last relationship that the key to an understanding of the first two levels is found, and it is this level with which we are in fact chiefly concerned in the present study. The Magus was not really interested in presenting an historically objective account of the life and work of Socrates (II, 65). In fact, at the time of writing his account he had not yet read Plato or Xenophon, but relied on secondary sources,[2] emphasizing those aspects of the life and work of Socrates which seemed to him most important for his own day. In considering Socrates as a prototype of the Christ, Hamann was by no means eccentric but was following the lead of such church fathers as Justin Martyr, Lactantius, and Minutius Felix. It is significant, however, that Christ is never mentioned by name but is alluded to only four times, and then indirectly by means of periphrastic expressions.[3] Yet, paradoxically, it is the nature of revelation in general, and of the biblical revelation in particular, which is most often being indirectly explicated on the second level.

I   *Title Page*

The title page of the *Socratic Memorabilia* bears the curious subtitle: "Compiled for the Boredom of the Public by a Lover of Boredom," followed by a "Double Dedication to Nobody and to Two" and a motto in Latin from Persius. The place of publication, "Amsterdam," is spurious in order to evade the censor, but the date, "1759," is correct. We have already recognized the great importance which Hamann ascribed to his titles and the care which he lavished on the "microcosmic seed" or "Orphic egg" which it represented for him. The following paraphrase of the title page seems to convey Hamann's meaning:

In the following pages, the author intends to discuss those aspects of the life and work of Socrates which he desires to impress upon the public and on two persons in particular (Berens and Kant). The work was composed to banish the boredom of the public by one who knows full well how to deal with that state, since he is himself a lover or connoisseur of leisure. At the same time, however, he must reveal his contempt for the anonymous and obtuse public by applying the term "Nobody" to it, for he knows that the work will find little echo among the general public. By quoting a bit of raillery from Persius the author indicates to his cultured readers that he by no means takes himself as seriously as he does his subject matter.

II   *Dedication*

The Dedication is divided into two parts. In the first, "To the Public, or Nobody, the Well-known," the author compares the public to an idol worshiped by his two friends. The first paragraph is largely a series of striking paradoxes concerning the nature of the public in the form of a biblical cento. In the remaining paragraphs, Hamann explains that, unlike Daniel, who destroyed an idol at Babylon by causing it to burst, he cannot destroy the idol representing the public, but at least he can hope that his Socratic treatise will act as a laxative "pill" to purge his two friends of their idolatry. The description of the anonymity and tyranny of the public is masterful, and is echoed in our own time by Heidegger in his remarks on "das Man."[4]

The second part of the Dedication, "To the Two," contains a statement, which we have already noted, to the effect that the essay is cast in "Socratic" form, and that the use of analogy and irony are central to his method. Unlike Plato and Xenophon, who lived at a time when they could openly show their reverence for Socrates, Hamann lives in such an excessively rationalistic age that he cannot overtly manifest any enthusiasm for his subject. He would prefer "to approach more closely the heathen in their ingenuousness," but finds it necessary to "veil" his work (II, 61). Varying the metaphor, he adds: "Where the ordinary reader might see only mold, the feeling of friendship, gentlemen, may perhaps disclose to you a microscopically tiny forest in these pages" (II, 61). Here Hamann exploits the double meaning of the word, which refers not only to the micro-forest in the form of mold, hidden to the naked eye, but also to the classical literary genre of the same name (*silvae*, cf. II, 100). Further, he compares his method of composition to that of Heraclitus, whose sentences often seem unconnected, but were joined beneath the surface "like a group of small islands for whose community the bridges and ferries of system were lacking" (II, 61). As Ernst Jünger has aptly put it: "Hamann thinks in archipelagoes with submarine connections."[5]

III *Introduction*

In the Introduction, Hamann gives his reasons for rejecting the school of historiography which seeks merely scholarly objectivity. For such a procedure involves the isolation or abstraction of parts from a living entity, a whole, in order either to create an artificial synthesis or to suppress those parts which do not fit a preconceived theory. He makes his meaning quite clear here by referring to the procedure of the Greek painter Zeuxis, who selected the best features from the most beautiful maidens of his city in order to create a portrait of the ideal beauty, Helen of Troy. Paradoxically, the "image of beauty" which Zeuxis attempted to create turned out to be "strange and incomplete" (II, 62). The scholars—in this instance historians of philosophy—follow a procedure analogous to that of Zeuxis, and therefore produce "fantastic growths and chimeras" (II, 62). Such are the multi-volume works by the British writer Stanley and the Swiss writer Brucker, which Hamann refers to as "colossi."[6] In spite of their size these works remain "strange and incomplete." As Hamann sees it, a French scholar by the name of Deslandes[7] has, in thrall to Charles Batteux's notion of "beautiful nature," shown a lighter touch in dealing with the same subject, but he has simply produced a "Chinese mantelpiece figurine" (II, 62). In their analytic tendencies all such writers go too far: "To dissect a body and an event into its primary elements means attempting to detect God's invisible being, His eternal power and Godhead" (II, 64). Ironically, even the composers of fables like Aesop or LaFontaine could do better. By this, Hamann means that such creators of fables start with animals and endow them with human attributes, whereas those who deal in abstractions reverse the process: they start with human beings, and thereupon strip them of their human attributes (II, 63).

Not only the historiographers, however, are to blame for the prevalence of such compilations, but also their admiring readers who could make better use of them: "A little enthusiasm and superstition here would not only deserve indulgence, but something of this leaven is necessary in order to put the soul in the ferment required for philosophical heroism" (II, 63). Earlier in the Introduction Hamann had related the anecdote of Peter the Great's offering to the statue of Cardinal Richelieu half of his kingdom if he would teach him to rule the other half" (II, 62). To drive his point home further Hamann refers to the legend of Pygmalion and his sculpture as evidence of the power of a warm response to even a lifeless artifact: as Pygmalion falls in love with the image he has created, the miracle happens and the image is transformed into a human being (II, 62).

For Hamann an important distinction between historiography and mythology is the power of the myth to penetrate to the core of historical truth and hence to manifest great power to move men. Not only ancient history, however, should be studied as a "poetic lexicon," as recommended by Bolingbroke, "but perhaps all history is more mythology than this philosopher thinks, and is, like nature, a book that is sealed, a hidden witness, a riddle which cannot be solved unless we plow with another heifer than our reason" (II, 65). Thus, when we respond to history with our whole being, not merely with our rational faculties, we will recognize the "subterranean truth that godly men did exist among the heathen, and that we should not despise the cloud of these witnesses" (II, 64). Hamann concludes the Introduction with the statement that he does not intend to be Socrates's historiographer, but is simply recording his memorabilia, i.e., those things concerning him which are most worth remembering. That the treatise is also to have the aspect of a sort of *roman à clef* is indicated by the reference to a minor French writer, who had written such a work.[8] We recall that in the Dedication Hamann had employed the metaphor of the "idol" for the public; here he has recourse to it again, this time equating it with the rationalistic approach to the study of history. His purpose, therefore, is to turn men away from the worship of the "idol in the temple of learning, which bears beneath its image the inscription, 'The History of Philosophy' " (II, 62).

IV   First Section

The bulk of the treatise is divided into three sections. In the First Section the author finds it significant that Socrates's father was a sculptor and his mother a midwife. For both parental professions are taken as symbolic of the method which the son was to adopt as a philosopher. His maieutic method, influenced by his mother's vocation, is described as follows: "Socrates was, therefore, modest enough to compare his theoretical wisdom with the skill of an old woman who merely comes to the aid of the mother's labor and her timely birth, and renders assistance to both" (II, 66). As for his father's example, we read: "Socrates imitated his father, a sculptor, who, by removing and cutting away what should not be in the wood, precisely in so doing, furthers the form of the image" (II, 66). But we should also note that Socrates became a sculptor in the literal sense, and we may infer that he was rather successful from the fact "that his three statues of the Graces were preserved at Athens" (II, 67). Having mentioned Socrates's activity as a sculptor, Hamann takes the opportunity to venture an explanation for the former's homosexuality: "Socrates's eye was, as a result of the art in which he had been trained, so accustomed to and practiced in beauty and its relationships that his taste for handsome youths should not surprise us" (II, 67). Further, "it is fatuous to attempt to absolve him of a vice which our Christianity ought to overlook," since it resulted from "the pagan age in which he lived" (II, 67).

Hamann defends Socrates's homosexuality on broader grounds by emphasizing the sensuous basis of all genuine human relationships: "One cannot feel a lively friendship without sensuousness, and a metaphysical love sins perhaps more grievously against the nervous fluid than does an animalistic love against flesh and blood" (II, 68). By "metaphysical love" is meant love devoid of real emotion, and by "nervous fluid" simply the nervous system. Then, in an unexpected but typically Hamannian tack, he interprets the flaws in Socrates's character as well as his lack of physical beauty, his childlessness, and poverty as a prefiguring of the incarnation. For when Christ appeared, the Jews were mortally "offended that the fairest of the sons of men was promised to them as a redeemer, and that a man of sorrows, full of wounds and stripes, should be the hero of their expectations" (II, 68). Even the poets of Greece, Hamann continues, those transmitters of the myths, were aware of the role of the paradox as the vehicle of religious truth "until their Sophists (i.e., rationalists), like ours, condemned such things" as subversive of "the first principles of human knowledge" (II, 68). The contemporary rationalists do, inconsistently, make an exception in their opposition to the paradox, when it comes to accepting the paradoxical pronouncement of the Delphic oracle to the effect that Socrates was the wisest of men because he confessed that he knew nothing (II, 68). Nonetheless, this exception does not convince them of the error of their fundamental hostility to all phenomena which cannot be explained away by human reason. A belief in miracles, oracles, comets, and dreams belongs, they maintain, to the childhood of the race. Yet, Hamann argues, to ascribe all that has arisen from such belief merely to "illusion" is, paradoxically, to believe in greater miracles than the miracles themselves (II, 69).

V *Second Section*

The nature and importance of Socratic ignorance is the dominant theme of the Second Section. At the outset Hamann makes the ironical observation that, although Socrates enjoyed a thorough education at the expense of his patron, Crito, he nevertheless not only remained ignorant but indulged in an "impertinent confession of ignorance" (II, 70). Here Crito's disappointment with Socrates is a veiled reference to Berens's disappointment and disgust with the results of his patronage of Hamann.

In a felicitous analogy, Hamann compares Socrates's preoccupation with his ignorance to the obsession of the hypochondriac. The hypochondriac is, of course, never as ill as he imagines, just as Socrates was never as devoid of knowledge as his confession of ignorance would imply. The confession was rather a device to lure his fellow Athenians to discover "a truth in the inward being" (II, 77). But not everyone has an affinity for Socratic ignorance: "Just as one must know this malady for himself in order to understand a hypochondriac and to make sense of him, so perhaps a sympathy

with ignorance is required in order to have an idea of the Socratic ignorance" (II, 70).

Everyone in Greece knew and admired the admonition "Know thyself," inscribed over the door of the temple of Apollo at Delphi, but only Socrates was proclaimed the wisest of men, even surpassing Sophocles and Euripides, "because he had advanced further in self-knowledge than they, and knew that he knew nothing" (II, 71). This painful first step nevertheless leads to true knowledge. On the religious level Hamann will assert a few years later: "Nothing but the descent into Hell of self-knowledge leads us to deification" (II, 164). Apollo's "leading his worshipers gradually to an understanding of his mysteries" (through his insistence on self-knowledge and the paradox) is interpreted by Hamann as confirming the observation of Paul and Barnabas[9] that, even among the heathen, "God had not left Himself without a witness" (II, 71). It is clear that Hamann saw Apollo's condescension to the needs of men as foreshadowing God's condescension to man in the revelation in Christ.

Hamann now inserts an excursus on the different meanings which may arise from the same sentence appearing in different contexts (anticipating, incidentally, the current emphasis in linguistic circles on the "word field" theory): "Like numbers, words derive their value from the position which they occupy, and their concepts are, like coins, mutable in their definitions and relations, according to time and place" (II, 71). Thus, when the serpent says to Eve, "You will be like God," and when God says, "Behold! Adam has become like one of us," the statements have quite different meanings (II, 72). In this excursus Hamann departs from the predominantly typological method of the essay and creates an extended analogy or parable designed to render the "energy" of Socrates's confession more "perceptible" (II, 71). Having initially castigated the scientific historians, he now, somewhat inconsistently, recommends a scientific approach to hermeneutical problems. We shall discuss the counterpart of this aspect of his philological procedure under the subject of his style (Chapter 6).

Hamann then proceeds to compare Socrates to an honorable man who is highly skilled at cards and at sleight-of-hand. When he is invited to play at cards with a company of clever swindlers, he answers, "I don't play." This statement is, of course, untrue in its literal sense, but is seen to be true when understood on another level, namely, that he does not play with swindlers. If invited under other circumstances, however, to a sleight-of-hand contest, he would perhaps accept the challenge. Analogously, when Socrates said to his Sophistical adversaries, "I know nothing," his words were a reproach to their pretensions, "a thorn in their eyes and a scourge on their backs," seeming "as frightful to them as the hair of Medusa's head" (II, 73). Hamann's enlightened adversaries profess a great admiration for Socratic ignorance, but their profession, he feels, is not really sincere:

If they know nothing, why does the world need a learned demonstration of it? Their hypocrisy is ridiculous and insolent (II, 73).

In contrast to such hypocrisy, the confession of Socrates was perfectly sincere. In a key passage of the essay Hamann expresses the matter thus: "The ignorance of Socrates was sensibility [Empfindung]. But between sensibility and a theoretical proposition is a greater difference than between a living animal and its anatomical skeleton" (II, 73).

Nevertheless, sensibility is not simply a matter of feeling but involves our basic cognitive powers as well. For immediately after equating the Socratic ignorance with sensibility Hamann introduces another excursus to the effect that all our knowledge, whether subjective or objective, rests on belief or faith: "Our own existence and the existence of all things outside of us must be believed and cannot be determined in any other way" (II, 73). Certainty does not arise from either empirical or logical proof, but from sensibility. As far as empirical proof is concerned, he writes: "What is more certain than the end of man, and of what truth is there a better attested knowledge? Nevertheless, no one is wise enough to believe it. . . ." As for logical proofs, he continues: ". . . a proposition can be ever so incontrovertibly proven without on that account being believed," and "there are proofs of truths which are of as little value as the truths themselves; indeed, one can believe the proof of a proposition without giving approval to the proposition itself" (II, 73). Faith and reason have their separate provinces, and when properly understood cannot encroach upon one another: "Faith is not the work of reason, and therefore cannot succumb to its attack" (II, 74). In his stress upon the basic epistemological role of faith or belief Hamann appeals to Hume, who is to remain his principal philosophical ally against both the Wolffians and Kant (II, 73). By no means does

Hamann denigrate reason when it is restricted to its proper sphere (see Chapter 5).

However, Hamann sees not only the rationalist as the victim of misplaced trust, but also the poet, who exalts the power of imagination over faith. If either the rationalistic philosopher or the poet undergoes a shattering experience, he is utterly downcast, for "in such a case the one disavows his reason and discloses that he does not believe in the best of worlds,[10] however well he can prove it, and the other sees himself robbed of his muse and his guardian angel. . . .[11] Even if the power of imagination were a steed of the sun-chariot and had the wings of the morning, it could not on that account become a creator of faith" (II, 74). We may note parenthetically here that, in renouncing excessive faith in the power of imagination no less than in reason, Hamann dissociates himself from the typically Romantic view of human nature, which was destined to come to full flower in Germany several decades later.

The Socratic indictment of those who make pretensions of knowledge while failing to recognize their own essential ignorance is, in Hamann's view, parallel to the Apostle Paul's statement: "If anyone imagines that he knows something, he does not yet know as he ought" (II, 74). As if to underscore this parallel, Hamann cites both the original Greek of the New Testament and Luther's German version (I Cor. 8:2–3). He then relates the Socratic ignorance as closely as possible to the Pauline conception:

But how the grain of all our natural wisdom must decay, must perish in ignorance, and how the life and being of a higher knowledge must spring forth newly created from this death, from this nothing—as far as this the nose of a Sophist does not reach (II, 74).

It is instructive to observe, however, that, though there is a parallel between the underlying meaning of Paul's statement and that of Socrates, they are expressed differently, for the Socratic assertion is essentially metaphorical (i.e., it is not literally true that he knows nothing, as Hamann makes clear with his parable of the card players), whereas that of Paul is a more literal statement. It is the nonliteral, metaphorical nature of the Socratic confession which led to the preceding excursus on language (II, 71–73), and which provides a kind of preview of Hamann's later preoccupation with the philosophy of language.

Immediately after relating the Socratic and Pauline views of ignorance, Hamann introduces the subject of Socrates's daimon or
tutelary spirit. As if to accommodate himself to the secular spirit of
the age, he underscores at first the aesthetic significance of that
daimon. Against the background of the contemporary debate concerning the validity of literary rules, especially the allegedly Aristotelian norms, he writes:

What for a Homer replaces ignorance of the rules of art which an Aristotle
devised after him, and what for a Shakespeare replaces the ignorance or
transgression of those critical laws? Genius [Genie] is the unanimous answer. Indeed, Socrates could very well afford to be ignorant; he had a
tutelary spirit [Genius], on whose science he could rely, which he loved and
feared as his god, whose peace was more important to him than all the
reason of the Egyptians and Greeks, whose voice he believed, and by
means of whose wind (as the experienced quack doctor Hill has proven to
us) the empty understanding of a Socrates can become as fruitful as the
womb of a pure virgin (II, 75).

After emphasizing the aesthetic aspect of the daimonic influence,
Hamann quickly shifts to its religious significance, for the tutelary
spirit is seen as a foreshadowing of the Holy Spirit. This fact is not
stated directly, but indirectly, and indeed by means of a facetious
simile: A Dr. John Hill had written a farcical treatise in which he
maintained that a virgin can conceive a child by the action of wind
rather than by the normal method. Likewise, "the empty understanding of a Socrates can become fruitful" as a result of the inspiration of his daimon. Despite the curious context in which it appears,
the phrase "pure virgin" is obviously intended to suggest the Virgin
Mary.[12] Kierkegaard once referred to Hamann as "the greatest
humorist in Christianity,"[13] and perhaps he was right, for here, as
indeed elsewhere, the Magus accomplishes the tour de force of
literally introducing the sublime by means of the ridiculous (reference to the theory of "the quack doctor Hill").

Following his discussion of the daimonic or nonrational side of
Socrates's nature, Hamann lists a number of the customary explanations of the phenomenon, as if to disarm in advance those critics who
would offer their own reductive explanations (II, 75). In order to
understand the main thrust of the Socratic essay one must recognize
that Hamann's emphasis is not primarily on human genius but on
divine action in the world accomplished through inspired individu-

als. It was a misinterpretation regarding this point which caused him
to become a fountainhead of the *Genie* cult in the eighteenth century.

Despite Hamann's deliberately unsystematic method of exposition we often encounter at crucial points, couched amid arabesques
and farfetched tropes, a remarkably succinct summary of his key
concepts. Such is the case in the present work when he returns to
the central subject of the Second Section:

From this Socratic ignorance readily flow the peculiarities of his manner of
teaching and thinking. What is more natural than that he always felt himself
compelled to ask and to become wiser; that he pretended to be credulous,
accepted everyone's opinion as true, preferred a mocking and humorous
exhibition to a serious investigation; that he made all of his logical deductions according to sensation and analogy . . . (II, 76).

There follows a castigation of the "present-day Socratics," because
they really do not emulate their model but "deviate infinitely from
the charter of his ignorance" (II, 76). Hamann laments that he does
not have the ability to bring to life as much as he would the historical
period in which Socrates lived, for "such a picture of the century
and the republic . . . would show us how ingeniously his ignorance
was calculated for the condition of his people . . ." (II, 76). The
Athenians were incurable seekers after knowledge, but only Socrates could cure them of their obsession with superficial or spurious
knowledge, for "he lured his fellow citizens out of the labyrinth of
their learned Sophists to a truth in the inward being, to a wisdom in
the secret heart . . . to the worship of an unknown God" (II, 77).
This divine mission of Socrates was sensed by Plato, who told the
Athenians frankly that Socrates was given to them by the gods to
convict them of their follies and to be an example of virtue. Hamann
then makes a plea to Christians to recognize the prophetic role of
Socrates (II, 77).

VI   *Third Section*

The Third Section of the *Socratic Memorabilia* is largely biographical, recalling well-known events in the life of Socrates.
Hamann's emphases are, however, significant: Socrates's bravery
and magnanimity as a soldier are stressed: he took part in three
campaigns, saving the life of Alcibiades in the first, turning over to

the latter the prize which he himself had won for bravery in battle. In the second campaign, when the Athenians were hard pressed, Socrates fought furiously in retreat and carried his friend Xenophon on his shoulders away from the battlefield. Having been dissuaded by his daimon from engaging in politics, he sat as a member of the town council only late in life. There "he is supposed to have made himself ridiculous on account of his clumsiness in collecting the votes and in other customs, and to have brought himself under suspicion of being a seditious person on account of the obduracy with which he had to oppose an unjust procedure" (II, 78).

As we have noted earlier, a central idea of the essay is that spiritual beauty may appear in unlikely form. Not only the "clumsiness" of Socrates in collecting votes in the town council and in carrying out other customs is further evidence of this phenomenon, but also his "impetuosity, which is said to have compelled him to pull out his hair sometimes in the marketplace and to act as if beside himself" (II, 79). Hamann sees in such behavior of Socrates vis-à-vis his adversaries a parallel to Christ's denunciation of the scribes and pious ones (II, 79). But more important than his overt behavior was his discourse, which was often criticized as crude. It was his friend Alcibiades, however, who, in summing up the nature of Socrates's discourse, most aptly described his true character: "Alcibiades . . . compared his parables to certain sacred images of the gods and goddesses, which were carried, according to the custom of that time, in a small case, on the outside of which only the form of a goat-footed satyr was visible" (II, 80).

In the remaining paragraphs of the Third Section, Hamann rehearses the main facts of Socrates's last days. Especially noteworthy is his insertion of an excursus on Xanthippe in which he exonerates her for her alleged shrewishness in dealing with her spouse. The exoneration takes on an ironical cast, however, when we realize that in this passage Hamann identifies Xanthippe's behavior toward Socrates with Berens's behavior toward him after his conversion; not only was Berens disgusted with the turn of events but he apparently threatened to become violent toward his friend.[14] "Because of Xanthippe's shortcomings and her disgust, the irritation he occasioned by his sudden ideas could not be more quickly checked than by means of uncouthness, insults, and her chamber pot. To a woman who has to keep house for a philosopher . . . time is too valuable to spend devising puns and employing figures of speech" (II, 79).

Charged with the serious crimes of dishonoring the gods and seducing the youth of Athens "because of his free and scandalous doctrines," Socrates conducted himself with great dignity at his trial, answering the accusations "with a seriousness and courage, with such pride and indifference, that, judging by his facial expression, one would have held him to be a commanding officer of his judges rather than an accused person" (II, 81). One is reminded of Dante's description of Farinata degli Uberti in the *Inferno,* who seemed majestic even in his torment. Socrates's bearing and his words, however, resulted in a unanimous verdict against him. Thus "Athens, which is said to have imposed a fine on Homer for madness, sentenced Socrates to death as a transgressor" (II, 80). Recognizing "his innocence and the wickedness of their own sentence of death," however, the Athenians later erected a monument to him. Although Plato saw in the voluntary poverty of Socrates a sign of his divine mission, Hamann, citing Matthew 23:29, finds a greater one in "his sharing of the final destiny of the prophets and the righteous" (II, 81).

VII *Peroration*

The *Socratic Memorabilia* concludes with a Peroration, proclaiming in impassioned and eloquent terms the belief that only those who are willing to sacrifice their all are "fit for the service of truth." Anyone unwilling to do so should "become forthwith a reasonable, useful, agreeable man in the world or learn to bow and scrape and to lick plates; in such a way he will be safe his life long from hunger and thirst, from the gallows and wheel" (II, 82). These words are not only directed against the "enlightened" bourgeois philosophy of a Christoph Berens but also against the secularized power-state of Frederick the Great's Prussia, as Hamann's French writings of the period amply attest (see Chapter 9). When one recalls that these words were written in a Prussia which Lessing once called the "most slavish land in Europe,"[15] the significance of Hamann's words is highlighted. The essay concludes with the observation that the fate of Socrates makes it clear that, if God were to appear in human form, death at the hands of men would also be His fate. In a typically Hamannian example of *Stilbruch* he stresses the severity of Christ's passion by stating that He "died a more ignominious and cruel death than the parricide[16] of the most Christian king, Louis the Beloved, who is a great-grandchild of Louis the Great" (II, 82).

A unique aspect of the Socratic essay is the fact that Hamann intended the *form* of the work to *conform* to both the appearance and the teachings of Socrates. Neither a Plato nor a Xenophon, nor in modern times a Nietzsche, makes such a claim for his account of Socrates, and, as far as I can tell, Hamann's claim is unique in the literature concerning the Greek philosopher. Elsewhere I have discussed at some length the idea of "Socratic form" as conceived by Hamann.[17] It will suffice here to say that for Hamann this notion meant that the reality always transcends its appearance, for the appearance is fragmentary, incomplete, and beckons beyond itself to a greater reality.

The form of the essay is not, however, consistently "Socratic" in the Hamannian sense. The matter is more complex. While it can be read simply as an essay whose parts are held together loosely by a common theme, it is equally true that it can be viewed from another angle as a sort of proto-drama, manifesting the Aristotelian requirement of a "beginning, middle, and end" or the pyramidal structure of rising and falling action. It was undoubtedly this aspect of the essay which inspired the young Goethe to consider composing a drama on the life and death of Socrates.[18] The underlying quasi-classical structure in the form of a proto-plot is hidden from view by the open, nonclassical, essayistic—in the last resort, intuitive—form. Thus, Hamann's metaphor of the veiled Graces is a fitting one for his practice of obscuring, not eliminating, the classical element which is also present in the structure of the work.

The use of irony, as I have noted, is central to Hamann's method in the present work. In it he employs both verbal and dramatic irony, though the latter preponderates. The most important example of verbal irony is, of course, the Socratic confession of ignorance with its interesting analogue in the declaration of the expert card player, who says to his would-be partners in a game, "I don't play." Otherwise, the treatise is shot through with so-called dramatic ironies, the greatest of all being that expressed in the Peroration that a good man cannot survive in the world, while those who adjust to its demands, who "bow and scrape and lick plates," will certainly prosper. It is important to bear in mind, however, the distinction between those contradictions which are merely ironical and those which are redemptive. For instance, that Christ appears in the form of a servant (Knechtsgestalt) is not ironical but is the form of the revelation which God has chosen for the redemption of man. The *coincidentia oppositorum* involved here is, of course, a basic theological and metaphysical principle of Hamann's thought. Nevertheless, irony may be *indirectly* redemptive if, as Hamann intended, its effect is to stab others awake to spiritual reality. In a letter to J. G. Linder written shortly before the *Socratic Memorabilia* he speaks of the Christian using irony "in order to chastise the Devil" (1, 339).

Another characteristic feature of the essay is Hamann's use of humor, which is often scurrilous or crude, at times appearing to border on blasphemy. The comparison of the treatise to laxative pills; the facetious reference to the Roman emperor Caligula's inability to swim (II, 61); the mention of an English quack doctor's theory regarding virgin births; Xanthippe's use of her chamber pot to chasten Socrates; the tasteless doggerel questioning Xanthippe's virtue (II, 79); the comparison of Socrates's invocation of the gods to an "enamored dandy" swearing falsely to his beloved or a knight-errant "swearing by the furies of his ancestors" (II, 80), and other similar remarks are typical. We shall note further on that the scriptural model was generally decisive for Hamann's style, but it is quite obvious that in his use of humor he departs radically from that model. Small wonder that his Pietistic admirers were often dismayed by his writings.

By way of summary we may say that Hamann's Socrates is the persistent seeker after both self-knowledge and knowledge of the external world, which can better be known *analogically* rather than *logically;* he is the arch-foe of the presumption of knowledge which is involved in the abstracting process. (In this regard, the Hamannian account of Socrates is diametrically opposed not only to that of the eighteenth-century Enlighteners but also to that of Nietzsche).[19] For this reason Socrates's confession of ignorance, with its underlying irony, became a "thorn" in the eyes of his adversaries, but at the same time it prefigures the New Testament or Pauline view of human knowledge. Socrates is always open to the promptings of his daimon or tutelary spirit, which for Hamann foreshadows the Holy Spirit. It is for this reason that he is independent of rules or rigidly prescriptive norms. That Hamann prefers to illustrate this independence by appealing primarily to aesthetic

examples (Homer and Shakespeare) represents his accommodation
to the prejudices of a secular age: his purpose is nonetheless essentially religious.

In the *Socratic Memorabilia* Hamann introduces—some in quite
embryonic form—almost all the major motifs of his later works:
pedagogy, history and myth, faith and reason, genius and inspiration, the imitation of nature, and the philosophy of language. Stylis-
tically, the essay is not yet vintage Hamann, for, despite genial
passages and striking formulations, he has yet to reach the zenith of
his literary powers.[20] The conception of man which emerges from
the work is clear: in spite of his shortcomings, Socrates represents
the ideal man in so far as he may flourish outside the biblical dispen-
sation. It is for this reason and because of the coherence of the
picture of the "daimonic" Socrates which it presents that the work is
one of Hamann's most important. Whether or not it is a faithful
portrait of the historical Socrates is an open question.[21] But Kierkegaard accepted it as such and wrote: ". . . my soul clings to Socrates, its first love, and rejoices in the one who understood him,
Hamann; for he has said the best that has been said about Socrates."[22]

As one would expect, the Socratic essay was not at all well received by the "Two"—Kant and Berens—to whom it had been dedicated. After all, they had acted from the best of motives in their
attempt to return him to sound reason, and he had answered with a
treatise, half pasquinade, half radical attack on their most cherished
spiritual and intellectual presuppositions. Somewhat surprisingly,
the review by Moses Mendelssohn in the *Literaturbriefe* was generally approbative. Quite the opposite was true of the review in a
Hamburg journal by one Christian Ziegra. Hamann suspected that
Berens and Kant were actually behind the latter review, since
Ziegra compared him to Jacob Böhme, something which they had
always been prone to do (2, 121). In the eyes of this reviewer,
Hamann appeared as a "mad enthusiast" (wahnwitziger Schwärmer). The real importance of the review, however, was the
reply which it evoked from Hamann, *Clouds: A Sequel to the Socratic Memorabilia* (1761).

The title is borrowed from Aristophanes's comedy about Socrates,
and also from Revelation 1:7, where Christ's triumphant return
"with clouds" is prophesied. Here again Hamann indicates the double meaning which the life and death of Socrates has for him, the

one having to do with the philosopher's literal existence, the other with his function as a foreshadowing of Christ. The treatise is divided into a "prologue," "epilogue," and three "acts." In the first "act" Hamann reprints the main part of the nugatory review by Ziegra, and annotates it. Thus he provides a review of the review. The second and third "acts" deal with the question of the relation of genius and inspiration to madness. Hamann reminds his readers of the long and impressive list of those who, in the course of human history, have been accused of madness: not only Jesus himself, but Saul, David, Elisha, and the disciples of Jesus, to name examples from the Scriptures; but there were also Hercules, Ajax, Orestes, Hamlet, and Ariosto. Neither Pharisaic legalism nor Greek philosophy—both of which share rationalistic assumptions—are able to distinguish between genial inspiration and true madness.

In the *Memorabilia*, the idea of the central role of sexuality in cognition was implicit; in *Clouds*, however, it becomes explicit. There the rationalists are compared to eunuchs, who are afraid to confess their impotence, as in the words of Scripture: "Behold, I am a dry tree,"[23] that is, to confess that they are really ignorant. If they did make such a confession, no one would consider them sincere. But Socrates could sincerely make such a confession, even though "it seemed immodest to expose the weakness of his cognitive powers without making use of an apron of fig-leaves or of coats of skins" (II, 97). Although *Clouds* is shot through with irony, wit, and persiflage, it elucidates further some of the basic ideas of the *Memorabilia*, and therefore constitutes an illuminating sequel to that work.

CHAPTER 4

Aesthetics in a Nutshell

THE year 1761 was in many ways a remarkable one for the young Hamann. Living at home in Königsberg, which was still occupied by the Russians, he devoted himself, in addition to his voracious and wide-ranging reading to the study of Greek, Hebrew, and Arabic. The study of Arabic must certainly have been the most time-consuming for him, for, although he had begun a reading of the Koran only in the spring, he had already finished it by the end of August (2, 103). It is interesting to note that, despite his disagreement with the Göttingen Orientalist Johann David Michaelis over the manner in which Arabic studies could be utilized to throw light on biblical Hebrew, he was obviously in agreement with the idea that it could contribute significantly to an understanding of the language and culture of the Old Testament. Michaelis had succeeded in persuading the King of Denmark to underwrite the expedition of Karsten Niebuhr, Peter Forskal, and others to Arabia (1761–66) for the purpose of studying the contemporary vernacular and culture of the natives in order to illuminate the "dead" languages of the Bible. In addition to the publication in that year of *Clouds* and *Chimerical Ideas*, Hamann took time out from his language studies to publish the *French Project* and the *Lettre néologique*. The latter is the opening salvo of his writings in French, in which he attacks root and branch the importation of the French culture of the *ancien régime* into Germany, and thus indirectly the King of Prussia, the head and forefront of the offense (see Chapter 9). His greatest achievement in this year, however, was the writing of the *Aesthetica in nuce*, which appeared in the collection of essays entitled *Crusades of the Philologist* (1762). ("Crusades" here refers not primarily to militant defense of the faith but—according to East Prussian folklore—to the zigzag sallies of the Teutonic Knights past the megaliths scattered throughout the Baltic area in order that they might avoid participa-

63

tion in an actual crusade against the Saracens; here the meaning is "labyrinthine wanderings of the philologist," namely, Hamann. See NB, 126–27 for an explanation of the play on words.)

If the purpose of the *Socratic Memorabilia* is to relate classical culture to Christianity, the purpose of the *Aesthetica* is to relate Oriental culture to Christianity, and further to show that its thought-forms are more congenial to that religion because they are more natural, hence less derivative. Hamann's intensive study of the Hebrew Bible and the Arabic Koran in the period just prior to the writing of the *Aesthetica* accounts for the impassioned, eloquent defense of the *form* in which the revelation must be couched. Although Mohammed was for him in the last analysis a "lying prophet" (II, 213), it was a little of the "leaven" of the genuine revelation in the Bible which made him one of the world's greatest figures (III, 145). Further background for the composition of the treatise is Hamann's paraphrase of the "Song of Solomon" in German (IV, 251–56). Though he never published this work or indeed mentioned it in his letters, its influence is palpable in his writings of the period and especially in the *Aesthetica* (cf. IV, 485).

The title of the work is in imitation of Christian Otto von Schönaich's book, *The Whole of Aesthetics in a Nutshell or Neological Dictionary* (1754). Schönaich, a Gottschedian rationalist, had in turn adopted the term "aesthetics" from the pioneering work of Alexander Gottlieb Baumgarten's *Aesthetica* (1750 ff.). For Baumgarten aesthetics meant not only the science of the beautiful, but it also embraced the sensory faculties of man in general. Hamann adopts this broader meaning of the term, a fact which should be borne in mind as one reads his treatise. Indeed the opening lines of the work emphasize the primacy of sensory over rational knowledge. The subtitle, "A Rhapsody in Cabbalistic Prose," is simply Hamann's way of stating that he is not going to argue with his "enlightened" adversaries in rationalistic terms, but that the treatise will be impassioned and cryptic. By the term "cabbalistic" he means that he is not adopting the univocal, literal language of his opponents, but that his discourse will involve the depth of meaning possible only with multivocal or symbolic language. Undoubtedly Jörgensen is right in saying that Hamann desired "with this expression to provoke the rationalistic exegetes and to anticipate their judgment" on his work.[1] The motto below the title proper contains a curious quotation in Hebrew from Judges 5:30: "a prey of diverse colors of needlework, of diverse colors of needlework on both sides, meet for the necks of them that take the spoil." Apparently Hamann is referring here to the works of Michaelis, for a continuation of which he waits impatiently like Sisera's mother waiting anxiously for the return of her treacherously slain son. The writings of Michaelis would thus constitute "prey" or "booty" for Hamann, but they are a poor substitute for the spiritual dimension of Scripture, which Michaelis neglects, just as the spoils of war were but a poor substitute for Sisera in the eyes of his mother. On the back of the title page there appears a quotation from Job, again in Hebrew, vividly expressing the necessity which Hamann feels for giving vent to his feelings. Adopting the role of Elihu over against Job, he declares: "Behold my belly is as wine which hath no vent; it is ready to burst like new bottles. I will speak that I may be refreshed: I will open my lips and answer."[2]

It is striking that the mottoes on the title page, despite the fact that they are drawn from Scripture, represent the human standpoint, whereas the verses from classical literature represent the divine. The opening lines of a famous Horatian ode (III, 1) introduce the text. With these lines the author establishes his authority as a "priest of the muses," avers that he shuns the rabble, and reminds his readers that God (here, Jove) is the almighty ruler of the universe. (Lines from another well-known ode by the Roman poet stand at the end of the text proper.[3]) Immediately following the cited verses, Hamann adopts in the exordium the sovereign stance of a "prophet of the muses":

Not a lyre!—nor a painter's brush—a winnowing shovel for my muse to sweep the threshing-floor of sacred literature! (II, 197)

Thus, after reminding his readers by means of the ode from Horace of the majesty of God, the author immediately turns to the matter at hand, namely, to cleanse the Scriptures of the chaff with which "materialistic" biblical exegetes like Michaelis have covered it in order to reveal its beauty and power. Punning on the name Michaelis, Hamann salutes the scholar for his mastery of the dead letter of Scripture, but predicts his own victory in the contest under the guise of Socrates:

Hail to the archangel who presides over the relics of the language of Canaan!—He that rides on white asses[4] is victorious in the contest;—but the wise layman of Greece borrows the steeds of Euthyphro[5] for philological discourse (II, 197).

Whatever Michaelis's achievements in the area of biblical scholarship, he has in Hamann's eyes no understanding for the essentially
poetic nature of the biblical revelation.[6] Hamann will invoke the aid
of a philosopher (Francis Bacon) just as Socrates, "the wise layman
of Greece," invoked the words of the priest Euthyphro in support of
his cause. With such an ally he will challenge the basic assumptions
of his adversary: "Poetry is the mother-tongue of the human race; as
gardening is older than agriculture; painting, than writing; song,
than declamation; parables, than deductions; barter, than trade" (II,
197). With these words we are thrust into the heart of the Hamannian polemic. It is advisable at this point, however, to abstract from
the treatise the main argument and to illustrate it as far as possible
with Hamann's own words. For the *Aesthetica in nuce*, unlike the
Socratic Memorabilia, cannot be adequately represented by a
paraphrase, but must be treated from the standpoint of its ideational
content. Like almost all of Hamann's important writings the *Aesthetica* contains many passages which resist interpretation, but what
is immediately clear, along with what has yielded to the patient
research of a number of commentators, amply vindicates its reputation as one of the Magus's most important works.

The key to an understanding of the *Aesthetica in nuce* may be
found in the following passage:

The opinions of the philosophers are readings of nature, and the dogmas
of the theologians readings of Scripture. The author [God] is the best interpreter of his words; he may speak through creatures—through
events—or through blood and fire and vapor of smoke, of which the language of the sanctuary consists.

The book of creation contains examples of universal concepts which God
desired to reveal to the creature through the creature; the books of the
covenant contain examples of secret articles which God desired to reveal to
man through man. The unity of the author [Urheber] is reflected in the very
dialect of his works; in all of them a note of immeasurable height and depth!
A proof of the most glorious majesty and the most complete divestiture. A
miracle of such infinite calm, causing God to resemble nothingness, so that
one must deny his existence either in good conscience or after the manner
of a beast,[7] but at the same time he is characterized by such infinite energy,
filling all in all, so that one can scarcely escape his most devoted attentive-
ness (II, 203–204).

It should be noted that Hamann uses the term "book" in both a
metaphorical and a literal sense. Thus, the expression "book of crea-

tion" is a figure of speech for nature or for natural events in general; the expression "books of the covenant," on the other hand, is a literal term referring to the Bible.[8] If one bears in mind the shift from the metaphorical to the literal use of the term "book" throughout the *Aesthetica*, the first step toward a discovery of the underlying symmetry in its conceptual framework is taken. For paralleling the "book of creation" or the "book of nature" is the metaphorical "book of history," and paralleling the literal Bible are other sacred writings such as the Koran and, above all, the myths of the ancients. Because of the perennial tendency of man in his fallen state to view the events of nature and history abstractly, he is not content to allow his writings on the subject to reflect their true character, but distorts them in the mirror of his abstraction. It is against such distortion that Hamann inveighs in the *Aesthetica*. But in order to do so effectively, he must first treat of the nature of God and man.

In the passage quoted above we find most of the important attributes of God in Hamannian thought already stated. Thus, God is characterized by a unity which embraces opposites: "the most glorious majesty" and "the most complete divestiture"; "immeasurable height and depth"; "infinite calm" and "infinite energy" (Kraft). Elsewhere, in a famous passage he declares: "The Poet at the beginning of days is the same as the Thief at the end of days" (II, 206). This statement is all too often quoted without the latter,—and necessary—half, which refers to the parousia or Second Coming of Christ.[9] Thus the God who *created* the light is the same as the One who *reveals* the "light . . . in Christ" (II, 206). Hamann's Trinitarian and eschatological views emerge further in the following passage near the end of the work:

After God had spoken exhaustively through nature and the Scriptures, through creatures and seers, through poets and prophets, he spoke to us in the evening of days through his Son—yesterday and today! until the promise of his future—no longer in the form if a servant [Knechtsgestalt] should be fulfilled.[10]

The doctrine of the coincidence of opposites, a basic concept in Hamann's thought, thus roots in his conception of a God in whom the greatest conceivable extremes are reconciled.

Central to an understanding of Hamann's view of man is his conception of the image of God in man:

Finally God crowned the sensible revelation of his glory with the master-piece of man. He created man in divine form—in the image of God He created him. This decree of the Creator solves the most complicated riddles of human nature and its destiny. Blind heathens have recognized the invisible nature which man shares with God. The veiled figure of the body, the countenance of the head, and the extremities of the arms are the visible scheme, in which we appear; yet they are really nothing but an indication of the hidden man within us (II, 198).

Hamann differentiates between the creation of the world and the creation of man, and, in so doing, has again recourse to literary metaphors:

The creation of the world-stage is related to the creation of man as the art of the epic is to the art of the drama. The former is created through the word; the latter through action . . . Hear the counsel: Let us make men in our image, after our likeness, and let them have dominion. Behold the deed: And the Lord God formed man out of the dust of the ground (II, 200).

The analogy between God and man, however, is not the analogy of *being* of the scholastics, but is an analogy of *speech* (cf. Chapter 5). Unlike the brute creation, man is endowed with the power of naming, i.e., of language, and it is this special endowment which constitutes the image of God in man. After mentioning the account in Genesis of Adam's naming the animals, which God had brought to him, Hamann writes:

This analogy of man to the Creator imparts to all creatures their content and character, upon which loyalty and faith throughout the world depend. The more lively this idea, the image of the living God, dwells in our heart, the more we are capable of seeing and tasting, of contemplating and of grasping with our hands his loving kindness in the creatures of the earth. Every impression of nature in man is not only a reminder but a pledge of the basic truth—who the Lord is. Every reaction of man toward the creature is a letter and seal of our participation in the divine nature, and that we are of his race (II, 206–207).

The analogy between man and God holds, however, only as long as man does not abuse the power of speech, whether on the ethical, philosophical, or aesthetic plane. In the seventh *Literaturbrief* Lessing had stated in effect that a man and his words are separate: "Of what concern," he asks, "is the private life of an author to us? I do

not imagine that we can learn from it anything about his works."[11]
In rebuttal of that opinion Hamann writes: "Of course one can be a
man without finding it necessary to become an author. But whoever
expects of good friends that they should regard the writer without
the man behind them is more inclined to imaginative than
philosophical abstractions" (II, 201). As we have seen earlier,
Hamann's idea of the whole man precludes any such separation of a
man from his words.

Immediately following his declaration that poetry is the mother
tongue of the human race and after establishing the priority of gardening (namely, the Garden of Eden), painting, song, parables, and
barter over their later developments, Hamann adopts Job as the
prototype of our ancestors, who were closer to the creational order
of things:

> The repose of our ancestors was a deeper sleep, and their movements a
> reeling dance. Seven days they sat in the silence of reflection or astonish-
> ment, and opened their mouths to speak winged words.
> Senses and passions speak and understand nothing but images. The en-
> tire treasury of human knowledge and felicity consists of nothing but im-
> ages. The first outburst of creation and the first impression of its historian,
> the first manifestation and the first enjoyment of nature are united in the
> word: Let there be light! (II, 197)

The seven days of silence on the part of Job and his friends ended
with Job's speaking his eloquent and moving lament,[12] which is cast
in the usual form of Hebrew poetry and is characterized by powerful
imagery. Although directed at the rationalists in general, Hamann's
words were evoked by Michaelis's criticisms of the use of imagery in
the Old Testament as contrary to sound reason. But it is not simply a
matter of language which interests Hamann here, for Michaelis's
rejection of poetry in favor of prose in the language of revelation is
symbolic of his rejection of the creational order of things. Parables,
which require imagery, are older than abstraction, which eliminates
imagery; but the latter is not therefore to be preferred to the
former. Nor are we moving toward any sort of Utopia through
"sound reason."

In Chapters 2 and 3 I have considered the strong emphasis which
Hamann places on the emotionality of man. In this connection I had
occasion to quote from the *Aesthetica* some of his most eloquent
statements on the subject, and therefore will not repeat them here.

In the discussion of other subjects which follows, additional light will be shed on the subject of the role of the emotions.

I *The Metaphorical Book of Nature*

Hamann's conception of nature is thoroughly biblical. For as important as nature is in his thought, it never becomes an end in itself, as it does, for instance, for many of the later romantics. Further, God is never immanent in nature but always transcends it. Yet the paradox remains that man never knows God apart from nature, i.e., apart from the created world in which he lives. The creation is like a scroll or a book in which are written the ways of God with man.[13] Consider the following passage:

Speak, that I may see you! —This wish was fulfilled through the creation, which is a speech to the creature through the creature, for day unto day uttereth speech, and night unto night showeth knowledge. There is no speech nor language, where their voice is not heard. Their line is gone out through all the earth, and their words to the end of the world.[14] No matter where the fault lies (whether outside us or within us), we have in nature nothing but disordered verses and *disiecti membra poetae* left for our use. It is the scholar's task to collect them, the philosopher's to interpret them, the poet's modest part to imitate them—or more audaciously—to put them in order.

Speaking is translating—from the language of angels into a human tongue, that is, thoughts into words, things into names, images into signs, which can be poetic or kyriological,[15] historical, or symbolic or hieroglyphic, and philosophical or characteristic. This kind of translation (or speech) is, more than any other, like the reverse side of carpets, "and shews the stuff, but not the workman's skill," or like an eclipse of the sun which is examined in a vessel full of water . . .[16] (II, 198–99).

The book of creation thus contains God's words to man, but they appear as "disordered verses and *disiecti membra poetae*." The Latin phrase from Horace[17] especially provides us with an important clue to an understanding of the divine order of things. With it the Roman poet avers that some of the verses of Ennius are so poetic that, even if one were to change the order of his words at random, you would still have the "dismembered limbs of a poet," i.e., you would still have poetry. In such an indirect way Hamann expresses a principle which we shall encounter in other contexts, i.e., the idea that behind the apparent contradictions of nature there is an invisi-

ble harmony. As each limb of the dismembered poet clearly belongs
to him, so each part of the creation is indelibly marked with its
divine origin, and this holds true no matter how confused the relation of part to part may appear to our limited vision.

Here we may anticipate the distinction between rational and intuitive order which I shall subsequently discuss (Chapter 6). The
expression "dismembered limbs of a poet" is obviously a metaphorical way of stating that the parts do not manifest a clear relationship
to each other, but do so with regard to the whole. It is important to
keep the distinction between God and the creation clearly in mind,
for in Hamann's theology nature is never to be regarded as God's
body, as in certain pantheistic conceptions. The term "poet" in the
phrase from Horace is thus simply a symbol for the unity of the
revelation, the Logos. Although the scholar (namely, scientist) and
the philosopher have important tasks to perform in the attempt to
discover some kind of order in the apparent chaos of the universe, it
is really the poet who is most nearly able to symbolize the hidden
unity of things.

According to Hamann, the book of nature is further characterized
by "beauty and riches," which the acids of reason completely destroy: "Behold! the great and small Masorah of philosophy has
flooded the text of nature like a deluge. Was it not inevitable that all
its beauties and riches should come to naught?" (II, 207). Hamann
sees the abstract view of nature as involving a kind of castration, for
he compares the discourses of the skeptical rationalists to the
falsetto singing of the *castrati* (II, 208). Continuing in this vein, he
writes:

If the passions are members of dishonor, do they therefore cease to be the
weapons of manhood? Do you understand the letter of reason any better
than that allegorical chamberlain of the Alexandrian church [Origen] understood the letter of the Scripture, who made himself a eunuch for the sake of
the Kingdom of God? (II, 208)

In what is undoubtedly an allusion to Frederick the Great and his
coterie of skeptical savants in Berlin, Hamann continues:

The prince of this aeon[18] makes favorites of the greatest villains against
themselves; his court-jesters are the worst enemies of beautiful nature . . . . Passion alone gives to abstractions as well as to hypotheses
hands, feet, wings, to images, and signs, spirit, life and tongue. Where are

swifter deductions? Where is the pealing thunder of eloquence produced and its companion—monosyllabic lightning?[19]

The abstract approach to nature, represented without exception by the *philosophes*, physicists, and mathematicians with whom the king surrounded himself, intellectuals like Pierre Louis Moreau de Maupertuis, Jean Baptiste d'Argens, Jean Offray de La Mettrie, and Voltaire, can never properly interpret nature. For they insist on reading the text of nature as if it were written only in mathematico-logical symbols.

II   *The Literal Books of Nature*

The figurative book of nature is reflected in the literal books which are created by man: "Speaking is translating—from the language of angels into a human tongue." But such "translation" is accomplished with varying degrees of fidelity. Subsequently I shall consider the formal reasons for the preeminence of the Bible in this regard (Chapter 5). One could, however, compile a long list of writings, sacred and profane, which in Hamann's view reflect the true state of things in nature, and which therefore tend, in varying degrees, to speak to the whole man. Numerous references of this sort are to be found in the *Aesthetica*.

It is Hamann's primary purpose in attacking Michaelis's hermeneutics to defend the *form* of the biblical revelation. In so doing, he invokes Mohammed as his chief witness against Michaelis. For, although Hamann considered Mohammed, insofar as he claimed a special revelation, to be a false prophet (II, 213), he recognized that the suras of the Koran are cast in poetic form. Michaelis had criticized both Augustine and Mohammed in the same breath for their overactive imagination and their inclination to poetry (II, 212–13). But it was precisely these characteristics which most distinguished the inhabitants of Arabia, the study of whose language Michaelis assiduously engaged in and promoted, indeed to the extent that he had instigated an expedition to Arabia for the purpose of studying the language. Hamann agreed that a journey to that land was needed, but a journey of quite a different sort, a "pilgrimage":

But how shall we awaken the extinct language of nature again from the dead?—Through pilgrimages to fortunate Arabia, through crusades to the lands of the East, and through the restoration of their magic, which we must capture by means of old wives' cunning, because that is the best (II, 211).

We have already observed that Hamann made his own arduous
pilgrimage to Arabia in his study of the Koran in the original language.

The other writings referred to in the *Aesthetica* which reflect, in
one way or another, the revelation in nature are drawn from Western literature, chiefly classical, and have to do with content rather
than form. Preeminent in this regard is Homer, who, although not
often mentioned in the text, towers impressively in the background.
The role which the young Goethe assigns to Homer in *Werther* as a
guide to the natural life is essentially in the Hamannian vein. But
Homer's writings are more important for the concept of history and
will, therefore, be considered further below. Scattered throughout
the *Aesthetica* are numerous references to poets who reflect some
aspect of the extrabiblical revelation in nature. Among them are:
Pindar, Horace, Ovid, Manilius, Petronius, and Ausonius. Among
the moderns Shakespeare and Klopstock are mentioned. As we shall
see below, the German poet is defended also for the open form of
his poetry.

III   *The Metaphorical Book of History*

Although the expression "book of history" does not appear in the
Aesthetica, the metaphor is clearly important for his thought. Earlier he had written in *Fragments:* "The book of nature and the book
of history are nothing but ciphers, hidden signs, which require the
same key which interprets the Scriptures, and which is the main'
point of its inspiration" (I, 308). The metaphor as applied to history
differs somewhat from its application to nature, for in the former
case its refers to all historical lore, whether written or oral, i.e., to
all tradition, which is essentially the experience of man embodied in
language. In order to take history or tradition seriously one has to
accept the principle that all ideas are timebound or conditioned.
This principle, however, contradicts a fundamental tenet of the Enlighteners, namely, that there are timeless or eternal truths, which
may be arrived at through autonomous reason. It was the acquisition
of such truths that constituted "progress" for the Enlighteners.
Since the earlier stages of man's existence were believed to be
clearly inferior to the present, one did not take them seriously. Or,
if one chose to concern himself with them, as, for instance, certain
philosophes did with the myths of the gods, it was for the purpose of
overlaying the absurdities of the past with a rational explanation.

As we have seen from Hamann's opening words of the *Aesthetica*, he inverts the notion of progress as held by his adversaries. In all the arts of civilization: language, agriculture, writing, rhetoric, philosophy, and commerce he holds the earlier stage to be the natural and therefore the more desirable one (II, 197). Thus with a clean sweep he rejects the whole idea of progress. In so doing he aligns himself with Rousseau. But there is a fundamental difference, for Hamann's idea of history is rooted in the biblical revelation, not in a hypothetical state of nature. The creation, fall, and redemption of man in the incarnation provides the fundamental typology which explains all human experience. Therefore he is able to speak of "the hieroglyphic Adam" as representing "the whole history of the race in a wheel" (II, 200). The term "wheel" obviously refers to the constant recurrence of this sequence in human life. In the same passage Eve becomes the prototype of philosophy, for just as Eve is derived from, and dependent on, Adam, so philosophy derives from, and depends on, history.[20]

IV *Literal Books of History*

If the Bible is necessary for an understanding of nature, it is equally so for an understanding of history:

> The first outburst of creation, and the first impression of its historian [Moses], the first appearance and the first pleasure in nature unite in the words: "Let there be light! Herewith begins the perception [Empfindung] of the presence of things (II, 197).

It is significant that these lines immediately follow Hamann's often-quoted statement concerning the importance of "images" (Bilder) for genuine cognition. Thus, Moses' account of the creation and God's subsequent dealing with man become the prototype for all valid historiography. Addressing those whom Schleiermacher was later to call the cultured despisers of religion Hamann writes: "Moses' torch illuminates even the intellectual world" (II, 199). Hamann is saying here essentially what he had said earlier in the Socratic essay, namely, that "perhaps all history is more mythology" than the rationalistic historian thinks (II, 65).

Homer is a prime example of an ancient writer who has conveyed historical truth through the medium of myth. For Hamann sees the Homeric epics as related to the general revelation in nature as the

Scriptures are to the special revelation to the Jews and in Christ. Unlike the Koran, which manifests the proper *form*[21] of the revelation without its *content*, the Greek epics foreshadow, by virtue of their mythologizing, the proper *content* of the revelation without possessing its specific *form* (cf. II, 215). Hamann finds, for instance, the *Knechtsgestalt* of Christ prefigured in the *Odyssey*. Using the word "translate" in a double sense, he addresses his adversaries: "You know the story of the beggar who appeared at the court of Ithaca [Odysseus], for has not Homer translated it into Greek and Pope into English verses?" (II, 211). Further evidence of the preeminence of Homer is found in Hamann's challenge to skeptical philosophers like Voltaire to read the text of the *Iliad*, while omitting all the alphas and omegas from the text. Such a procedure is analogous to the process of abstraction, through which all its "riches and beauty, like those of nature, would come to naught" (II, 207). More important, however, is the religious implication: by eliminating the alphas and omegas, the reader is eliminating the hidden, but very real, foreshadowings of Christ, the "Alpha and Omega" of the Scriptures.

Although Ovid is only briefly alluded to in the text, his *Metamorphoses* are cited at great length in a footnote (II, 209–10). The verses in which the importance of mythology for the history of man is attested refer to the myth of Narcissus:

> We deal with the ancients like a man, who, after beholding his natural face in a glass,[22] goes away and from that hour forgets how he looks. But a painter who takes his own visage as a subject acts quite differently. Narcissus (the narcissus[23] of beautiful spirits) loves his own image more than his life (II, 209).

Thus, the myths of the ancients tell us much about ourselves, but we do not really heed them. Instead we project our own image onto the past, and, like a painter who is doing a self-portrait, we concentrate on it. The "beautiful spirits" (Hamann's term for those who "beautify" the myths, i.e., make them more conformable to their own ideas) are, however, like Narcissus, who loved "his own image more than his life."

Myths do not simply belong to a time long past, but, when properly understood as bearers of the Logos in secular history, they are seen as necessarily belonging to the present. It is inadmissible to

reject them as irrational after the manner of Bernard de Fontenelle.[24] Nor is it acceptable to rationalize them by means of
naturalistic explanations. There are, indeed, those who value the
classics in their own way, but nevertheless succeed in falsifying
them. In the *Aesthetica,* Hamann attacks Lessing for doing precisely
this in his youthful poetry (II, 201). Hamann's criticism of the
refined eroticism of Anacreontic poetry is that it adopts an artificial
attitude toward love and sexuality, both of which have a much pro-
founder effect on human life than the poetry of dalliance suggests. It
is in this context that he writes:

> Therefore do not undertake to delve into the metaphysics of the fine arts
> without being initiated into the orgies and Eleusinian mysteries. The senses
> are, however, Ceres, and Bacchus the passions—old foster-parents of
> beautiful nature (II, 201).

Immediately following these words Hamann cites in Latin verses
from Tibullus, invoking the blessing of Bacchus and Ceres, as if to
underscore the importance of his preceding statement. The truth
about the depth aspects of human nature can thus be learned
from the Greek fertility cults.

In spite of his admiration for the myths of classical antiquity,
Hamann issues a caveat concerning the heresy of excessive venera-
tion of the Greeks. In an accusatory question directed at
Graecophiles like J. J. Winckelmann (whose greatness he elsewhere
acknowledges[25]) he writes: "Why does one remain with the broken
cisterns[26] of the Greeks, and abandon the most living springs of
antiquity? We ourselves may not realize that we admire the Greeks
and Romans even to the point of idolatry" (II, 209). In criticism of
Lessing and Denis Diderot's attitude toward Greek literary models,
Hamann writes: "If one would discover the documents of nature,
the Greeks and Romans are broken cisterns" (2, 84). With the expression "documents of nature" (das Urkundliche der Natur)
Hamann makes it clear that he does not consider the *literature* of the
Greeks and Romans as being as close to nature as that of the Hebrews. Here, as elsewhere, "salvation comes from the Jews" (II, 210).

V *Commentaries on the Book of Nature and History*

God is not only the author of the book of nature and the book of
history, but is also the constantly active interpreter of both. In the

former case, "he may speak through blood and fire and vapor of smoke" (II, 203) or through "oak trees" and "pillars of salt"[27]— through natural, indeed supernatural, events. Nature is not to be understood only in mathematical or physical terms after the manner of the Newtonian philosophers, but in terms of the biblical account. Unlike the mature Goethe, who opposed Newton's theory of light on scientific grounds, Hamann rejected the whole rationalistic approach to nature. God, for him, is not the cosmic Mathematician or Logician, but the cosmic Poet. Earlier he had written:

> It would be as ludicrous to ask that Moses should have interpreted nature according to Aristotelian, Cartesian or Newtonian concepts as to expect God to have revealed himself in the universal philosophical language, which has been the philosopher's stone for so many learned men (I, 12).

But not all natural philosophers approach nature on purely rationalistic grounds. Francis Bacon, Hamann's "Euthyphro," is the example of a scientist who, by virtue of his empiricism, achieves insight into the correspondences between the revelation in nature, in Scripture, and in history. Further, his employment of intuitive, as opposed to abstract, reasoning makes him a more trustworthy guide to a genuine understanding of nature than a Newton, however great the latter's stature as a physicist.

But God is not only the great interpreter of nature, he also continues through "creatures, through events," through history, to provide commentaries on the biblical revelation. In considering the typological themes of the *Socratic Memorabilia*, we saw to what extent Hamann considered the events of secular history, both before and after Christ, to provide instructive parallels to those recorded in Scripture. Hamann's emphasis in the present work precludes his dealing specifically with history as the divine commentary on the revelation proper. Nevertheless, the principle is clearly stated. Further, insofar as mythology is history, we have seen to what extent Hamann regards it as an important part of the general revelation, and one may safely consider all extrabiblical revelation as both divine text *and* commentary for Hamann.

As far as human interpreters of nature and the Scriptures are concerned, the *Aesthetica* teems with references to them. They divide roughly into two categories: first, those who, because of Hamann's approbation, we may call "canonical," and those of whom

he does not approve, whom we may call "heretical." Heading the
former list would be Bacon, and heading the latter, Michaelis. The
list of those who, implicitly or explicitly, draw Hamann's fire is a
long one. Among them are: Epicurus, Lessing, Mendelssohn,
Christian von Schönaich, Alexander Gottlieb Baumgarten, George
Benson, Fontenelle, Newton, Georges Buffon, and Frederick II.
Hamann's canon, on the other hand, includes, among others: Plato
(on Socrates), Horace, Cicero, Manilius, Augustine, Mohammed (as
an exemplar of poetic form), Photius, Luther, and Johann Albrecht
Bengel. As elsewhere, Hamann further delights in quoting those he
considers enemies of the truth against themselves, as in the case of
Voltaire, Caiaphas, and Herod (II, 205).

VI *Aesthetic Problems*

The paradox concerning the historical influence of the *Aesthetica
in nuce* is that, while it addresses itself so little to specifically aesthetic questions, it nevertheless had enormous influence on the development of German literature. Yet certain definite aesthetic principles do emerge. Particularly important is Hamann's idea of imitation. We have seen that Hamann conceived of man as dependent on
sources outside himself not only for genuine self-knowledge, but
also for his artistic creativity. "Nature and Scripture," he writes,
"are therefore the materials of the beautiful, creative, imitative
spirit" (II, 210). We have already noted that, though the scholar and
the philosopher have their special tasks with regard to the *disiecti
membra poetae* of nature, it is the poet's all-important task "to imitate them—or more audaciously—to put them in order."

There is no question here of Hamann's "overcoming" (Unger's
term[28]) of the Aristotelian theory of imitation. The Magus does, of
course, reject the neoclassical idea that art must be subject to rules
derived from the ancients. Modern writers, no less than ancient,
must look to nature as their model: "Perhaps," he writes in the
second *Clover Leaf of Hellenistic Letters*," the ancients have the
same relation to nature as the scholiasts do to their author. Whoever
studies the ancients without knowing nature is reading notes without the text . . . " (II, 117). The fact that Hamann, following Shaftesbury, shifts the emphasis from the work of art itself to the creative process does, it must be admitted, represents a break with the
Aristotelian tradition, and it was this emphasis which was to become
so influential in the *Sturm und Drang* and, indirectly, in later

Romanticism. Shakespeare was for Hamann the great exemplar in the modern world of a dramatist who engages in true mimesis but by no means allows his imagination to be shackled by the traditional rules.

In a treatise on aesthetics one logically expects to find a discussion, if not a definition, of the nature of beauty. One will look in vain, however, for such a formulation in the *Aesthetica*. Nevertheless, it is possible to discover Hamann's underlying assumptions. It is important to note that he uses the word "beautiful" (schön) with two distinct meanings. It is used first as a straightforward description of that which he considers to possess the attribute of beauty; secondly, in an ironical sense, denoting that which he considers fictitious, affected, superficial, or in any way unnatural. For example, when he complains that the rationalistic approach to nature robs it of "all its riches and beauties" (II, 207), he is using the term straightforwardly, but when he refers to the "aesthetic beauty of Aesop the Younger [Lessing],"[29] the term is clearly ironical. At times it is difficult to determine whether he is being ironical or not, but on the whole the usage is clear enough.

Perhaps the best way to understand Hamann's idea of the beautiful is to compare it with that of Moses Mendelssohn, whom Hamann calls "the Levite of the most recent literature" (II, 200) and elsewhere the "aesthetic Moses" (II, 163). Hamann predicts that Mendelssohn will, if he reads the *Aesthetica*, recoil from it as the Apostle Peter recoiled from the vision of the unclean creatures which he was commanded by the Lord to eat.[30] Mendelssohn believed in the perfect harmony of the cosmos, which is, however, not immediately apparent to us. For we find scattered throughout nature various objects, which the artist selects and forms into an artistic whole. The resulting work of art is precisely what nature would have produced had it been her intention to express beauty through the given object. Obviously there is a close parallel between Hamann's and Mendelssohn's ideas with respect to the apparently chaotic data of ordinary experience: the task of the Mendelssohnian artist is to "form a whole" out of such data; the task of the Hamannian artist "to put them in order." But when the question is asked as to *how* the artist is to accomplish his task, a considerable difference emerges. For Mendelssohn, abstract reason is required; for Hamann, faith and its twin, intuitive reason. Mendelssohn's rational norm of beauty excludes from the work of art everything which disrupts its harmony; therefore, mathematical clarity, symmetry, and precision become the ideals. For Hamann, on the other hand, a work of art involves antitheses which are not resolved, but which point beyond themselves to a resolution. As we have seen, for Hamann it is God alone who ultimately reconciles all opposites. Therefore, the artist may not usurp the role of deity by imputing to his autonomous reason the power to harmonize all antitheses. Mendelssohn, Lessing, and other Enlighteners, however, did not conceive of God in such dialectical terms. What has been called Hamann's "biblical realism" is relevant here, for the Bible reflects the heights and depths, the glory and shame, the admirable and contemptible in human experience, all with a sovereign impartiality. In short, one may say that Hamann's concept of beauty is of the kind found, above all, in the "regular disorder" of the Bible.

Near the end of the *Aesthetica* Hamann appends a brief and probably ironical excursus on the question of prosody. The occasion is his defense of Klopstock's unrhymed free verse against his traditionalist critics. In Hamann's eyes, Klopstock is "the German Pindar" and "the great restorer of lyric song" (II, 215). As an authentic genius he has the right to do away with rhyme and meter (II, 214). Hamann takes the part of Klopstock against Lessing, who had charged that Klopstock's poetry was no more than artistic prose, ordered in symmetrical lines, but possessing no meter. The Magus counters this objection with the statement that Klopstock's poetry is "presumably an archaism, which felicitously imitates the enigmatic mechanics of the sacred poetry of the Hebrews" (II, 215). Yet Michaelis had admitted that Hebrew poetry *was* poetry, albeit without meter, and maintained, in contradiction of Lessing's idea, that it was quite different from ordered prose. In such a way Hamann cleverly played off the two "profound critics," Lessing and Michaelis, against each other.

In granting genius the right to dispense with rhyme and meter, Hamann does not disparage their use. On the contrary, he finds that they both have a natural origin, rhyme springing from the nature of language, and meter, for example, from the rhythm of men at work. In the latter connection he speaks of understanding the reasons for "Homer's monotonous meter" better after hearing, while on a journey through the Baltic area, Latvian workers singing at their work in such a way as to suggest the natural origin of metered verse. He indicates further that, if a poet were to arise among such people, his verses would naturally accord with their rhythm (II, 215–16). But it is obvious that Hamann considers the free form of Hebrew poetry, as well as its echo in modern poets like Klopstock, to be superior to the restraints of rhyme and meter. For, after all, it is the form in which the revelation proper is cast, and which is more congenial with intuitive reason (cf. Chapter 5).

The technically aesthetic questions to which Hamann briefly addresses himself in the *Aesthetica* are, however, subordinate to his main concern, namely, the proper interpretation of the Scriptures. For it is only by such hermeneutics that man can do justice to his need of religion, the most important of all his needs. Therefore, he concludes the work with an "Afterword" (Apostille):

As the oldest reader of this rhapsody in cabbalistic prose, I feel myself obligated by virtue of the right of the firstborn to bequeath to my younger brothers, who will come after me, still another example of a merciful judgment as follows:

Everything in this aesthetic nut smacks of vanity!—of vanity! The rhapsodist has read, observed, pondered, sought and found pleasant words, faithfully cited them. Like a merchant ship he has fetched his provisions from afar. He has added sentence to sentence, as one counts arrows on a battlefield, and has measured his figures of speech as one lays out the pegs for a tent . . .

Let us now hear the sum and substance of his latest aesthetics, which is the oldest: Fear God, and give glory to him; for the hour of his judgment is come: and worship him that made heaven, and earth, and the sea, and the fountain of waters (II, 217).

CHAPTER 5

The Limits of Reason

ONE of the indispensable clues to an understanding of Hamann's thought is his concept of reason. In fact, there is no subject with which he is more concerned throughout his entire career subsequent to the London conversion than the question of the powers and limitations of human reason. A glance at the concordance of the Roth-Wiener edition of his works reveals, for instance, that there are more references to the terms "Vernunft" and "Verstand" than any other subject including the next most frequently occurring terms such as "Gott" and "Natur." (Despite the fact that this particular edition is incomplete, there is no reason to suppose that a concordance to Hamann's complete works and letters would yield a different result.) It is ironical that a thinker whose primary concern was to underscore the importance of faith should actually have addressed himself more frequently to the question of the nature of reason, and in so doing have become the counterpart of his compatriot and friendly adversary, Immanuel Kant, a thinker who had deliberately ruled out faith in order to deal with the problem of reason. Further, it is interesting to note that, long before Kant turned his attention to the question of cognition, Hamann had been wrestling in his own way with the problem of the nature and limits of reason. That these two great thinkers came to radically different conclusions should not obscure the fact that they were largely concerned with the same problem.

Unlike Kant, however, Hamann offers no systematic analysis of the function of reason. Indeed, his highly impassioned indictments of reason as "an *ens rationis*, a dumb staring idol, to which a clamorous superstition of unreason attributes divine attributes" (III, 225) and statements to the effect that "all abstractions are, and must of necessity be, arbitrary" (III, 190) might easily mislead the reader into the belief that Hamann's contribution to the subject amounts to no more than a virtuoso performance resulting only in highly colored and supercharged invective. The fact is, however, that underlying all his remarks on the subject is a remarkably self-consistent and clearly definable concept of reason.

In order to comprehend Hamann's understanding of reason it is necessary to distinguish between two modes of cognition, namely, the intuitive and the abstract. Although he does not employ the term *intuitive* (anschauend) in programmatic fashion to designate a mode of reasoning, he nevertheless speaks, in an important context, of "intuitive knowledge," which, he argues, alone renders possible a true understanding of the nature of man. Thus, in *The Wise-Men from the East at Bethlehem* (1760) he wrote that "human living seems to consist of a series of symbolic actions by means of which our soul is capable of revealing its invisible nature, and produces and communicates beyond itself an intuitive knowledge (anschauende Erkäntniβ) of its effective existence."[1] We may therefore confidently adopt the term as descriptive of his thought. Further, it was none other than Immanuel Kant who, writing to Hamann in 1774 to ask the latter's help in the interpretation of an obscure passage of Herder's *Oldest Document of the Human Race*, requested that Hamann reply "in human language, if possible," adding, "for I, poor mortal, am not at all organized to understand the divine language of *intuitive reason*" (3, 82). Though Kant is, no doubt, here using the phrase "intuitive reason" (anschauende Vernunft) as a bit of raillery, it is a very accurate and felicitous one to describe Hamann's procedure. The term abstract, on the other hand, is frequently used by Hamann to denote the rationalism of the Enlightenment and kindred movements.

The characteristics of Hamann's use of reason emerge most clearly when we investigate the effects of his thinking upon language. Since in his view there is no thought apart from language, it seems quite appropriate that we should look to language for the earmarks of reason. It will be seen that there are six salient features which characterize the language of *anschauende Vernunft* or intuitive reason, i.e., reason functioning within its appropriate limits. To be specific, we may say that intuitive reason manifests itself in language by the following: (1) the abundance of concrete images (Bilder); (2) the employment of analogical reasoning; (3) the frequent recourse to paradoxes; (4) the presence of multiple levels of meaning; (5) paratactic sentence structure; and (6) the presence of affec-

tive terminology. Of these six characteristics Hamann lays down, at
one point or another, the principles which govern all except the
fifth, which is, however, clearly manifested in his use of language.
As we shall see in the sequel, abstract reason affects language in
precisely the opposite ways from intuitive reason. It is true that
Hamann does not subsume the six characteristics listed above under
one heading as defining a mode of reasoning. Nevertheless, it is
clearly advantageous to see these characteristics in their essential
relationship to one another and to the problem of reason in
Hamann's thought. Adopting this procedure will help us to understand his otherwise contradictory statements regarding reason. Let
us now briefly consider each of the characteristic earmarks of intuitive reason as they manifest themselves in language.

I Imagery (Bilder)

Hamann maintains that natural language is, to adopt Henri
Bergson's phrase, "molded on reality." Ordinary language or "the
language of nature" (die Sprache der Natur, II, 211) is for him the
historically developed vernacular of a people, which has been "un-
improved" by grammarians or the creators of technical jargon. It is
this kind of language which can be raised to the level of poetic
expression. Opposed to it is the "unnatural use of abstractions" (II,
207) on the part of the philosophers. Such abstract terms are "wax
noses [i.e., deceivers], concoctions of sophistry and of academic
reason," again "fancies" and "air-castles" (G, 16). Abstract terminology can never be transformed into poetry, inasmuch as it has
forsaken the wellsprings of all inspiration, "the language of nature."
To say that the abstract word can never become the poetic word is to
say that it can never speak meaningfully of spiritual matters. It is a
striking fact that Nietzsche, whose religious views are diametrically
opposed to those of Hamann, should have composed lines which
accord so perfectly with Hamann's sentiments regarding the relation
of poetry to truth:

The sphere of poetry does not lie outside of the world as a fantastic possibility conceived by the brain of a poet; it strives to be precisely the opposite,
the unadorned expression of truth, and must for just that reason reject the
deceptive finery of the alleged reality of the man of culture.[2]

Hamann's conviction, unlike Nietzsche's, is grounded in the essential nature of both God and man. Hence, God, "the Poet at the beginning of days" (II, 206), always speaks to man in poetic language:

The Scriptures cannot speak with us as human beings otherwise than in parables because all our knowledge is sensory, figurative, and because understanding and reason transform the images of external things everywhere into allegories and signs of more abstract, more intellectual, more lofty concepts (I, 157–58).

It is clear from this passage that Hamann conceived of the abstracting process as one which, among other things, removes the "external images of things" and replaces them with empty terminology. This process is fatal to language as a vehicle for the expression of veridical knowledge. Thus he says in the *Aesthetica in nuce:* "Senses and emotions speak and understand nothing but images [Bilder]. The entire treasury of human knowledge and felicity consists in images" (II, 197).

Rationalistic theologians like Michaelis had objected that the earthy, picturesque language of the Scriptures, particularly the Old Testament, could not possibly be regarded as the Word of God in any literal sense, since it would be unworthy of Deity to speak in the unpolished and imprecise vernacular. If God were to speak directly to man, He would choose more intellectual, more abstract language, that is, the language of the philosophers. Such a view of revelation fails, according to Hamann, to take into account the fact that God's infinite love for man is revealed precisely in His willingness to condescend to man's estate. God has humbled himself to the extent of speaking in the everyday idiom of the people by means of "little, contemptible events" (II, 43) and "humanly foolish, indeed sinful actions" (I, 99). God has not seen fit to couch His revelation in a form "which a Voltaire, a Bolingbroke, a Shaftesbury, would find acceptable, which would most nearly satisfy their prejudices, their wit, their moral, political, and magic whims" (I, 10). To speak in the rarefied language of these philosophers would be to ignore the needs of the "whole human race" including, ironically, the rationalistic philosophers themselves, who fail to recognize their own deepest spiritual needs. For Hamann does not subscribe to any form of the double-truth theory: spiritual truth does not require two forms, one for the philosopher, another for the masses. "To say that

Moses wrote only for the common people is either meaningless or a ridiculous view of the matter," he wrote in *Biblical Reflections* (I, 12).

Philosophically speaking, the "images" (Bilder) of natural language represent for Hamann "objects" (Gegenstände), which may be defined as uncritically perceived entities of ordinary experience, principally visual in nature. Abstract or discursive reason has the power, however, to eliminate such objects and to replace them with terms which actually stand for relations.[3] Therefore, he may say that "academic reason" (Schulvernunft) deals in "nothing but relations, which cannot be treated as absolutes . . . not things, but simply academic concepts, signs for understanding, not for admiring, aids in arousing and holding our attention" (G, 513). "Existence [i.e., concrete existence in a world of real objects] is realism," he wrote to Jacobi in 1787, "and must be believed; relations are idealism and rest upon connective and discriminatory procedures" (G, 507). In his indictment of the Kantian critical philosophy, he writes that metaphysics misuses "all the word-signs and figures of speech of our empirical knowledge" (III, 285) by transforming them into "nothing but hieroglyphs and types of ideal relations" (III, 385). In other words, the language of nature deals in the relations of objects, whereas abstract language deals only in the relations of relations, a procedure which can only result in "a violent divestiture of real objects, rendering them naked concepts and merely conceivable signs, pure appearances and phenomena" (III, 385).

Another fundamental aspect of imagery is, of course, its strong appeal to the emotions, a quality which is lacking in the case of abstract terminology. Our concern in this section has been to consider briefly the epistemological implications of Hamann's insistence that language robbed of its imagery is inauthentic. I shall return below to the subject of the affective aspect of natural language.

II   *Analogy (Analogie; Analogon)*

The second characteristic of Hamann's use of reason is his preference for *analogical*, as opposed to purely *logical*, thinking. Whereas the rationalist establishes a principle, whether deductively or inductively, and thereupon proceeds to draw inferences from it, the intuitive thinker establishes a model on nonrational grounds, as, for example, instinct or faith, and thereupon proceeds to draw parallels to the model. This latter procedure accords, in Hamann's view, with the proper use of reason, despite the fact that reasoning from analogy does not yield the certainty one might desire. Thus, he writes that "reason cannot grasp anything but analogies in order to obtain a very ambiguous light" (l, 302). We have already seen that he quite consciously adopted the analogical method at the beginning of the *Socratic Memorabilia*. Following the lead of Francis Bacon, Hamann maintains that man, in his original state, thought analogically rather than logically. This idea is clearly stated in the famous passage at the beginning of the *Aesthetica in nuce:* "Poetry is the mother-tongue of the human race; as gardening is older than agriculture; painting than writing; song than declamation; parables,— than deductions; barter,—than trade" (II, 197). Thus, Hamann places analogical thinking, as opposed to the later development of discursive thinking, within the framework of his general anthropology with its emphasis on man's retrograde development away from his primordial state. It is more natural for man to think in metaphors or parables (Gleichnisse), which involve analogical thinking, than to arrive at deductions (Schlüsse) based on rational principles. Early in his career Hamann wrote in *Biblical Reflections:* "All mortal creatures are able to see the truth and essence of things only in parables" (I, 112).

The fundamental importance of analogical thinking in Hamann's philosophy is underscored by the fact that it furnishes us with one of the few instances in which he felt it necessary to label his procedure with an abstract term, namely, "metaschematism." The word derives from a term used by the Apostle Paul in writing to the members of the church at Corinth exhorting them to cease from quarreling among themselves. But instead of addressing himself directly to their situation Paul draws an analogy between his relationship to his followers, on the one hand, and the relationship of Apollos to his followers on the other (I, Cor. 4:6). The Apostle uses a Greek word which is translated in the Revised Version as "transfer in a figure." From the Greek original Hamann created both the abstract noun "Metaschematismus" (II, 150) and the verb "metaschematisiren" (III, 144). For Hamann, to metaschematize means, then, to substitute one set of objective relationships for another, analogous set of subjective, personal, or existential relationships in order to throw some light on their meaning. One of the best examples of his use of metaschematism is the *Socratic Memorabilia*.[4] For in this treatise he adopts the role of Socrates, while assigning the role of Socrates's adversaries, the Sophists, to his own philosophical adversaries. Metaschematism is, of course, a form of indirect communication, a method which was subsequently to be made famous by Kierkegaard.

Still another way in which Hamann exploits the possibilities of analogical thinking is his use of typology. This ancient hermeneutical device is to be carefully distinguished from allegory. Whereas the latter clothes an abstract idea in concrete form, the former involves the establishment of a parallel or analogy between a given concrete historical event and another which succeeds it in time. In biblical hermeneutics this means the foreshadowing in the Old Testament of important events in the New: thus, the Paschal Lamb foreshadows the Sacrifice of Christ on the cross, or again Adam foreshadows the Christ. In his interpretation of Scripture Hamann uses this method consistently. However, he also sees in the events of his own life (as that of a typical believer) a sort of recapitulation of the history of the Jews, both collectively and individually (cf. II, 41). So enamored of this method is Hamann that he transfers it from sacred to profane history. Interesting instances of this procedure may be found in his *Socratic Memorabilia*, where Socrates is seen as foreshadowing the Christ, or the general public in the Athens of Socrates's day as foreshadowing the general public in eighteenth-century Germany. In fact, scattered throughout the essay are at least twelve typological themes.[5] Typology differs from metaschematism in always involving the historicity of the events which it connects. Further, metaschematism always involves the existential moment, whereas typological relationships may, or may not, do so.

Apart from typology and metaschematism, however, Hamann also recognizes the uses of analogical thinking in connection with *ideas* or *ideals* which may also anticipate the historical event. Thus he writes in *Golgotha and Scheblimini*:

Not only the whole history of Judaism was prophecy, but the spirit of that history occupied itself more than all other nations, to which one perhaps cannot deny the *analogon* of a similar obscure intimation and anticipation, with the ideal of a Savior and knight, a man of power and of miracle, a goel, whose origin according to the flesh should be from the tribe of Juda, his procession from on high, however, from the bosom of the Father (III, 311).

In this important Christological passage Hamann has doubly emphasized the term "analogon" by utilizing the Greek form and then italicizing it.

But it is not only these devices which characterize Hamann's variations of the analogical method; there are others which would merit closer attention if space permitted. We may note in passing, however, that an interesting and illuminating book has been written by Wilhelm Koepp, *The Magus and His Masks*.[6] The book deals with Hamann's tendency to adopt numerous suggestive and often provocative masks, as well as his habit of veiling his references to others. Since in each case the mask, while concealing an identity, reveals at the same time a particular quality of the person or thing masked, a likeness or analogy is therefore established between the mask and that which it conceals.

Although the abstract thinker is ready to admit that the appeal to analogy may yield genuine knowledge, he is quick to point out that "arguments from analogy are . . . precarious unless supported by considerations which can be established independently."[7] Such considerations are, of course, those which may be established on purely logical or empirical grounds, hence acceptable to the thoroughgoing rationalist. For Hamann, however, "the considerations which can be established independently" are those which are grounded in faith. Bolstered by Hume's insistence on faith or belief as the basis on which our propositions are ultimately grounded, Hamann maintains that the most certain kind of knowledge is that which derives from the revelation in nature, history, and Scripture, and he thereupon proceeds to draw analogies to the truths there revealed. It must be conceded that Hamann makes excessive use of the analogical method and that his philosophy would undoubtedly have profited by greater concession to discursive thinking and by a somewhat higher regard for academic reason or "Schulvernunft." On the other hand, it is interesting to note that recent philosophical thought is moving toward a higher evaluation of the analogical method even in the realm of pure science. In a recent work, Wilfrid Sellars argues, somewhat against Kant, that analogy is even more fruitful for modern science than it has been traditionally for theology, holding that it is "a powerful tool for resolving perennial problems in epistemology and metaphysics."[8] This would seem to constitute one more compelling reason why it is misleading to label Hamann an "irrationalist."

III   *Paradox (Widerspruch)*

An important aspect of Hamann's conception of reason as it
emerges from his use of language is his acceptance of the paradox as
a vehicle for the expression of spiritual truth. His reason for such a
positive view of the paradox is, in the last resort, theological. Since
God has condescended to reveal Himself in lowly, even contemptible form—as the Scriptures everywhere attest—the paradox
possesses the highest possible legitimation. "One must view with
astonishment," he writes in the *Biblical Reflections*, "how God
accomodates Himself to all small circumstances, and prefers to reveal His government through the everyday events of human life
rather than the singular and extraordinary events . . . (I, 36). Or
again:

What man would, like the Apostle Paul, venture to speak of the foolishness
of God, of the weakness of God. None but the Spirit which searches the
deep things of God would have disclosed this prophecy to us, the fulfillment
of which is evident in our own day more than ever: that not many wise after
the flesh, not many mighty, not many noble are called to the Kingdom of
Heaven, and that God willed to reveal His wisdom and power in that he
chose the foolish things of the world to confound the wise, that he chose the
weak things of the world to confound the things which are mighty, that he
chose what is low and despised in the world, even things that are not, to
bring to naught things that are . . . (1, 6, after I Corinthians 1:25–29).

The supreme paradox of Christianity is, to be sure, the incarnation
in Christ, the appearance of the Creator of heaven and earth in
Knechtsgestalt, in the form of a servant. Although the main source of
Hamann's emphasis on the paradox is certainly the biblical revelation, he is also conscious of carrying on the tradition of Luther in this
regard (cf. II, 247, 249). Later, Kierkegaard would draw strong
inspiration from Hamann's emphasis on the paradox of faith. As the
natural idiom of the spirit, paradoxical language stands in strong
contrast to logical discourse, which seeks to eliminate the paradox
entirely, and in so doing becomes in Hamann's eyes merely empty
discourse.

It is not only in the biblical revelation, however, that the
paradoxical nature of spiritual truth is manifested. In the *Socratic
Memorabilia* Hamann stresses, as we have seen, the principle that
the religiously inclined among the Greeks accepted the paradox as a

matter of course when they spoke of the gods, and that it was only the rationalists among them who rejected it. Since Hamann believed in the essential continuity of classical culture and Christianity,[9] it is not surprising that he found in its religion, at what he considered to be its healthiest stage, an anticipation of the Christian dialectical view of reality.

Hamann's insight into the paradoxical nature of ultimate reality was reinforced by his keen awareness of the contradictions within his own nature. Thus, at the beginning of his career he spoke of "the innumerable contradictions which we find in our own nature, and whose resolution is impossible for us" (1, 224), and many years later, only a few weeks before his death, he wrote to Jacobi: "To do what one hates, and having to hate what one does, and having to carry these contradictions about with oneself is a real cross to bear" (G, 657). At the same time, however, he realized that his was not a unique case: "Such contradictions [namely, the cross-currents of his own impulses] everyone experiences more or less in his own nature or in his fate . . ." (G, 1). Hamann's dialectical view of reality derives, then, not from a theoretical proposition, as for instance in the case of a Hegel, but from experience, both subjective and objective.

There is one important exception to Hamann's general refusal to appeal to a metaphysical principle, namely, the idea of *coincidentia oppositorum*. Stressing, as he did, the contradictory nature of experience and its reflection in the conceptual opposites with which the honest thinker is constantly confronted, it was but natural that he would require a principle by means of which the opposites might be reconciled. In 1782 he wrote to Herder: "Giordano Bruno's principle of the coincidence of opposites is in my opinion worth more than all Kantian criticism" (4, 462). A year earlier he had requested Herder's assistance in finding a copy of a work by Bruno in which he (erroneously) believed that the principle was treated, stating that the idea had been in his mind for some years.[10] Nicholas of Cusa rather than Giordano Bruno was the real formulater of the principle of the coincidence of opposites, but this fact was unknown to Hamann as well as to most of his contemporaries. Unlike Hegel, who sought to specify in what manner the contradictory elements of experience are reconciled, Hamann never departed from the conviction that such antitheses can only be reconciled in God, and hence the need for faith is not eliminated by his appeal to the principle.

IV   Multiple Levels of Language
(Einheit mit der Mannigfaltigkeit)

The fourth characteristic of intuitive reason is that it may produce multiple levels of language, whereas abstract reason may not. Again the biblical revelation is central, for the Hamannian conception of the authentic use of language was determined almost entirely by it. Just as Christ had assumed lowly human form, so had the Holy Spirit assumed in the Scriptures the lowly form of ordinary human language. "God an Author [Schriftsteller]!" he wrote in *Biblical Reflections*. "The inspiration of this book is just as great a humiliation and condescension of God as the creation was for the Father, and the Incarnation for the Son" (I, 5). From this standpoint it was natural that Hamann should repudiate the strictly rationalistic exegesis of scholars like Michaelis. In fact, the *Aesthetica in nuce* is principally an attack on Michaelis's method of biblical interpretation, which requires that all levels of meaning except the literal be rigidly excluded from biblical exegesis. Such an approach to the Scriptures leaves one, however, merely with "the dead body of the letter" (II, 203).

The British biblical critic George Benson (1699–1762), whose exegetical views were shared and disseminated in Germany by Michaelis, also came under Hamann's fire. In an essay on the unity of sense in the Scriptures Benson had written: "It appears to me that a critical interpreter of Holy Scripture should set out with this as a first principle; viz. that no text of Scripture has more than one meaning. *That one true sense* he should endeavor to find out as he would find out the sense of Homer or any other ancient writer."[11] Such a method of interpretation was in Hamann's eyes simply "exegetical materialism" (II, 239). As the passage cited from Benson clearly shows, the rationalistic exegetes allowed no room for a genuinely religious dimension of Scripture, since in their view, it had to be interpreted like any other piece of ancient literature, as, for example, the *Iliad* and the *Odyssey*. Further, the hermeneutics of Benson and Michaelis sets up an abstract norm in place of the rule of faith as the last court of appeal in biblical interpretation. Hamann was by no means ready to concede that even Homer, let alone the Bible, could be properly interpreted by means of Benson's "just rules of interpretation" (II, 203).

As we have already seen, Hamann's method of biblical interpretation is, generally speaking, typological, although it is on occasion allegorical. To what extent he accepted the traditional hermeneutical principle of the four-fold sense of Scripture, the literal, allegorical, moral, and anagogical, is debatable. Nevertheless, it is clear that both the literal and figurative or spiritual meanings are equally important for him. Therefore his objections to Michaelis's "materialistic exegesis" by no means imply an underrating of the literal sense of Scripture, but only dismay and indignation that Michaelis should deny the figurative, and therefore the spiritual, sense. The two meanings cannot be separated. Thus Hamann says of the Bible in a letter to his brother written in 1760: "The more the Christian recognizes that this book was written about himself, the more his zeal for the literal word grows . . ." (2, 9). By itself, however, the literal meaning is nothing. In a typically Hamannian thrust at the rationalistic exegetes he writes that "the external appearance of the letter is more like an ass's colt which has not been broken in" than "the proud steeds which caused disaster for Phaethon" (II, 171).

The rationalistic critics had repudiated the principle of the multiple sense of Scripture in the interest of preserving its unity. In the *Aesthetica in nuce*, however, Hamann poses the question "whether it is not possible for unity to exist along with multiplicity" (II, 203). He had, as a matter of fact, already answered this question to his own satisfaction a few years earlier, in the weeks just prior to writing the *Socratic Memorabilia*. In a letter to his friend J. G. Lindner, dated June 1, 1759, he reports that a remarkable passage in Augustine's *Confessions* has come to his attention wherein the great theologian speculates on why the scriptural revelation manifests different levels of meaning. The Magus does not quote the passage from the *Confessions*, but it is illuminating to examine Augustine's own words. Imagining himself in the place of Moses, with a commission to transmit God's message to man, he writes:

I should then, had I been at that time what he [Moses] was, and enjoined by Thee to write the book of Genesis, have wished that such a power of expression and such a method of arrangement should be given me, that they who cannot as yet understand how God creates might not reject the words as surpassing their powers; and they who are already able to do this, would find, in what true opinion soever they had by thought arrived at, that it was not passed over in the few words of Thy servant; and should another man by the light of truth have discovered another, neither should that fail to be found in these same words.[12]

So impressed with this doctrine was the young Hamann that he undertook in the essay on Socrates, as indeed in most of his later writings, to follow its precept. It suffices for our present purpose, however, simply to note that his idea of the multiple sense of "the language of nature" is quite basic to his thought, since it stems ultimately from his idea of deity.

V *Parataxis*

A fifth effect of Hamann's use of reason manifests itself in a technical but highly important aspect of language, namely, the tendency to produce parataxis as opposed to hypotaxis. Paratactic sentences are characterized by brevity and the absence of long, involved dependent clauses; the word order tends to be natural or to follow an elementary logic in that the subject and predicate are expressed at or near the beginning of the sentence with the other elements following generally in the order of their importance. Aphorisms, epigrams, etc., because of their laconic nature, are necessarily paratactic in structure. Hypotactic sentences, on the other hand, are characterized by greater length, involving , as they do, longer dependent clauses (or, their equivalent in German, the so-called long attribute); the word order tends toward a certain artificiality in that the full disclosure of the meaning of the sentence may be suspended until the end. Because of its frequent use of dependent clauses, hypotaxis involves the *subordination* of certain elements within a sentence, whereas parataxis involves their *coordination*. Historically, parataxis is associated with Senecan or "Silver Age" Latin prose, hypotaxis with Ciceronian or "Golden Age" Latin prose.

Growing to maturity in the mid-eighteenth century, Hamann was heir to the so-called *Kanzleistil* or Chancery Style, a wooden—and peculiarly German—imitation of the style of Cicero. The fact is that he never completely abandoned the Chancery Style. Since it has been customary to describe him as an "aphoristic" writer, and to cite him along with Lichtenberg, Nietzsche, and others, as a prime example of that literary species, a clarification is in order. For the question arises as to how he could be both a practitioner of the Chancery Style and a master of aphoristic prose.

In order to answer this question one must recognize that both styles do occur in Hamann's writings, and, while the Chancery Style precedes the looser Senecan type prose, he never really abandons it but returns to it on a number of occasions even in his later writings. A study of the works in which the two styles occur reveals that in his most characteristic and influential writings, such as the *Socratic Memorabilia* and especially the *Aesthetica in nuce*, the aphoristic mode dominates, more consistently, however, in the latter. It is precisely in these works that we find him employing intuitive, as opposed to abstract, reason since all the other criteria for determining its use are present. When he does enter the lists against the abstract thinkers, however, he is quite capable of arguing to a great extent on their own terms, as, for example, against Moses Mendelssohn in *Golgotha and Scheblimini!* (1784) and against Kant in the *Metacritique of the Purism of Reason* (1784). Despite the fact that Hegel considered the former to be Hamann's most important writing, and despite the growing appreciation of the cogent argument he employs against Kant in the latter, one scarcely considers the prose of these works as examples of Hamann's best or most characteristic style. It is in writings such as these, however, that his recourse to abstract reason most clearly manifests itself. Here is also evidence that, while he was primarily an intuitive thinker, he also shows considerable power when he does turn to the abstract mode. One must conclude with Eric Blackall, however, that Hamann "tended towards the aphorism as his natural means of expression."[13] His use of the Chancery Style was, therefore not natural, but an acquired manner, into which he fell when he had recourse—as he did on occasion—to an abstract mode of thought.

VI   *Affective Terminology (Donner der Beredsamkeit, der einsylbichte Blitz)*

Perhaps the most obvious of all the earmarks of intuitive reason is its affinity with the affective or emotional elements which characterize ordinary language, and which are present to a heightened degree in poetic language. As I have already noted, discursive reasoning effectively eliminates this aspect of language and therefore robs it of its natural richness. Thus against the philosophers who adopted the point of view of Newtonian physics, Hamann wrote:

O for a muse like the fire of the goldsmiths and like the soap of the fullers!—She will dare to cleanse the natural use of the senses from the

unnatural use of abstractions, by which our concepts of things are as muti-
lated as the name of the Creator is suppressed and blasphemed. . . . Behold! the great and small Masorah of wordly wisdom has flooded the text of
nature like a deluge. Was it not inevitable that all its riches come to naught?
(II, 207)

Natural language, whether the everyday vernacular or its transmu-
tation into genuine poetry, addresses itself to the whole man, to
feeling as well as to intellect, for "nature works through senses and
emotions. How may anyone who mutilates her instruments be capable of feeling?" (II, 206). Language divested of its affective appeal
cannot stir the heart or the imagination: "Emotion alone gives to
abstractions as well as to hypotheses hands, feet, wings;—to images
and signs spirit, life, and tongue.—Where are swifter deductions?
Where is the pealing thunder of eloquence produced, and its companion—monosyllabic lightning" (II, 208). The basic reason that
language must not be robbed of its capacity to appeal to the affective
and poetic side of man's nature is that God Himself, "the Poet at the
beginning of days," has chosen to speak to man in the vernacular
and in poetry, as the Scriptures abundantly testify. Here, as we saw
in the case of the imagistic nature of ordinary language, the reason
for Hamann's view is fundamentally theological.

The emasculation of language is not only a by-product of the
abstract world-view of the physicists and philosophers who would
adopt their method, but it is also a result of the deliberate effort of
the prescriptive grammarians and indeed of all rationalistic arbiters
of language (see Chapter 7).

VII   Conclusion

Although Hamann does not subsume all the characteristics of his
use of reason under the head of *anschauende Vernunft* or indeed of
any other definitive term, it is clear that in the case of each of the
characteristics save one he has provided us with both a general
principle and an abundance of examples illustrating the principle.
Since perceptive thinkers from Immanuel Kant to Georg Lukács[14]
have recognized that Hamann was not an irrationalist, but that, on
the contrary, reason plays an important role in his philosophy, however different it may be from the one it customarily plays in the case
of more abstract thinkers. A superficial analysis of Hamann's prose

may result in the conclusion that its all too frequent obscurity is rooted in sheer irrationalism. This is, however, by no means the case. Its obscurity derives for the most part from an excessive use of intuitive reason rather than from true irrationalism—quite a different matter.

Having seen to what extent Hamann is committed to intuitive or analogical reasoning, while at the same time rejecting the abstractions of the *Aufklärer*, we can more readily understand why he alternates between praise and vilification in his references to *Vernunft*. Thus, when he makes such statements as: "Faith has need of reason just as much as reason needs faith" (G, 504); "without language we would have no reason, without reason no religion . . . (3, 231); "as soon as one knows what reason is, all conflict with revelation ceases" (G, 406), he is obviously referring to what he considers the legitimate use of reason. Or again when he speaks of the "the most natural use of reason" (II, 190), which the rationalists have transformed into "Schulvernunft" with disastrous results, he patently has in mind his own use of reason. On the other hand, the long series of pejorative epithets which he scornfully applies to "exalted reason" (III, 225), are aimed not only at the philosophical pretensions of the *Aufklärer* but also at their official, therefore privileged, position in the Prussia of Frederick II, indeed at the king himself. Having now examined the principal evidence for the ambivalence in his concept of reason, we are in a better position to understand how he could write the following lines to his friend Jacobi in 1787:

Reason is the source of all truth and of all errors. It is the tree of knowledge of good and evil. Therefore, both parties are right and wrong which deify it and which vilify it. Faith, likewise, is the source of unbelief and of superstition. "Out of the same mouth proceed blessing and cursing" (G, 513).

Three decades earlier Hamann had written to another friend, J. G. Lindner, lines which summarize effectively the conception of reason to which he adhered throughout his career: "We make deductions as poets, as orators and as philosophers. The former are often closer to reason than those in the logical form. When the heart declares itself, our understanding is mere rationalization (klügeln, 1, 201). These lines are by no means the typical romantic assertion of the priority of blind emotion over intellect, but are to be taken quite literally as the most concentrated summation possible of the Hamannian conception of reason.

After recognizing that Hamann's use of reason is quite different from that of more orthodox thinkers, one must still come to terms with the fact that there are general tendencies of his thought which bespeak underlying, hidden assumptions which, if spelled out, are revealed to be quite abstract. A striking illustration of this fact is his idea of language, which, if full justice were done to it, would require a whole new metalanguage for its precise exposition. Perhaps the most important of all the underlying principles of his philosophy, and one which he is quite willing to acknowledge, is, as we have seen, the metaphysical principle of the coincidence of opposites. But Hamann's general aversion to giving abstract formulation to his ideas cannot be considered simply perverse. For his purpose was to avoid what he held to be the arbitrariness, the mendacity, the arrogance, and the dehumanization which he believed invariably accompany the tendency to abstraction in philosophy, with its resulting unfortunate effects radiating out into all areas of human existence.

It is clear from the foregoing that there exists a close parallel between the operation of the Hamannian "intuitive" reason and the operation of what today would be called "unconscious mind." It would, however, be quite misleading to psychologize his thought at this point. For not only was he keenly aware of the existence of the unconscious aspect of mind—which he describes as "that monstrous hole, that monstrous, murky abyss"—but explicitly warns against dealing *directly* with it: "Not that I have any doubts," he wrote to Jacobi, "about the depths of human nature, but to explore those chasms or to communicate to others such visions is hazardous" (G, 6). It is the central characteristic of his approach that he equates the "depth" (die Tiefe) of the human psyche with the depths to be found in the poetic view of the universe as crystallized in genuine poetry, definitively, of course, in the Scriptures. Thus instead of gazing *directly* into the "subterranean" recesses of his own psyche, he views them *indirectly* as reflected in the mirror of the Scriptures (cf. esp. I, 75–76). This shift from pure introspection to a consideration of the given facts of the "mirror" means a shift from subjectivity to objectivity, and is a fact of primary importance for an understanding of his philosophy. Hamann's concern was consistently epistemological, namely, to discover the conditions of intuitive knowledge. Since there is no thought apart from language, such conditions have to be sought in language. It is obvious that Hamann's thought, despite definite parallels with depth-*psychology*, is chiefly concerned with depth-*epistemology*. Perhaps nowhere is his thinking in this regard more succinctly summarized than in a letter to Jacobi written about a year before his death:

The truth must be dug out of the earth, and not drawn from the air, from artificial words [Kunstwörtern], but must be brought to light from earthly and subterranean objects by means of metaphors and parables, which cannot be *direct* but only *reflected rays* . . . .[15] Besides the principle of cognition ("principio cognoscendi") there is no special principle of being ("principium essendi") for us. In this sense, *cogito, ergo sum* is true (G, 497).

Thus Hamann indicates how genuine access to the unconscious, or in his terminology, "subterranean," mind may be gained, namely, by the proper use of language. The implications of this idea are far reaching not only for his own thought but also for the philosophy of the *Sturm und Drang* in general as well as for the later development of Romanticism.

CHAPTER 6

The Style Is the Man

WHOEVER deals with Hamann's thought must perforce come to terms with the difficult but fascinating subject of his style. Whether or not it is true, as Salmony maintains, that "no work in the German language is as difficult to understand as every one of the writings of Hamann,"[1] certainly there is no German *Klassiker* whose prose style is more opaque than that of his formal writings. Yet such a statement must be immediately qualified by a recognition of the fact that scattered throughout his generally obscure prose are many succinct, epigrammatic, and very quotable expressions. The existence of numerous anthologies and other collections of his sayings is proof enough of that. Further, it is true that Hamann's letters are by no means as difficult to understand as his formal writings. Nevertheless, the forbidding aspect of the body of his prose remains.

As Goethe wrote in *Dichtung und Wahrheit*, the Hamannian writings are characterized by

a sort of double light, which appears to us highly agreeable; only one must completely renounce what is ordinarily called understanding. Such leaves merit to be called sybilline, for this reason, that one cannot consider them in and for themselves, but must wait for an opportunity to seek refuge with their oracles. Every time that one opens them one fancies one has found something new, because the sense which abides in every passage touches and excites us in a curious manner.[2]

These words are an excellent characterization of Hamann's style, but like all such generalizations they require some qualification, which, it is hoped, the present study will provide. Hegel, who was obviously fascinated with the Hamannian writings, nevertheless speaks of them as "an enigma, indeed an exhausting one."[3] But one does not need to invoke the authority of Goethe, Kant, or Hegel to

100

recognize the extraordinary difficulty of deciphering Hamann's meaning. Except for the aphorisms, which may be more or less extended, one invariably needs a commentary to make sense of Hamann's formal writings.

Generally speaking, it is Hamann's practice to compress as much meaning as possible into a word, phrase, or sentence. "I have written according to the strictest natural law of economy . . ." he writes in the *Monologue of an Author (Selbstgespräch eines Autors,* III, 73). As Kierkegaard says in the *Concluding Unscientific Postscript:* "With all his life and soul, to the last drop of blood, he [Hamann] is concentrated in a single word. . . ."[4] Concentration is quite often attained, however, by omitting the conceptual link between sentences. Although Hamann's style is quintessentially aphoristic, we have already noted the fact that in some of his writings he reverts to the "Ciceronian" style which had predominated in his youth.[5]

In the preceding chapter we have seen the effects produced upon language by reason operating within the limits which Hamann considered legitimate. In that case language was employed as the prismatic medium by means of which the chief characteristics of intuitive reason might be detected. For the present purpose the matter is reversed. We are now in a position to see that Hamann's style flows inevitably from his conception of reason. It is true that he exploits the possibilities inherent in his approach to an unheard-of degree, thereby causing difficulties for himself and his readers. At the same time, it is true that the perennial fascination and challenge of his style for many commentators stem from the same source. In the present chapter we can do no more than consider certain aspects of Hamann's style which are well adapted to reveal its singularity.

Since God has not simply revealed Himself to the Jews and Christians but in some measure to all men, Hamann can write

that godly men did exist among the heathen, and that we should not despise the cloud of these witnesses, that heaven has anointed them as its messengers and interpreters, and consecrated them to precisely that vocation among their people which the prophets had among the Jews (II, 64).

It is thus Hamann's recognition of "the cloud of these witnesses" who have existed, and indeed continue to exist, apart from the biblical revelation that forms the basis for his extraordinary concern with secular history. Here are the roots of his famous (or notorious)

polyhistorical allusions, and it is this concern, we may note in passing, which makes him a foremost critic of culture in the eighteenth
century.

One of Hamann's favorite ideas is that an individual may "preach
the truth even in jest and without his knowledge and intention,"
even though he be the greatest skeptic like the philosopher Hume
(1, 380; cf. 356). As a result of this conception, Hamann's writings
become interlarded with the most unexpected and often astonishing
parallels and comparisons drawn from secular as well as sacred history. Although he is ready to draw his parallels and illustrations from
all periods of the past and even from the present, the great majority
are drawn from classical literature and history. In fact, one of the
most striking things about the Magus is his profound concern with
and knowledge of Greek and Roman literature.

The fact that Hamann lived at a time when the opponents of
Christianity often invoked the classical poets and philosophers to
discredit that faith was another important reason for his strategy of
turning their own weapons against them. One must concede that
there was also an element of pride, of the display of erudition, at the
root of the matter. But to recognize the presence of these motives is
by no means to impugn the basic Hamannian principle that the
divine revelation was not limited to the Word as revealed in the
Scriptures and incarnated in Christ. As greatly as he treasured the
classics, however, there could be no question but that they must
always be subordinate to the sacred literature of the Hebrews.
Hence he inveighs against the undiluted philhellenism of Winckelmann and Lessing in the *Aesthetica in nuce*.[6]

Hamann was always concerned with the format, the physical
makeup, of his publications, and as a result gave detailed, often
eccentric, instructions to his printers. Of primary importance to him
was the title page. "For me," he wrote to Jacobi, "the title is not
simply a sign to hang out, but the *nucleus in nuce*, the mustard seed
of the whole growth" (G, 137–38). On another occasion he speaks of
the title as "a microcosmic seed, an Orphic egg" (III, 373). This
does not mean, however, that the title is so conceived and expressed
that the content of the pages which follow can be readily inferred
from it. For the most part, Hamann's titles, in fact, pose a riddle and
thus from the very beginning he challenges the reader. In speaking
of the title of a work he actually had in mind the entire title page,
including the title proper, subtitle, mottoes, dedications, place of

publication, publisher and date, in short, any material appearing on the face of the page (he also often records a motto or quotation on the back of the page).

Since the titles of his works were of such extraordinary importance to Hamann, it will not be amiss to observe certain of their characteristic features. We shall also find that they do in fact afford a special insight into his use of language. It is, however, the entire material appearing on the title page in addition to the title proper which is of particular interest. First, it is illuminating to note the type of motto which he adopts for his writings, for he rarely fails to inscribe on the title pages one or more quotations intended to serve as mottoes. An examination of the title pages of twenty-three of his works (including all the major formal publications and some minor works as well as a few posthumously published ones) reveals the following distribution: twenty-five classical quotations (some works containing none, some more than one); of these, eleven are from Horace, four from Persius, two from Virgil and Cicero respectively, one from each of the following, Apuleius, Juvenal, Petronius, and Manilius—all in the original Latin. There are two Greek quotations, namely, from Aristophanes and Pindar. Although quotations from the Bible serving as mottoes appear thirteen times on the title pages examined, only four of them are in German, the remainder being in Latin and Greek, with one in Hebrew.[7]

It is evident that with such a generous use of classical references, and even in the use of the scriptural quotations where they are cited in the original language or in Latin, Hamann is "metaschematizing," for he is thereby adapting himself to the literary taste or scholarly interests of his readers. Obviously Hamann was not addressing himself to the unlearned multitude in these instances, but to those whom Friedrich Schleiermacher was later to call the "cultured despisers" of Christianity. Yet the metaschematism of the title pages is more than normally complex, for it turns out that even if the reader understands the motto quite well, he is most often at a loss to understand why it is cited: frequently the quotation appears to have no connection with the title proper or with the other material on the page. True, there are a few whose appropriateness is immediately obvious, but by far the greater number appear to be at one time mere persiflage, at another a riddle, and at still another simply an offense to good taste.

One should not suppose that we are here dealing simply with a stylistic matter, as important as the question of Hamann's style is in itself, for he played an important role in the development of modern literary German.[8] The truth is that we have here in symbolic form the most important clue to an understanding of how Hamann absorbed and related the classical heritage to his faith. Perhaps not since the Patristic age has a Christian thinker dealt so extensively and earnestly with the heritage of Greece and Rome. Certainly none of the early Church Fathers was in a position to deal as sympathetically with that heritage, for the threat to the fledgling church posed by the state and vested hostile religious interests was still too real and too powerful in their day for a sympathetic appreciation of the elements common to both Christianity and Hellenic-Roman religion. Further, in the age of the Renaissance and the Baroque, classical culture was understood as more of an adornment and enhancement of the faith than as being somehow related to its very essence.

A word should be said about the biblical quotations which appear on the title pages of Hamann's works. Of the thirteen scriptural verses occurring there only three are found in major publications; five quotations are in the Latin of the Vulgate, three in the Greek of the New Testament, and one in Hebrew. Thus Hamann, an apologist for the Christian faith, is here most sparing of biblical allusions, and when a verse from the Bible is cited, it is rarely clothed in the straightforward vernacular of Luther but in translations which only the learned could read. In citing the Greek and Hebrew texts Hamann is manifesting his positive attitude toward the accomplishments of the biblical scholarship of the Renaissance, and simultaneously addressing himself to a scholarly audience.

One will find, of course, in the texts of Hamann's works themselves an overabundance of quotations from the classics, from the Bible, from contemporary writers, indeed from all imaginable sources. Some quotations are literal, others paraphrases, still others are veiled allusions, many of which he himself could not clear up after the passage of time (4, 202). His art of quotation is a large and difficult subject, and one on which a great deal of work remains to be done. However, if we are to take him at his word, we will not go far astray in assuming that, like the overture to a Wagnerian opera, Hamann's title pages announce the important motifs of what is to follow, and give us a hint of the way in which they are related to one another. For the true author, Hamann believed, "the superscription of his work [the title] is at the same time the signing of his name" (III, 372). There are, to be sure, other eccentricities appearing on Hamann's title pages, such as the grotesque head of Pan adorning the *Crusades of the Philologist* and the *Essais à la Mosaïque:* the absurd localities sometimes alleged as the places of publication, e.g., "à Bedlam"; "à Tyburn Road"; "La Bourse d'Amsterdam"; in other case simply remote or foreign cities, if indeed the place of publication is specified at all, e.g., "Thorn!"; "Halle"; "Pisa"; "Altona"; "Amsterdam" (the latter practice an understandable one in view of the prevailing censorship).

Hamann's own name is never printed on the title page. On one occasion he uses his sobriquet "Magus of the North." Otherwise the following expressions appear instead of his name: "A Lover of Boredom") "The Philolgist"; "Aristobulus"; "Most Learned German-Frenchman"; "Abaelardus Virbius"; "A Fifty-Year-Old Clergyman in Swabia"; "A Prodigal Son of the Albertina" (Königsberg University); "Savage of the North"; "A Reader, Who Has No Desire to Become a Critic or Writer"; "Knight of the Rose-Cross"; "Christianus Zacchaeus Telonarcha"; "Vettius Epagathus"; "One Crying in the Wilderness"; "Pelican of the Wilderness." Particularly striking about the pseudonyms or "masks" which Hamann adopts is the fact that even the few that are of classical provenance bear scarcely any relation to the type of classical pseudonym so popular in certain circles in the eighteenth century. Each of Hamann's pseudonymous expressions would, of course, have to be considered specifically in its own context for a full understanding of its import. Nevertheless, it is possible to generalize that, even when they have an obviously religious import, they are characterized by the peculiarly Hamannian wit or irony.

An important feature of Hamann's style is his use of the cento. So pervasive and important is this characteristic that Arthur Henkel refers to his manner in general as an "abbreviated cento-style."[9] The term "cento," the Latin word for patchwork, is an appropriate one for a literary composition made up by collecting passages from various works. The use of this literary device is an old tradition in the religious and moral literature of the West. For instance, the Byzantine empress, Eudoxia, following a widespread practice of late antiquity, composed a cento on the life of Christ and several other biblical subjects entirely from verses gleaned from Homer. In addition to Homer, Euripides and Virgil were also mined for images, figures of speech, segments of verse, and sometimes even whole verses to recount biblical narratives or to express a spiritual or moral truth. As late as 1634, one Alexander Ross, chaplain to Charles I of England, wrote a work entitled *Evangelizing Virgil, or the History of Our Lord Jesus Christ Described with the Words and Verses of Virgil.*

In adopting the cento style Hamann is thus renewing an age-old Christian tradition. But his use of the method is radically different from the traditional practice in works of the type mentioned, for such compositions, however ingenious, do no more than present familiar subject matter in a new form. Hamann, on the other hand, employs the device to create, as it were, a dialogue between individuals often remote from each other in time, place, and philosophical or the theological orientation. Here again we see how tradition and contemporaneity, the past and the present, are often creatively interwoven in Hamann's writings. Thus, the cento is involved in the *substance* of Hamann's discourse as well as in its *form.* It should also be noted that the cento style often affords him an opportunity for a virtuoso display of wit and irony, especially when citing his adversaries. Since the words of another may often be used against him, obviously the cento style is closely allied to metaschematism.

The frequent use of the cento becomes, of course, one of the chief reasons for the difficulty of Hamann's prose, for it presupposes familiarity on the part of the reader with the material which the author is "mining." Since modern readers are no longer as familiar with classical literature—and in many instances with the Bible—as were the cultivated readers of the eighteenth century, and since Hamann had the habit of citing writers often obscure even to his contemporaries, it is obvious that, if the modern reader wishes to understand more than the apothegms encountered here and there, a commentary is absolutely necessary. Any careful commentary on Hamann's works will render quite graphic the extent to which even a short passage may bristle with expressions borrowed from other sources, but which nevertheless form just as integral a part of the whole as the individual pieces which make up a mosaic.

A highly characteristic feature of Hamann's style is his employment of the traditional rhetorical devices of antonomasia and periphrasis. His use of antonomasia, that is, an epithet or another noun in place of a proper name or a class of persons, is often conventional, as when he refers to Christ as "The Galilean" or to an Aristotelian as "A Peripatetic." More often, however, he creates original antonomastic expressions, which may, if the context is clear, be quite intelligible. In the writings concerning Frederick the Great, for instance, Hamann's use of antonomasia is a virtuoso performance, for there the meaning of almost every epithet or "mask" is clear enough, and, taken together, they yield a masterfully limned portrait of the king as Hamann saw him (see Chapter 9). Unfortunately, the reference of many of his antonomastic expressions elsewhere is by no means so clear. Hamann's original and masterful use of language is nowhere better illustrated than in his use of periphrasis, which involves the substitution of a whole phrase, sometimes quite long, for a proper name or a class of persons. A number of the pseudonymous phrases on the title pages of his works are periphrastic, as we have seen above. Elsewhere, we read that Louis XIV was "a monarch . . . whose name became the name of a whole century" (II, 62); in a long and complex example Peter the Great becomes "the Scythian . . . who traveled in the interest of his trade, and, like Noah or the Galilean of the schemer Julian, became a carpenter in order to be the god of his people" (II, 62); Lessing is referred to on one occasion as "a *petit-maître* of the seven unprofitable arts" (II, 100).

That Hamann consciously utilized various traditional rhetorical devices of classical literature has been amply demonstrated by recent research. As one commentator has said, his style is "hermetic, learned, rhetorical, ironic, and is in the fullest meaning of the word, traditional: it presupposes a tradition, it appeals to it, and can only be understood on the basis of it."[10] Such a description of Hamann's style contains an element of exaggeration, since it fails to account for its uniqueness, but it nevertheless has the virtue of calling attention to a fact which has largely been overlooked, and may therefore serve as a corrective to those who regard his formulations as the result of his inability to express his thoughts in simpler, more conventional fashion.

In the previous chapter we noted that two important aspects of Hamann's style, metaschematism and typology, necessarily involve analogical thinking. But with regard to the two literary devices, antonomasia and periphrasis, which we have just examined, such is not the case, for unless metaphor is present in the first instance, and simile in the second, we are dealing with logical, not analogical, reasoning. Thus, when Hamann speaks of Jesus as "The Galilean" he is using a generic term which could be used by the most rigorous logician, but when he refers to Frederick the Great as "The White Bull," the term is based on the analogy which Hamann would draw between Zeus's abduction of Europa in the form of a bull and Frederick's rape of Europe. Both terms are antonomastic, but the former is essentially logical, the latter metaphorical, hence analogical. On the other hand, the closeness of periphrasis to purely logical thinking may be underscored by reference to Bertrand Russell's "theory of descriptions,"[11] according to which the descriptions are simply more abstract and rigorously logical versions of the type of metaphorical periphrases or descriptions that Hamann employs. Since both antonomasia and periphrasis are thus not confined to purely analogical thinking, they have been considered here along with the other peculiarities of Hamann's style which actually tend more toward abstract than toward intuitive reasoning.

Another characteristic of Hamann's attitude toward language which accords more with rationalistic than intuitive thinking is his espousal of a principle consciously modeled on the procedure of experimental science. Thus in seeking the meaning of the Delphic pronouncement "Know thyself" in its relation to Socrates he writes:

A careful interpreter must imitate the natural scientists. Just as the latter place a body in all sorts of arbitrary combinations with other bodies, and devise artificial experiences in order to determine its properties, so the former does with his text . . . (II, 71).

It is obvious that the experimental combination of words in order to derive new meanings is quite a different matter from the expression in as many ways as possible of a truth or principle already firmly established. Normally Hamann's procedure calls, as we have seen, for the exploitation of all the resources of language in order to witness to a firmly held truth. In the present instance, however, he endorses a procedure of empirical science which appears to be at odds with his basic principle. On account of this aspect of Hamann's stylistic procedure one commentator has referred to his "chemical style"![12]

It must not be assumed, however, that Hamann's combinative procedure is always as serious as the cited passage would suggest. For there is unquestionably an element of playfulness at the bottom of it. Hence, even in the period when the *Socratic Memorabilia* was gestating in his mind he could write to his friend J. G. Lindner: "There are people who play with ideas just as I play with words" (l, 34). Undoubtedly this aspect of his style has led to the observation that deciphering his writings is often like working a crossword puzzle. In the attempt to understand the complex phenomenon that was Hamann it is important to bear in mind that, along with his dead seriousness in matters of faith, there is a lighter side in what one might call his philological play. We see this in the frequent occurrence of *Stilbruch,* which often involves a mixture of the sublime and the ludicrous or the offensive. We have seen that Hamann's *Stilbruch* involves, after the model of the Scriptures, a mixture of the sublime and the lowly. What is not scriptural, but purely Hamannian, however, is his juxtaposition of the sublime with the ludicrous or the crude and obscene. It was this side of his nature which caused offense to his Pietistic admirers, who thereby revealed the gulf which existed between his conception of Christianity and theirs. On the other hand, it was this aspect of Hamann's faith which caused Kierkegaard to refer to him as "the greatest humorist in Christianity."[13]

As we have seen, Hamann inaugurated his career as a writer firmly committed to the notion that the proper vehicle for the expression of his thoughts was the multidimensional, concentrated language of the type found preeminently in the Bible. Rejecting the Enlightenment idea of a language whose chief characteristic is the clarity which springs from strict conformity to rational norms as espoused in literature by Gottsched (or Mendelssohn and Lessing) and in religious matters by Christian Wolff or Michaelis, he wrote to Lindner: " . . . if I could think and record my thoughts in ever so orderly a way, ever so rationally and conclusively, God grant me the grace to divest myself of such ability as far as possible" (1, 344). A few weeks later he wrote to Kant: "In my mimic style there prevail stricter logic and closer connections than in the concepts of more lively minds" (1, 378).

But in contrast to these defenses of his style he regrets, especially later in life, his singular mode of writing. "I have accustomed myself to a manner of writing which neither pleases me nor is natural," he wrote in 1780.[14] Some years later he wrote to Jacobi that it was his "firm intention and desire to write differently, in a more composed manner and more clearly," adding the lament that he is too old to change his ways.[15] It is thus clear that, in certain moods, Hamann deplored the style for which he had become famous. Yet he was certainly in error when he asserted, as he did on several occasions, that he had adopted a manner which was alien to his nature. To be sure, whether any style of writing is second nature for a given individual is an open question. What is certain, however, is that, having, as a young man, cast his lot on the side of religious faith and intuitive reason (unlike, say, Thomas Aquinas, who cast his lot on the side of religious faith and discursive reasoning), it was inevitable that he would become an aphoristic thinker, and that his style would, in spite of certain inconsistencies, manifest the general characteristics which it does. That he intensified those characteristics to an unheard-of degree constitutes of course the essentially Hamannian element in the amalgam which his style represents.

This conclusion is confirmed by his own statement in endorsement of Buffon's principle that "the style is the man." In a footnote to a German translation of Buffon he remarks apropos of this dictum that "the vitality of one's style depends on the individuality of one's concepts and passion . . ." (IV, 424). Or again, in the first *Clover-Leaf of Hellenistic Letters*, discussing the nature of the Koine of the New Testament in relation to classical Greek, he writes: "Every mode of thought which becomes fashionable, every imperceptible modulation of the passions colors the expression of our concepts" (II, 170). Since a primary characteristic of intuitive reason is its affinity for the affective side of human nature, it is not surprising to find Hamann's prose often serving as the vehicle of strong pathos. "I am not one," he wrote to J. F. Reichardt in 1778, "to demonstrate truths and lies *ad oculum et unguem* [with great exactitude]. With me it is a matter of tempests whose roaring one hears without being able to see them otherwise than in their effects and which prevail in the air without one's being able to discern their configuration, their beginning and end" (4, 2).

Hamann's remarks concerning the kind of order found in nature and in the Bible may with equal justice be applied to his own writings:

We find in the Bible precisely the orderly disorder [regelmässige Unordnung] which we find in nature. All [abstract] methods are to be regarded as the go-carts of reason and as its crutches. The imaginative power of the poets possesses a thread which is invisible to the common eye, but which appears as a masterpiece to those who understand. All hidden art appears to the common eye as nature. The Scriptures are in this matter the greatest model and the finest touchstone of all human criticism (I, 229–30; cf. 243).

If Hamann's oxymoron, "orderly disorder," be applied to his own writings, we find that the aspect of "disorder" (Unordnung) derives from his rejection of rational method—according to which the parts may be said to relate clearly to the whole and always to each other. On the other hand, we find that the "orderly" (regelmässige) aspect derives from his use of *anschauende Vernunft,* according to which the parts may be said to relate clearly to the whole but not always to each other.[16] We have seen that it is necessary to exert oneself considerably to discover the "hidden art" in Hamann's prose, for the surface appearance manifests often the same aspect to the "common eye" as the apparent chaos of nature. The order is there, but it is rarely easy to descry at first glance.

One may generalize about the style of Hamann's formal writings to the effect that he is a profound philosopher who has chosen to express his most abstract thoughts in poetic or metaphorical language rather than in abstract or literal language. Just as the content of poetry is inseparable from its form, so is the content of the Hamannian writings inseparable from its singular, often eccentric form. This is why Hegel could quite aptly say: "Hamann's writings do not *have* a characteristic style so much as they *are* style through and through."[17] Unger also emphasizes that in Hamann's writings "content and form, conceptual subject matter and stylistic representation, spirit and form" are uncommonly fused (U, I, 482). Certainly this fusion is due to the poetic nature of his prose. Gerhard Nebel goes so far as to say that there is more poetry on any page of Hamann's than in the entire corpus of Lessing's works.[18] But it is precisely Hamann's consistency in undertaking to express abstract conceptions metaphorically which makes him more difficult to understand than, for instance, Plato or Nietzsche. To create our own metaphor here, we may say that his meaning lies deeper beneath the surface than that of other philosophers who share his poetic feeling—often, one feels, deeper than necessary.

CHAPTER 7

Language and the Spirit of Man

THE fact that Hamann was not a systematic philosopher does not mean that his philosophy lacks coherence. For despite the centrifugal effect of his widely ranging interests and polyhistory, his abiding concern with language provides the center around which his thought revolves. It should be borne in mind that the term "language" (Sprache) has, however, three distinct meanings for Hamann: (1) language proper—a historically developed vernacular such as Latin, French, German, etc., or such languages collectively; (2) language as one of the three essential "capacities" or "constituents" (Bestandtheile, III, 231) of the human mind; and (3) the divine revelation, the Logos in time and space. In the present chapter we shall consider how Hamann relates language in the first sense to his conception of genius, revelation, and individual freedom.

We have already seen that for Hamann certain facts of ordinary language are crucial. In the *Aesthetica in nuce* the imagery and metaphors of a vernacular are, particularly when raised to the level of poetry, a reflection of the Logos. But whenever they are replaced by abstract terminology and purely literal language, they negate an essential aspect of the medium in which God has chosen to speak to man. If, as Bertrand Russell asserts, it was characteristic of Leibniz to draw "inferences from syntax to the real world,"[1] the same may be asserted of Hamann, with the qualification that Leibniz was primarily interested in the mathematico-logical aspect of language, which of course Hamann was not.

One of Hamann's early essays may be taken as typical of his procedure, namely, *Miscellaneous Notes on Word Order in the French Language*. Though published independently two years earlier, it was included in the *Crusades of the Philologist* in 1762. If one were to conclude from the title—as he very well might—that the essay is simply a dry-as-dust treatment of one aspect of French grammar, he would be quite misled. Instead he will find that, although the author does indeed deal briefly with the subject of the title, the real import of the essay is quite different. Characteristically, Hamann's name as author is missing from the title page; instead he states that the work was "thrown together (zusammengeworfen) with patriotic freedom by a learned German-Frenchman." On the back of the title page Hamann printed the illustration which was to cause so much consternation and dismay among his Pietistic admirers: a woodcut of a rooster, with a musical score in its claws, leading two cockerels in the singing of church music (II, 128).

Hamann was aroused to write the essay by the publication of a work entitled *Master and Servant* (1759) by Friedrich Karl von Moser.[2] Moser, first minister of the landgraviate of Hessen-Darmstadt, was, despite his sincere Pietism, an advocate of the enlightened despotism of rulers like Joseph II and Catherine the Great. His book is greatly indebted to the political thought of the French Enlightenment, especially the ideas of Montesquieu. Therefore, Hamann was quite correct in asserting that it was "partly spun out of French silk" (II, 135). It was the "French silk" in the work which provoked Hamann to criticize its author, who was, nevertheless, later to become his ardent admirer, and who was to bestow on him the epithet "Magus of the North."[3] The latter indicated on the very title page of his essay that he had Moser in mind in composing the work, since he had borrowed the phrase "with patriotic freedom" verbatim from the title-page of Moser's book.

Miscellaneous Notes is also especially interesting because of the analogy which the author draws between language and money. In the opening lines he writes:

Money and language are two objects whose investigation is as profound and abstract as their use is universal. Both stand in a closer relationship [to each other] than one might presume. The theory of the one explains the theory of the other; therefore they seem to flow from common sources. The wealth of all human knowledge rests on the exchange of words; and it was a theologian of keen wit[4] who declared theology—this oldest sister of the higher sciences—to be a grammar of the language of Holy Scriptures. On the other hand, all the goods of civil or social life have reference to money as their universal standard . . . (II, 129).

Subsequently Hamann refers to philologists and rhetoricians as "bankers of the republic of letters" (II, 130).

In addition to the analogies mentioned above, however, there is still another way in which the worlds of money and of language resemble each other. When Hamann asserts that "the theory of the one explains the theory of the other," we are not to conclude that men are in fact capable of arriving at viable theories in either case. On the contrary, when they convince themselves that they have, they fall into grievous error. By way of illustration he cites the case of "the famous stockbroker," John Law, who "had studied money as a philosopher and a statesman," but who, despite his great ability, foundered in the end (II, 130). Hamann reminds us, however, with not a little irony, that most merchants are not John Laws, i.e., they pay little attention to theory, a fact which is fortunate for them and for society in general (II, 130). These references to the world of finance are, of course, intended to illuminate the nature of language. For language, like money, is so constituted that men subject it to theoretically concocted rules at their own peril.

After initially discussing the parallel between money and language, Hamann abruptly turns to the grammatical subject announced in the title, word order in the French language. The German language, he argues, is like Latin in providing greater freedom in word order, and this is the case, because German has preserved the case-endings which make such flexibility possible. Because of the complete lack of case-endings and therefore of declensions in French, however, that language lacks the freedom which the German rule of inversions allows. The closer a language is related to the character of a people, the more freedom it will allow in its syntax (II, 131). The fact that French is more rigid than German or Latin Hamann obviously ascribes to the (historically conditioned) inclination of the French to rationalism, hence their penchant for rules. But slavish obedience to rules robs a language of its pristine power.

Returning, at the end of the essay, to the parallel between money and language, Hamann writes concerning the French Academy:

The purity of a language diminishes its riches; a too strict correctness diminishes its strength and manhood. In as large a city as Paris are foregathered annually, without expense, forty learned men who know infallibly what is pure and decent in their mother-tongue and what is necessary for the monopoly of this second-hand trade. Once, however, in centuries it happens that a gift of Pallas—a human image—falls from heaven, empowered to rule the public treasury of a language with wisdom—like a Sully, or to increase it—like a Colbert (II, 136).

In the passage cited Hamann again uses metaphors and expressions from the area of finance: "riches"; "without expense"; "monopoly"; "second-hand trade"; "public treasury." Instead of naming literary geniuses as examples of the "gift of Pallas," he mentions, with obvious admiration, two financial geniuses of the *ancien régime* in France, Maximilien de Béthune Sully and Jean Baptiste Colbert. It is worth noting that Hamann's examples here reveal to what extent his earlier interest in political economy retained its hold on him.

As in the *Socratic Memorabilia*, the emphasis is, however, on the freedom of genius from abstract rules. In this connection Hamann makes it clear that he believes all languages to be equally capable of responding to the touch of genius. Refuting Rousseau's claim that the characteristics of the French language preclude the attainment of excellence in music, Hamann writes: "The deficiencies, however, which are laid to the charge of a language always derive from the incapacity of an author or a composer in the choice of his material and in the manner of treating it" (II, 135). In the *Essay on an Academic Question* he makes his position on this point even clearer: "There must exist similarities among all human languages, which are based on the uniformity of our nature, and similarities which are necessary in the smaller spheres of society" (II, 121–22).

The *Clover-Leaf of Hellenistic Letters*, begun in 1759 and completed in 1760, was published for the first time in the *Crusades of the Philologist*. It is a defense of the Koine of the New Testament, the version of the Greek language used throughout Greece and the Near East from the time of Alexander to that of Justinian. It was written in the period immediately following publication of the Socratic essay when Hamann was pursuing Greek, Hebrew, and Arabic studies, and is directed at biblical scholars like G. D. Kypke, Albert Schultens, and Michaelis. It is, however, chiefly Michaelis's *Criticism of the Means Employed to Understand the Extinct Hebrew Language* (1757),[5] which draws Hamann's fire here as in the *Aesthetica in nuce*. If in *Miscellaneous Notes* he had restricted himself to the secular plane, in the *Clover-Leaf of Hellenistic Letters* the religious aspect is evident.

In countering the views of those who considered Koine a debased language and therefore unworthy to be considered the vehicle of divine revelation, Hamann writes in the first *Hellenistic Letter*:

> The dispute over the language and style of the New Testament is not entirely unknown to me. I doubt therefore that philology alone will suffice to resolve contradictory opinions. One must not only know what good Greek is, but what language in general is, not only what the eloquence of the classical author is, but what style in general is. Philosophical insights on both subjects are rare. The lack of general principles, however, is usually responsible for academic feuds (II, 169).

It is inevitable, he argues, that a language adopted as an international medium of communication will undergo changes in different localities and among different peoples:

> French is as common in our day as Greek was formerly. How could it fail to degenerate in Berlin and London just as Greek was spoken imperfectly in Jewish lands, especially in Galilee? (II, 172).

Critics had charged that Koine was a hybrid language, mixing Hebrew and Roman elements with the Greek. But for Hamann this fact speaks *for* rather than *against* the trustworthiness of the books of the New Testament, for it is precisely their style that is "the most authentic proof of the authorship, time, and place of these books" (II, 170). After all, the superscription on the cross on which Christ was crucified was written in Greek, Hebrew, and Latin, thus accurately reflecting the makeup of the populace of Judaea. Hamann astutely turns the tables on the critics of the hybrid nature of Koine by stressing that, in the last resort, it is the Hebrew element which gives religious vitality to the language:

> Every mode of thought which becomes somewhat fashionable, every imperceptible transition of the emotions colors the expression of our concepts. . . . Enter any congregation of Christians you will, the language of the sanctuary will betray their fatherland and genealogy, that they are heathen branches grafted *para phusin* [against nature] onto a Jewish stem. The more edifying the speaker is, the more his Galilean shibboleth is discernible to the ear. . . . In short, the Oriental element in our pulpit style leads us back to the cradle of our race and religion, so that one should not take offense at the aesthetic taste of some Christian spokesmen (II, 170).

In addition to the purely rational arguments which Hamann adduces
in defense of Koine in the New Testament, he introduces a theological justification, again appealing to the idea of divine condescension:

It belongs to the unity of the divine revelation that the Spirit of God
humbled itself and divested itself of its majesty in inspiring the writings of
the holy men who were moved by the Spirit just as the Son of God appearing in the form of a servant [Knechtsgestalt] and the whole creation is a
work of the greatest humility. . . . If therefore it is the divine style to
choose the foolish, the commonplace, the ignoble in order to put to shame
the strength and ingenuity of all profane writers, it requires the illuminated
and inspired eye of a friend, of an intimate, of a lover armed with jealousy,
to recognize through such a disguise the radiance of heavenly glory (II,
171).

Hamann thereupon reminds his readers of the words of Paul, that
we have the treasure of revelation in earthen vessels,[6] and that the
power of the Word comes from God, not from its outward form. For
"the external appearance of the letter is more like an ass's colt which
has not been broken in than those proud steeds which caused the
disaster of Phaethon" (II, 171). In his defense of the language of the
New Testament Hamann has revealed two of its dimensions, the
one historical, the other spiritual: on the purely historical plane it
leads us back in time to "the cradle of our race and our religion"; on
the spiritual plane, and therefore outside time, it leads upward to
God. These two aspects of the revelation cannot, of course, be
separated, as attested above all by the Incarnation or *Knechtgestalt
Christi*.

   If the first *Hellenistic Letter* is a defense of the language in which
the revelation is cast, the second is primarily a statement of how it
should be read, for God speaks through the past, through history, to
us in the present:

Sagacity and *vis divinandi* [the power of prophecy] are almost as necessary
for reading the past as for the future. Just as one begins the New Testament
in school with the Gospel of John, so the historians are regarded as the
easiest writers. But can one know the past if one does not understand the
present? And who will have proper ideas of the present without knowing
the future? The future determines the present, and the present determines
the past, just as purpose determines the nature and use of any means we
employ. Nevertheless, we are accustomed here to a *hysteron proteron* in
our manner of thinking (II, 175).

Thus, we cannot simply turn to historical records and, with the aid of reason or common sense, properly interpret them. If we try to do so, history remains a closed book for us. When, however, we know in advance the end toward which all events are moving according to the divine purpose, we can reason from such a purpose to the present, and from the present, in turn, to the past. This of course is the method of biblical prophecy, but Hamann holds it to be the proper method of any meaningful interpretation of history.

Taking such an eschatological view of history means that the historian is no longer dealing with a skeleton. In a vein reminiscent of his remarks on historiography in the Socratic essay, Hamann writes:

I would sooner regard anatomy as a key to *gnothi seauthon* [know thyself!] than to seek the art of living and governing in our historical skeletons, as I was taught to do in my youth. The field of history has always seemed to me like that wide field which was full of bones—and behold! they were very dry. No one but a prophet can prophesy of these bones that veins and flesh will grow upon them and that skin will cover them. There will be no breath in them until the prophet prophesies to the wind, and the word of the Lord speaks to the wind (II, 176).

Hamann concedes that poetry can aid us in understanding the present, for after all poetry speaks to the whole man, and not merely to his intellect. Insofar as it does this it is "helpful in a synthetic way." By "synthetic" here he apparently means a combining of the elements which make up the total response of the human being to present experience. At the same time he maintains that philosophy is "helpful in an analytic way" in understanding present experience (II, 176). Further, he warns that those who look to ancient literature alone for wisdom concerning the past will find it lacking: "Perhaps the ancients bear the same relation to nature as the scholiasts do to their author, Whoever studies the ancients without knowing nature is reading the notes without the text . . ." (II, 177). Hence, poetry, philosophy, the study of ancient literature combined with a knowledge of nature are all helpful in their way, but only the *vis divinandi* can bring the dry bones of history to life. We may say that in Hamann's prophetic view of history time's arrow is reversed: it flies from the future through the present to the past, thus from the end of time to the beginning of time.

In the third *Hellenistic Letter* Hamann returns to the more strictly philological concerns of the first. Although he leaves open the question how much light is actually shed on biblical studies by men like Schultens and Michaelis, he also makes it quite clear that they will never speak the final word concerning its meaning. Addressing such exegetes he charges: "You do not understand the Scriptures or the power of God, neither its inspiration nor its interpretation, which is not dependent on philosophical reasons" (II, 182). Even though the Hebrew language be as dead as the womb of Sarah, it can still be as miraculously fruitful as that wife of the patriarch when past the age of childbearing (II, 182–83).

Although Hamann's attitude toward Michaelis is somewhat ambivalent, in the end the Göttingen biblicist becomes his main adversary here as elsewhere:

> With all the merits of this author I find a fundamental error in his earliest and most recent writings which I have read up till now. . . . It has to do with his whole manner of thought so that it is just as impossible for me to point it out as it would have been for one to point to the field of Jezreel and say: "This is Jezebel" (II, 179).

Here the Magus is referring to the fate of Jezebel as recorded in the Old Testament, who, after being hurled from the window of her palace, was run over by the chariot of her enemy Jehu, and thereupon eaten by dogs. When the order to bury her was given, the remaining parts of her body were found to be scattered across the field of Jezreel.[7] Hamann does not equate Michaelis with Jezebel, the fanatical worshiper of Baal and slayer of prophets, but the import of his reference to her in connection with Michaelis's scholarly activity is not lost on the reader.

Perhaps the most significant aspect of the *Clover-Leaf of Hellenistic Letters* is the tension it manifests between the claims of reason as expressed in rigorous philological procedure, on the one hand, and the claims of faith, on the other. True, faith is "not dependent on philosophical reasons" in the final analysis, but, as we have seen, Hamann takes such reasons quite seriously, and seeks as far as possible to refute them on rational or "philosophical" grounds. The manner in which he does this—reasoning from the historical context of Koine and from the internal evidence of its mixed nature; his partial acceptance of the necessity of studying Arabic as the sister-language of Hebrew for light on the biblical text; his stress on the necessity of a knowledge of nature as an aid to an understanding of the classics—all of this reveals him to be to a great extent also a child of the Enlightenment, not simply its adversary.

We now turn to a writing of the second period of Hamann's literary productivity entitled *New Apology of the Letter h, or Extraordinary Reflections on the Orthography of the Germans* (1773). This work is not only the best sustained example of Hamann's irony and humor but is at the same time remarkable for its combination of micrological detail with the broadest of metaphysical principles. Nowhere else has Hamann so successfully balanced so weighty a topic on so narrow a base. The occasion for its composition was the publication of a work by one Christian Tobias Damm entitled *Reflections on Religion* (1773), in which the author takes occasion to inveigh against the retention of the silent h in German orthography, an orthographic detail which had become a "stumbling-block" for him. He suggests that only audible sounds be written, and blames the existence of the silent h on the arbitrariness of the chancelleries. Damm was an unimaginative disciple of Wolff, and Hamann would doubtless have ignored his book, had he not seen the opportunity afforded by the author's ideas on spelling for yet another, albeit different, sally against his old foe, programmatic rationalism (III, 91). So delighted was Kant with *The New Apology* that he expressed the hope that Hamann would continue to write in this vein.

The work is divided into two parts: the first is a defense of the silent letter h, allegedly by a Königsberg schoolmaster named Heinrich Schröder, whose initials "H.S." appear on the title page along with the (fictitious) place of publication, Pisa; the second part represents the letter h as speaking "with a human voice" in order to reproach the "transgressions" of presumptuous orthographers like Damm (III, 105). In censuring the aspiration of the rationalists to become the magisterial arbiters of what is right and wrong in language, Hamann is adopting the same position we have observed earlier with regard to the nature of language as a guide to the nature of reality, but with an added dimension.

Damm boasts that he was always concerned with the "most stringent clarity of thought," asserting that he "would have nothing to do with any proposition whose reasonableness was not apparent" (III, 91). From this lofty intellectual position he launches his crusade against the lowly aspirate, the letter h, which Hamann calls "an innocent breath that some ponderers on language have not even

wanted to recognize as a letter of the alphabet" (III, 92). Damm
justifies his undertaking with a remark worthy of Molière's Alceste:
"Whoever is not faithful in the orthography of the small letter h is
unfaithful and unjust in the great revelations and mysteries of universal, sound, and practical human religion."[8] Further, he alleges
that the German use of the silent h was a "disgraceful habit," which
appeared "barbaric" in the eyes of all foreigners (III, 91). The unin-
tended humor in these exaggerations was of course an open invitation to satire, and Hamann accepted it readily.

The Magus thereupon proceeds to demolish Damm's arguments,
first on purely rational grounds. He charges the author with incon-
sistency in not arguing against *all* silent letters, and further maintains that pronunciation cannot be the sole guide to spelling (III,
94). Moreover, he accuses Damm of indulging in bad child psychology (III, 97). But the most important arguments against the orthographic reformer are specifically Hamannian. The Magus argues that
Damm's ideas would result in the castration or perversion of language (III, 97); that the demand for "a universal, sound practical
human language, reason and religion without arbitrary principles" is
"a baking-oven of ice,"—a sheer impossibility (here Hamann adopts
Damm's own expression against him);[9] that the rationalist is incon-
sistent in so far as he opposes tradition, since his kind of rationalism
is based and dependent on tradition (III, 107). Moreover, the clear
implication of such programmatic rationalism is that the right of the
individual, whether a mere letter of the alphabet or an individual
human being, to exist *qua* individual is denied.

It is not, however, the logical or philosophical arguments in *The
New Apology* which are most significant but the indictment uttered
by the letter h itself, for here Hamann seizes the opportunity which
such personification offers to assert that the least of created things, a
mere breath, is the effective sign and seal of God's invisible working
in the world:

You little prophets of Böhmisch Breda![10] Do not be amazed that I speak
to you with a human voice like that dumb beast of burden [Balaam's ass] to
punish your transgression. Your life is what I am—a breath. Do not think
that I will grovel before you, whine for my preservation or lament being
completely banished or extirpated from your writings . . . . My existence
and preservation is the affair of Him who bears all things with His powerful
word, and who has sworn and said: "Till heaven and earth pass away neither
the smallest letter or tittle will pass."

You little prophets of Böhmisch Breda! I see that in all things you are too superstitious. The God who is invisible, and therefore unknown to you, is indeed the Father of reason and religion, which are, however, spirit and truth, and therefore these are just as much of a mystery to your perceptions as the God who is invisible, and therefore unknown to you (III, 105)

Continuing in this vein, Hamann charges his rationalistic adversaries, "the little prophets of Böhmisch Breda," with the substitution of an abstract term like "universal human reason" for God, that is, an artificial construct, which thereupon becomes the object of their "reflections and devotions" (III, 106). Further, it is from the mouth of the personified letter h that Hamann taunts his adversaries with ignorance of what he considered the most basic of metaphysical principles: "Is the famous principle of *coincidentia oppositorum* completely unknown to you? It is the spirit which gives life; the letter is flesh, and your dictionaries are straw" (III, 107).

In defending the silent letter h Hamann has made it into a symbol for (1) the individual human being and (2) the invisible but life-giving spirit of God. He conceived of the natural development of language as paralleling the activity of the spirit in that both lie well beyond the control of man. One may imagine that the spirit is subject to rational control, but it is not. In *Two Small Contributions to the Most Recent German Literature* (1780),[11] in which he was to resume the attack against the language reformers (this time even against the otherwise so venerated Klopstock, who had joined their ranks) he makes it clear that they are, wittingly or not, in the service of those who would tyrannize over the spirits of men.[12] In his keen awareness of the potentialities of language as an instrument of political and cultural oppression Hamann was a forerunner of men like George Orwell.

CHAPTER 8

The Dignity of Man

IT is in the controversy with Herder over the origin of language that Hamann's ideal of human dignity emerges. In order to understand his idea, therefore, it will be necessary to trace briefly the main outlines of the dispute which arose as a result of the publication of Herder's prize-winning *Treatise on the Origin of Language* (1772).[1] Hamann would doubtless never have concerned himself with the problem, had he not been aroused to do so by the appearance of Herder's work. Stemming as it did from his close friend and, in many ways, faithful disciple, the essay inevitably aroused the Magus to a vigorous and well-reasoned rebuttal. One could not, of course, declare either side the victor in the encounter, for the premises on which their arguments are based are quite dissimilar.[2] What does emerge from the dispute, however, is a deeper understanding of the thought of both men, and thereby a clearer understanding of the gulf between Hamann's thought and the first stirrings of German idealism, of which Herder's essay is a noteworthy harbinger. Here, however, we are primarily interested in the light which it throws on the Hamannian notion of human worth or dignity.

Herder composed his treatise in response to a question posed by the Berlin Academy in the competition for 1769, but the events leading up to its formulation are significant. In 1754 Pierre Moreau de Maupertuis, the president of the academy, famous as a mathematician, geographer, and as formulator of the principle of least action in physics, had given a lecture in which he conceived of language as a tool which man had invented for practical purposes. In his argument he made no mention of the "higher hypothesis," i.e., that God had created language, but simply took its purely human origin for granted. His thoroughly pragmatic and secular approach aroused a German member of the academy to counter Maupertuis's thesis with the argument that language was imparted directly to man by Deity. Although a Lutheran theologian, Johann Peter Süssmilch approached his subject in a thoroughly rationalistic way. In essence, he maintains that, since language is perfectly orderly and rational, it was necessary for a rational being to have created it. But, since reason is dependent upon the prior possession of language, the only way out of the dilemma is to assume divine intervention. However far apart their premises and conclusions, both Maupertuis and Süssmilch argue their case on strictly rationalistic grounds.

As a result of the bitterness within its ranks which the debate between Maupertuis and Süssmilch had engendered, the academy decided on a topic for the prize essay for 1759 which was so framed as to avoid the question of the origin of language,[3] namely, the reciprocal influence of language and opinions. The prize-winning essay was submitted by Michaelis, which in turn elicited from Hamann the "Essay on an Academic Question" (1760). In that "Essay" Hamann scores the ambiguity in the key words of the prize topic, and in general is more critical of the academy than of Michaelis, a criticism which will be considerably heightened in the case of Herder's treatise.

A decade later the Berlin Academy resumed the topic of the origin of language, offering as a prize question: "Supposing that men are abandoned to their natural faculties, are they in a position to invent language? And by what means might they arrive at this invention by themselves?" Herder, who had long been interested in the subject, immediately felt that the topic was made to order for him, and hurriedly composed his *Treatise on the Origin of Language* in December 1770 in Strassburg, sharing its freshly written pages with the young Goethe.[4]

It is Herder's thesis that "while still an animal, man already has language."[5] This animal language or, as Herder calls it, "language of nature"[6] (quite different from Hamann's use of the same term!) is designed to express feeling—passion, joy, pain, distress, etc.—and not to represent or depict. It can never become, as Herder believed Condillac to have held, the basis for human language. The human being, however, is characterized by a capacity which Herder calls "reflection" (Besonnenheit), which is not a special faculty, separate from man's other powers, but an organization of all of them, "a disposition of his nature."[7] Human language arises when man, confronted with "the vast ocean of sensations," singles out, by means of reflection, one wave, concentrates on it, and is at the same time conscious of doing so.[8] Herder then uses the example of a man singling out the bleating of the sheep as its "distinguishing mark" (Merkmal).[9] With such a distinguishing mark the name of the sheep is established. (For Herder, the sense of hearing is primary, for so much of nature "sounds.") "The first distinguishing mark, a result of reflection, was a word of the soul. With it human language was invented."[10] It is illuminating to note that Herder *interiorizes* the whole process: "The hermit living alone in the forest would have had to invent language for himself, even if he had never spoken it. It was an agreement of his soul with itself. . . ."[11] Thus reflection has a dual function for Herder: (1) it organizes the forces of the human psyche or "soul", and (2) represents the outer world inwardly. In such a way the subject-object dualism is overcome by the absorption of the object into the subject. It was this complete interiorization of the process which led Hamann to impute Platonism to Herder's theory.[12]

Hamann's disappointment with Herder's essay was all the greater, since he had a few months earlier, in a review of an inferior work on the same subject by Dietrich Tiedemann,[13] expressed the hope that Herder's forthcoming work would give "more substance and pleasure in investigations of this sort" (III, 16). When Herder's treatise did appear, the attack proceeded slowly, at first with an anonymous review in the *Königsbergsche Gelehrte und Politische Zeitungen* (1772). It consists chiefly of quotations from Herder's essay, interlarded with Hamann's own comments and an ironical use of Herder's own words. Herder, for example, speaks of his "disobedience" in answering the question posed by the academy. By this he means that he had not offered an hypothesis, as required, but had instead "collected firm data from the human soul" and had demonstrated his thesis to be "the strictest philosophical truth."[14] In Hamann's eyes Herder was being "disobedient" to the truth to write in the spirit of the Berlin Academy at all. That Herder did not violate that spirit is indicated by the fact that his deviation from a strict construction of the question was in the end deemed a "merit" by the academy (III, 17). Hamann sees in Herder's refutation of the higher hypothesis simply a glorification ("apotheosis") of the autonomous human being (III, 18). Finally, he expresses the hope that a compatriot—by which he means himself—will come forward later

to express his "doubts and oracle" concerning the whole matter,
even though the defense of the higher hypothesis in his day is
comparable to the "avenging" of Dulcinea by Don Quixote (III, 19).
(At the time of the Herder-controversy Hamann's style was much
influenced by Cervantes and Rabelais.) At the very end of the review Hamann takes an unexpected tack by asserting that even the
"new Babel" (Berlin Academy) draws its strength from language,
but that it will eventually suffer "dissolution and destruction" for its
abuse of language, reducing it to abstract "systems" (III, 19). What
is now a cloud no bigger than a man's hand will become a storm of
indictment in the end, not only of the academy, but also of the king
himself.

Hamann's first review was followed in the next year by an essay
with the curious title, *The Last Will and Testament of the Knight of
the Rose-Cross concerning the Divine and Human Origin of Language*,[15] and a second review appearing under the pseudonym
"Aristobulus," which purported to "dispose of" the first negative
review, but which in reality took back none of its substantive criticism. In it Hamann parodies contemporary hypotheses concerning
the origin of language by utilizing, tongue in cheek, the Cartesian
method of reasoning to eliminate all the possible ways in which
language could be acquired except by "animal instruction" (III, 29).
Thus he "disposes of" the ideas expressed in the first review. This
second review was intended to reassure Herder of Hamann's continuing friendship and esteem. Two further works, which form a
unit, were also composed in the same year, but were not published
during Hamann's lifetime because of the highly explosive content of
the second part. The first part, *Philological Ideas and Doubts about
an Academic Prize-Essay*, is written in German, and the second, *To
the Solomon of Prussia*, in French.

It cannot be my task in the present chapter to go into any detail
concerning Hamann's criticism of Herder's ideas on the origin of
language. I shall, however, trace the major outlines of what is
perhaps the most important aspect of Hamann's thought to emerge
in the course of the controversy: his concept of human dignity
(Würde). In the opening lines of the *Knight of the Rose-Cross*
Hamann opposes to Herder's anthropocentric theorizing a solemn
religious declaration. He cites again the first words of the Horatian
ode with which he began the *Aesthetica:* "Fauete linguis!" (Observe
a religious silence), and thereupon continues:

If one presupposes God to be the origin of all effects, whether great or small, in heaven or on earth, every numbered hair of our head is just as divine as the Behemoth, that beginning of God's ways. The spirit of the Mosaic laws extends, therefore, even to the most disgusting secretions of the human corpse. Consequently everything is divine, and the question of the origin of evil amounts only to word-play and academic chatter. Everything divine, however, is also human, because man can neither act nor suffer otherwise than according to the analogy of his nature, however simple or complicated a machine it is. This *communicatio* of divine and human *idiomatum* is a basic law and the master-key to all our knowledge and the whole visible economy (III, 27).

Hamann had placed on the title page a motto from the Latin Bible: "I believed, therefore have I spoken" (2 Cor. 4:13). With these words he underscores the fact that, unlike the members of the academy who framed the prize question, he does not believe that one can approach the subject of the origin of language without presuppositions, and that he is quite ready to acknowledge his own at the outset. At the same time he is obviously indicating Herder, albeit indirectly, for accommodating himself to the thinking of the skeptical Enlighteners, who, though presupposing a mechanistic philosophy and thinking strictly in terms of physical causation (III, 29), nevertheless pretend to presuppositionless thinking. The very word "invent" in the prize question, he argues, is evidence of the scientific bias of the academicians. To the dilemma posed by the assumption that language must have either a divine or human origin, Hamann opposes the traditional Christian doctrine of the *communicatio idiomatum,* which was formulated to describe the relation of the two natures of Christ.

It is clear that Herder's idea of the invention of language by means of "reflection" (Besonnenheit) is at the opposite pole from Hamann's as we have seen it explicated in the *Aesthetica.* But it is in the *Knight of the Rose-Cross* that Hamann directly counters Herder's theory by a positive statement:

Adam was, therefore, God's, and God himself introduced the first-born and oldest of our race as the vassal and heir of the world which was created by the word of his mouth. . . . Every phenomenon of nature was a word— the sign, symbol, and pledge of a new, inexpressible, but all the more intimate union, communication, and community of divine energy and ideas. Everything that man heard in the beginning, saw with his eyes, contemplated, and his hands touched was a living word, for God was the Word. With this word in his mouth and in his heart, the origin of language was as natural, as near, and as easy as child's play (III, 32).

Herder had stressed the primacy of the sense of hearing in language,[16] and Hamann, too, accords it first place in the above statement: "everything that man heard. . ., saw. . ., contemplated . . . touched. . . ." Despite the central significance of the book metaphor in the *Aesthetica,* Hamann always conceived of God as a speaking God, for even in that work he quotes the paradoxical saying: "Speak, that I may see you!" adding: "This wish was fulfilled by the creation, which is speech to the creature through the creature. . ." (II, 198).

For Herder the human psyche or "soul" (Seele) is the real creator of the word; for Hamann, on the contrary, "every phenomenon of nature *was* a word . . . intimate union, communication of divine energy and ideas" (my italics). In other words, Herder's theory of the origin of language firmly establishes man's autonomy, whereas Hamann's biblically derived theory establishes man's heteronomy. Hamann's paradox that the origin of language involves the *communicatio idiomatum* or intimate togetherness of the divine and human elements in the language process is paralleled by the paradox that man is described as both "vassal" and "heir" of the created world. Normally these terms are mutually exclusive, for it was contrary to feudal custom for the vassal to become the heir of his liege-lord. Thus the *Knight of the Rose-Cross* foreshadows the unequivocal statements of the dignity of man which we will encounter in *Philological Ideas and Doubts.*

Herder maintains that man differs from the animals "not in degrees of more or less, but in kind."[17] To this Hamann responds:

Man not only has his life in common with the animals, but resembles them more or less, that is, in degrees in their organization as well as in their mechanism. The main difference must therefore have to do with their manner of life . . . [Lebensart]. I presume therefore that the true character of our nature consists in the judicial [richterlich] and the magisterial [obrigkeitlich] dignity of a political animal, and that consequently man bears the same relation to the animals as the prince does to his subjects. This dignity, now, like all posts of honor, presupposes no worthiness or merit of our nature, but is, like our nature itself, a direct gift of grace from the Giver of All Things. No hero or poet, whether he be a type of the Messiah or a prophet of the Antichrist, lacks a period in his life when he has ample justification to confess with David: "I am a worm and no man" (III, 37–38; cf. Psalm 22:6).

Thus Hamann shifts the whole question from the biological to the social or, as he expresses it, the "political" sphere, and draws important conclusions from that position.

In speaking of the "judicial and magisterial dignity of a political animal" (elsewhere "judicial" is replaced by "critical"[18]), Hamann is invoking with some irony but more seriousness both Aristotelian and biblical thought at the same time. With regard to the latter he has in mind God's charge to Adam and Eve: "Be fruitful and multiply, and replenish the earth, and subdue it (Gen. 1:28). In the *Knight of the Rose-Cross* he had given a poetic account, in the form of a biblical cento, of God speaking to Adam and Eve concerning "the development of their political destiny to populate the earth and to rule over it through the word of their mouth" (III, 31).

It was no doubt Herder's mention of the relationship of man to the animals at the beginning of his treatise that led Hamann to draw the ironic analogy that man bears the same relationship to the animals as the prince does to his subjects. Here again he shifts the emphasis from the biological to the "political" level, and thereby challenges us to cease thinking, for the time being, of animals in biological terms. Herder had assumed a physical or biological *discontinuity* between man and the animals; Hamann, on the other hand, citing Aristotle as his authority,[19] maintains biological *continuity*, but argues for social *discontinuity*, for a difference in "the manner of life." The prince, as ruler of his people, necessarily manifests the same social discontinuity with his subjects as man normally does with the animals. Hamann then proceeds to make the crucial statement that what characterizes man as man is his "judicial (or critical) and magisterial dignity." This dignity is, however, not innate, but is a gift of God to those who respond to the revelation through faith, and indeed may be forfeited; as it had been forfeited in Hamann's own time. Thus, while exculpating somewhat Herder's "accommodation" to the spirit of the age,[20] he charges it with "critical and magisterial weakness," hence with a lack of true worth or dignity (III, 50). For all its pretense of being "a moral century" it lacks the foundation for genuine morality.

Human dignity involves for Hamann both freedom and responsibility:

> Without the freedom to be evil, there is no merit, and without the freedom to be good, no imputation of personal guilt, indeed there is even no knowledge of good and evil. Freedom is the maximum and minimum of all our natural powers and the basic motivation and ultimate purpose of its whole direction, development, and return.[21] Therefore neither instinct nor sound reason governs the human being; neither natural law or international law governs the prince. Each is his own lawgiver, but at the same time the first-born and neighbor of his subjects. Without the perfect law of freedom man would not at all be capable of any imitation, upon which all education and invention depend, for man is by nature the greatest pantomimist among the animals. Consciousness, attention, abstraction, and even moral conscience seem for the most part to be energies of our freedom (III, 38).

The preceding passage is essentially Hamann's answer to Herder's idea of "Besonnenheit." Herder had contrasted animal instinct with the freedom which, according to his theory, is made possible through reflection.[22] But human freedom, Hamann replies, is not to be understood in terms of Herder's categories, but rather in terms of good and evil, namely, ethical categories. Each man is his own lawgiver in the sense that he is free to act morally or not, just as the prince is not really constrained by any externally imposed law. All men, whether subject or prince, stand in a dual relationship to their fellow man both as a superior ("first-born") or equal ("neighbor"), a paradoxical relationship resolved only by faith. All culture ("education and invention") depends on imitation, which comes naturally to man, but man has to be free to choose what and how he will imitate. Finally, the attributes of mind necessary for intellection ("consciousness, attention, abstraction") are products of human freedom; to this list, which is so far in agreement with Herder's conception, Hamann adds yet another attribute which, in our present context, is the most important of all: "moral conscience."

In an often-quoted statement Hamann complains that "the philosophers have always given truth a bill of divorcement in that they have separated that which nature has joined together and vice versa. . . ."[23] In Herder's theory of the origin of language those things which nature has separated—the five senses—have been joined together to create artificially "a single positive power or entelechy of the soul."[24] In order to give his readers "a comprehensible notion of the fullness in unity of our human nature," i.e., an idea of the complexity of human relationships which cannot be separated, he offers in an extended metaphorical statement "several distinguishing, earthly characteristics" (Merkmale):

> Man is not only a living field, but also a son of the field, and not only field and seed (according to the system of materialists and idealists), but also king of the field for the cultivation of good seed and hostile weeds; for what is a field without seed and a prince without a country and revenues? These three in us are therefore one, namely, *theou georgion* [God's husbandry],[25] just as three spectres on the wall are the natural shadow of a single body, which has a double light behind it (III, 40).

The mixture of metaphors is, of course, intentional and is actually an apt vehicle for the expression of the close-knit complexity of discrete relationships. As "a living field," man is cultivated, i.e., determined to a great extent by external experience; but, paradoxically, he is also a "son of the field," that is, the product or fruit of the cultivated field. Again, he is a "field" insofar as he, in turn, is fruitful, and "seed" insofar as he contains within himself that which ultimately flowers or bears fruit. Hamann parenthetically indicates that the metaphor "field" represents the "system of the materialists" and the metaphor "seed," the system of the idealists. Man is also "king of the field," i.e., he is posessor of the "critical and magisterial dignity of a political animal," whose duty it is to rule over his dominion. Further, he is "to cultivate good seed and hostile weeds," i.e., to rule wisely and fairly over the good and the bad in society. His dominion necessarily includes territory and revenues, the former representing that which is fixed, and the latter that which, as indicated by the word "seed," is capable of growth. The three relationships represented figuratively are held together in a concrete, living union, and cannot be separated, for thus they were created as "God's husbandry." The illustration of the three shadows cast by a single body reinforces the idea of complexity in unity.

In the second review of Herder's treatise, the *Disposition (Abfertigung)*, Hamann refers to what he had written as "partly learned, partly political" (III, 24). This statement may very well apply to all of his writings with which we have dealt in this chapter, for they are all, to some degree, aimed at two targets at once. The main target is the "institutionalized Enlightenment," to borrow a phrase of Josef Simon's,[26] with Berlin as the center, the "new Babel" (III, 19), and

Frederick II as the moving spirit. Herder, however, becomes the
target to the extent that he had moved within the orbit of the Berlin
Academy, thus subjecting himself to the influence of the king's
philosophical bias.

Hamann's task was, therefore, two-fold: to refute in "learned"
terms Herder's thesis, and, at the same time, to impugn the ideas of
the Enlightenment as they were expressed in "political" terms in
Prussia. Since Frederick the Great was an absolute ruler, any negative criticism of the state meant an attack, directly or indirectly, on
the monarch himself. In the writings against Herder's language
theory the Magus seizes every opportunity to divert the attack
against the king, not by name, but unmistakably. The attack proceeds on the ideological, institutional, and personal levels. On all
three the indictments are scathing, but on the personal level they
become drastic indeed. Since the following chapter is devoted to
Hamann's relationship to the king, a consideration of *To the Solomon of Prussia* is deferred to that chapter. Space does not permit
mention of the numerous direct and indirect allusions to Frederick
II and his followers in *The Kinght of the Rose-Cross* and *Philological
Ideas and Doubts,* but the importance of such allusions can scarcely
be exaggerated.

The Prussia of Frederick II was known throughout the civilized
world for its religious tolerance. One might surmise from this that
the king's tolerance stemmed from his respect for the rights of individuals and groups, thus constituting evidence of his regard for
human dignity. Quite the contrary, in Hamann's view,[27] for the king
and his philosophical followers completely ignored the spiritual aspect of man's existence or reduced it entirely to the physical plane.
Connecting sexuality and politics in a way anticipatory of certain
ideas of the twentieth century Hamann reasons thus: the king's
tolerance grows out of his materialistic and cynical philosophy and
his own perverted sexuality, namely, homosexuality. Rejecting the
biblical view of sexuality, i.e., that its purpose is the propagation of
the race, and that it cannot be divorced from a religious context, the
king can see no reason why sexual behavior should not be subject to
the inclination or whim of the individual.

Hamann accepted as genuine a work in French, entitled *Royal
Morning Devotions or Discourses on the Art of Governing* (c.
1763),[28] purportedly written by the king himself, and containing the
statement that one is free to worship God in Prussia as he wishes or

to engage in sexual intercourse as he is able.[29] In Hamann's eyes it was quite natural and logical for "those warm brothers [homosexuals] of the human race, the Sophists of Sodom-Samaria [Berlin]," to link religious tolerance with sexual license (III, 27). In this connection he proceeds to make a scarcely pardonable scatological attack on the king (III, 29). The drastic nature of the attack was certainly not due to Hamann's indignation at the alleged homosexuality of the king alone (he was quite willing to exonerate Socrates, and did not hold it against Winckelmann). But a homosexual relation between human beings is sterile and therefore unfitting for a monarch whose duty it is to represent the divine order of things (III, 58). Such sterility becomes for Hamann also a symbol of the spiritual sterility of the Enlightenment as it was institutionalized in Prussia.

In the "learned" or theoretical part of the writings considered in this chapter we have seen that the Hamannian idea of human dignity is meaningful only within the context of the Judaeo-Christian revelation. For within the context of Herder's anthropocentric assumptions the opposite would be true: Man achieves dignity precisely through his unique ability to "invent" language. But Hamann's view is nourished by the Old Testament idea of prophecy, and is a counterpart of the *vis divinandi* which he invokes as necessary for an understanding of history (cf. above, pp. 117–19). It was precisely the office of an Old Testament prophet like Nathan to rebuke the king of Israel for his sin in the name of Jehovah. Hamann's idea, however, goes further, for, as we have seen, the "judicial" or "critical" aspect of man's dignity empowers him to judge or criticize not only political ideologies and practices but also their underlying assumptions. This aspect of his thought is of course historically conditioned. The Age of Enlightenment was preeminently the age of ideas, and Hamann was an adherent of the Enlightenment to the extent that he took ideas seriously and engaged in radical criticism of those he deemed important. In addition to adding the intellectual dimension to his prophetic Christianity, however, Hamann believed that he remained well within the framework of the biblical revelation, however much some of his Pietistic contemporaries might demur.

It is illuminating to compare Hamann's idea of human dignity with that of Schiller in his famous essay, *On Grace and Dignity* (1793), for the light it sheds on the positions which both Hamann and Herder occupy in German *Geistesgeschichte*. Hamann's idea of dignity arises from man's relationship to God, and is developed within the context of biblical theology and Humean skepticism. Schiller's idea, on the other hand, arises out of the relationship of man's instincts to his rational nature,[30] and is developed within the context of Kantian critical philosophy. When man's recalcitrant sensuous nature is, according to Schiller, held in check by the will, man appears under the aspect of dignity, adumbrated as the sublime or noble, but never the beautiful.[31] Beauty is adumbrated only when man's inclinations accord naturally with his duty, and is called, in terms of Schiller's moral aestheticism, "grace" (Anmut). Those who are characterized by grace are referred to, therefore, as "beautiful souls" (schöne Seelen).[32]

For Hamann, on the other hand, there exists no such *natural* goodness in man at any time, hence there can be no naturally "beautiful souls." Dignity, the highest state which man may attain is imparted to man, as we have seen, as "a direct gift of God's grace."

> Our dignity [he wrote to J. G. Scheffner] is, according to better concepts, not dependent on understanding, will, and activity, but remains the gift of a higher choice, not an innate, but an acquired merit, yet not self-acquired or independent, but absolutely dependent and precisely for that reason more firm and abiding.[33]

Therefore dignity is not a harmony of man's reason with his sensuous nature, effected by an act of the sovereign will, as in Schiller's thought, but a reconciliation of God with man through faith. Like Herder's idea of the origin of language, Schiller's idea of dignity and grace involves a relation of man to himself, not a relation of man to God. Insofar as this is true, both Herder and Schiller (however far apart they otherwise are) stand within the tradition of German idealism and thus take up a position quite different from Hamann's.

It would be wrong to conclude from the general tenor of Hamann's remarks in the course of his reckoning with Herder that his attitude toward his age was pharisaical or self-righteous. The fact is that he acknowledged his solidarity with what he called "his tragi-comic century" (III, 52), and desired its salvation. In the last lines of *Philological Ideas and Doubts* he writes:

> Do not weep, compassionate readers, for the Magus of the North, whom you see before you with a small half-year-old muse or grace on his right arm

and a small three-year-old Apollo in his left hand. . . . Suppose the Magus dies today or tomorrow, then know, readers, that he dies as a Magus who has loved his God, his king, and his fatherland—and as one who is outraged at their similar fates—NON OMNIS [No, not entirely][34] because he bequeaths to his friend Herder a small male and female to rear. . . . To my Herder, the worthiest of all my friends in the North and in Germany, I bequeath my joy and my crown, indeed, as surely as I die as Magus, father, friend, the genuine blood of my heart. May he give to you bread and wine, but to me no monument of stone. EXEGI.[35]

In thus concluding his essay Hamann intertwines in his inimitable way existential motifs with the main thread of the work. By "bequeathing" to Herder in the case of his death his two children, his "joy and crown," Hamann expresses symbolically in the warmest possible way his esteem for and trust in "the worthiest" of all his friends. In affirming his "love" for the king, despite all he has written against him, along with love of God and country, Hamann is making a declaration of loyalty to the monarchy not as it is, but as it should be, an attitude which becomes abundantly clear in the sequel, *To the Solomon of Prussia.* In the wish concerning "bread and wine"[36] he undoubtedly expresses a dual hope: that the king will reward Herder as he deserves and grant the conditions in Prussia for a spiritual renewal.

CHAPTER 9

Hamann contra Frederick the Great

H AMANN'S relation to his monarch was a most singular one. For, as we have seen, Frederick II was the real, though generally unnamed, adversary in Hamann's incessant attacks on the Berlin Enlightenment. "My hatred for Babel [Berlin]," he wrote to Jacobi in 1786, only seven months before the king's death, "that is the true key to my writings."[1] Frederick had ascended the throne in 1740 when Hamann was only ten years old, and died when the latter had less than two years to live. Thus the Magus lived out his life in the shadow of an absolute monarch whose deeds on the field of battle astonished an incredulous world, but who at the same time aspired to be the arbiter of the arts and sciences within his domains. Although Hamann always remained a faithful subject, conscientiously discharging his duties as a minor civil servant in Königsberg for many years, he chafed mightily under the yoke of his employment. He suffered even more, however, under the influence of a ruler who represented everything he abominated in religion, philosophy, literature, ethics, and statecraft. It is therefore not surprising to find him engaged in a running literary battle with the king and his ideological cohorts, a battle which had begun interestingly enough with his early treatise on the role of the merchant in society (*Supplement to Dangeuil*), and which continued until the death of the king. There is perhaps a rare irony in the fact that Frederick II, who was always so sensitive to the movements of his military adversaries, whether overt or covert, actually seems to have known nothing of Hamann's devastating verbal assaults on himself and his coterie of imported "enlightened" philosophers.

Hamann's attacks were, to be sure, camouflaged, for he was well aware that what he had to say about the king and his influence could not be said openly.[2] Freedom of speech in Frederick's Prussia meant essentially the freedom to attack religion and to speculate on

philosophical matters, never the freedom to question the policies of
the king or his ministers.[3] But the fact is that the corpus of the
Hamannian writings against the king, embracing both those appearing during his lifetime and those posthumously published, constitute a remarkable, and indeed remarkably courageous performance with regard to both form and content.[4] Until recently German scholars have generally played down these attacks on Frederick
the Great as somewhat embarrassing. It is the merit of Josef Nadler
especially—significantly of Austrian provenance—to have sketched
the main outlines and thrust of the Hamannian polemic against the
king.

Although numerous references to Frederick II are scattered
throughout Hamann's German "Autorschaft," the essays which
focus on the king and his philosophical allies were composed in
French. Therefore it is imperative for an understanding of his opinion of the king to study these essays. We shall find that they present
us with a striking paradox, for here we observe an ardent champion
of his mother tongue writing in a foreign language. It is true that in
the eighteenth century the French language was, as Nadler says,
"the Koine of the enlightened world,"[5] but that fact alone would
surely have prompted Hamann to avoid its use. In order to explain
why he chose French for his polemic in this area one must recognize
that the young Hamann had tacitly accepted Frederick's estimate of
the cultural importance of that language, and had by the time he left
the university become fairly proficient in it. Many years later he
wrote that "a secret instinct for this language above all others" had
motivated him in his youth.[6] Be that as it may, there is no question
but that the cultural ascendancy of French in mid-eighteenth-cen-
tury Germany was decisive. However, it should be noted that
Hamann is unique among the German *Klassiker* in adopting French
to the extent he did, a fact which is all the more surprising when one
realizes that the direct influence of the French language in East
Prussia was negligible. It was only in his later years, after a decade
of onerous labor translating into and out of French, and using it in
daily intercourse with his superiors in the tax administration that he
developed an aversion to the language.

More important than the general cultural reasons for choosing
French, however, were the practical and metaschematic possibilities which it offered. Since the king considered French the only
appropriate medium for serious discourse (he never read a book in

German and spoke the language "like a coachman"[7]), Hamann would address his monarch in French. Further, since the catchwords and slogans of the hated *ancien régime* as well as the terminology of the *philosophes* offered rich opportunity for the employment of his favorite literary device, there was apparently never any question in Hamann's mind but that French was the only proper vehicle for remonstrating with the king. That the use of French meant a sacrifice for him can be gleaned from his words in the *Essay on an Academic Question:* "He who writes in a foreign language must, like a lover, know how to adapt his mode of thinking; he who writes in his mother tongue has the domestic authority of a husband, provided he is capable of asserting it" (II, 126).

But Hamann did not doubt for a moment that the cause for which he contended fully justified the sacrifice. As to the quality of his French, one may only say that all the familiar difficulties of his German prose are present with the superadded problem of the foreign language.[8] Grammatically and idiomatically the quality of the essays varies from those with few, if any, outright errors to those with a high proportion of them. But it is not the grammatical or syntactical difficulty which poses problems in Hamann's prose, whether in French or German, but his complex and all too often obscure allusions. Nevertheless, as in the German writings, the general drift of his meaning is obvious enough, and in a number of instances particular passages are quite clear and telling in their effect. The fact is that there are certain felicitous formulations of his thought here and there in these writings which Hamann scholars have neglected.[9]

The first of the French-language writings to appear in print bore the title *Lettre néologique et provincial sur l'inoculation du bon sens*, 1761 (Neological and Provincial Letter on the Inoculation with Sound Reason) with the motto "for fools, angels, and devils." Both the title and the motto are metaschematic, for Hamann has adopted certain watchwords of his philosophical adversaries and turned them to his own use: "neological" refers here to the coiners of new terms for a new and rationalistic theology and philosophy, while Hamann is infusing it with a still newer meaning; "provincial letter" announces that he is writing from the provinces, and it further calls to mind Pascal's *Provincial Letters*, which were highly regarded because of their style even by rationalistic skeptics; "inoculation," a genuine step forward in the science of immunology, was naturally welcomed by all enlightened persons (in this instance including Hamann himself); "sound reason" or "common sense" (bon sens) is of course the all-embracing watchword of the Enlightenment, and for Hamann it is, in a philosophical sense, to be equated with *Vernunft* and, in a theological sense, with law (Gesetz).[10] The motto "for fools . . ." is quoted from Voltaire's poem on the epic poets where he speaks of Milton. Thus Hamann has given ample evidence in the title and motto that he desires to attack his ideological adversaries on their own ground and with their own weapons. On the verso appears a quotation from an ode of Horace's to the effect that the penates or household gods will be appeased by a simple offering. Apparently Hamann regarded the *Neological and Provincial Letter* as his simple offering designed to help set matters straight in his own household (Prussia). The quotations can be regarded as meta-schematic since Horace was a favorite poet of Frederick's and of the Enlighteners in general (as indeed of Hamann himself).

Hamann was moved to compose this brief essay after receiving from an anonymous donor a treatise by a native of France, one Nicholas Josef Selis, entitled *Inoculation du bon sens,* 1761 (Inoculation with Sound Reason). In it the author deplores the sick condition of his country and suggests that it might be cured by an inoculation of the predominant characteristics of the other nations of Europe: England, Spain, Italy, and Germany. Hamann makes it plain that the author of the treatise (which he translated into German and included in the *Crusades of the Philologist,* 1762) is on the wrong track, inasmuch as the other nations of Europe are just as sick as France: their "belle nature" has also been corrupted. "A bird's-eye view of the map of Europe reduces it to three climates . . . Genius (Génie) and liberty overarches the horizon of Great Britain; taste (le goût) and luxury that of France; but "sound reason" (le bon sens) that of Germany" (II, 282). But even the British appreciation of genius cannot render the proposed mixture wholesome. Hence Hamann's advice to the author: "Physician, heal thyself" (II, 281). Further, he relishes the opportunity to play off one French critic against the other. For André Premontval, a member of the Berlin Academy, rejects German philosophy, while his compatriot Selis would inject the French brain with it. The most important fact about the *Neological and Provincial Letter,* however, is that it constitutes a public attack on both Frederick II, "le philosophe de Sans Soucy," and above all on Voltaire, his "grand vizier." The

Letter ends with the bold and ominous words: "Sleep well, Sir!—
Tomorrow I shall await you at Philippi . . ." (II, 285).

In the following year Hamann reprinted the *Neological and Provincial Letter* together with another diatribe in French, the *Glose
Philippique* (Philippic Gloss). The latter is thus a "gloss" on the
former as well as a redemption of the promise at the end of that
letter. In the *Philippic Gloss* he develops more explicitly the theme
of ideological opposition to the monarch. The two essays were published under the collective title *Essais à la Mosaique*, with the
ironical motto, borrowed from a poem by Voltaire on Frederick II:
". . . there is nothing a philosopher should fear; Socrates is on the
throne and truth reigns supreme." Just below the title and motto
appears the same grotesque head of Pan which appears on the title
page of the *Crusades of the Philologist*. On the verso is an anecdote
from the works of Francis Bacon in Latin about a humble woman's
petition to Philip of Macedon: when the king refused to accept her
petition as beneath his dignity, she replied: "Then cease to be king!"
(Desine ergo rex esse! II, 278). Hamann has emphasized the woman's challenge to the king by capitalizing all the letters. On the
title page of the *Philippic Gloss* itself Hamann again borrows his
motto from Voltaire's ode to Frederick: "Barbarian! Open your
eyes" (Barbare! ouvres les yeux.). The "barbarian" thus exhorted is
of course the "unenlightened" German of the eighteenth century.

Josef Nadler maintains that Hamann was inspired to write such an
indictment of his monarch by the example of François Fénelon in
his letter of 1695 to Louis XIV and by Jacques Bossuet's treatise, *La
Politique tirée de l'Ecriture Sainte* (Politics Based on the Holy Scriptures), in which the great ecclesiastic sketches his idea of a theo-
cratic monarchy (NB, 142). Behind these modern churchmen, however, is the example of Demosthenes attacking Philip of Macedon in
the original "philippic," as Hamann's title makes clear. But more
important is the towering example of the prophets of the Old Testament in their relation to the kings of Israel. Nadler is no doubt
correct about the influence of Fénelon and Bossuet as literary models, but certainly wrong in implying that Bossuet's conception of
absolute monarchy, with its proscription of the right of the subject
to criticize the king, coincided with Hamann's conception. For, as
we have seen, he conceived of man as possessing, by virtue of the
gift of language bestowed upon him at the creation, "the critical and
magisterial dignity of a political animal." Hamann was by no means a

"political" writer in the strict sense of the word. But if culture is the
true matrix of political thought and feeling, his ideas are of considerable importance for their political implications.

The main theme of the *Philippic Gloss* is the "poverty of sound
reason (bons sens) and the riches of good faith (bonne foi)" (II, 297).
The king may imagine he owes his greatness—and Hamann does
acknowledge him to be the "Genius of Germany" (II, 291)—to *bon
sens*, but even his accomplishments on the field of battle must stem
from another and deeper source: "Is it," Hamann asks, *"bon sens*
which teaches 'Solomon of the North Wind' [Salomon de l'Aquilon]
to perform marvels? Is it *bon sens* which has made him prosper in
the face of the mutiny of all the nations and against the vain projects
of all the peoples?" (II, 292). Thus *bon sens* cannot produce a Frederick the Great any more than it could produce a Moses, a Draco, a
Lycurgus, or any of the other great lawgivers of history. At best it
can produce a Hobbes, a Macchiavelli, a Hume, and the like (II,
293).

Adopting the role of John the Baptist, Hamann indicts the king in
language drawn almost entirely from the Bible:

> It is not permitted for you to foreswear the faith of the fathers and your
> nephews with the *bon sens* of the whores of Ashdod, Ammon, and Moab. It
> is not fitting to take the bread from the children and cast it to the little dogs,
> to neglect your vineyard in Baalhamon, and to dally with foreign muses
> (whose mouths bring forth mere froth and whose right hand is one of lying
> and deception).—Solomon, the king of Israel, did he not sin in this way?
> (II, 293).

The plea to the monarch is to dissociate himself from his rationalistic
favorites at court and in the Berlin Academy, and to remember that
even as great a king as Solomon became guilty of whoring after
foreign gods. At the same time Hamann cannot resist the
opportunity to let fly, by means of a scriptural quotation (Mark
7:27), a barb at the king for pampering his favorite dogs while his
loyal subjects go hungry. Hamann appeals to his readers to have pity
on him as the dullest of men. For there are three things that are too
wonderful for him to comprehend: a man of *bon sens* who seeks the
philosopher's stone; the squaring of the circle; the longitude of the
sea; and a man of genius who proudly displays the religion of *bon
sens* (II, 294).

The *Philippic Gloss* is aptly named, for, although it is a philippic against the king, it is to a remarkable extent a gloss or commentary on the salient features of the *ancien régime*, especially as imported into Prussia. The central thought of the essay, that genius is more important than reason in the affairs of men, springs from Hamann's belief that God Himself is the Supreme Genius, who does not reveal Himself in the form of precepts or rules but in the historical events recorded in Scripture: "His memoirs which serve as the history of heaven and earth" (II, 294). This truth can, however, only be apprehended through faith in the crucified Christ. Hamann has singled out the features of a foreign culture which he abominated, and set over against them those features of the Christian faith which they have replaced. In so doing he metaschematizes the doctrine of the Trinity. Thus the French *Encyclopédie*, that veritable "code of *bon sens*" (II, 296), is but a barren substitute for the "Encyclopaedia of the Genius-Creator," namely the Holy Scriptures (II, 294). The witty and sophisticated men of the age, the "beaux esprits,"[11] value few things higher than the clever word, the *bon mot*, but there is One who is able to "call forth all things from nothingness and to return them to nothingness," all by the power of His Word, which constitutes His "bon mots" (II, 294).

Prussia was above all a military state, and Hamann does not neglect this aspect. In an extended metaphor drawn from the profession of arms he deals with the office of the Second Person of the Trinity: he speaks of God's "stratagem" of appearing in the "uniform of human nature" on behalf of the "cadets of the material and spiritual world" (II, 294). Thus the accent is on the redemptive work of Christ as the "Genius-Mediator" (II, 294). The wits of the age also lay great store by literary style, but the style of the Third Person of the Trinity, the "Genius-Author" or Holy Spirit, surpasses their limited talents, for it embraces the greatest possible extremes, both the majesty and the humility of God (II, 294–95). Aristocratic adherents of the *ancien régime* had a word to express the great contempt they felt for the rabble, namely, "canaille," but Christians willingly become the "*canaille* of the republic of letters" for the love of Christ (II, 295). Believers are referred to as the "*chargés d'affairs* of Jesus Christ" (II, 295). The Enlighteners cherish the "code of *bon sens*," and, in a phrase reminiscent of Bossuet, they reject "la politique du S. Evangile" (II, 295). In so doing they expose themselves to the dread "lettres de cachet" of worldy despots instead of the spiritually captivating "lettres de cachet" of the Apostle Paul (II, 297). (Hamann uses the same terminology in speaking of the Gospel as a whole as "mysteriously hidden ["mystérieusement cachée"] to unbelievers.)[12] It is the "age of Voltaire" which prevails (II, 293), when the "Academy of Satan" flourishes in Berlin, whose members claim to be "authors of taste" and of "bon sens" but are not so (II, 297).

The composition of the *Philippic Gloss* is especially striking, for the metaschematic expressions found in it are drawn from the philosophy, literature, learning, law, and military affairs of the ideological adversary. The essay was written in 1761 when Frederick's fortunes were at their lowest ebb, and when many in Russian-occupied Königsberg, indeed throughout Europe doubted that he would ever recover his easternmost province. A skeptic might conclude that this fact accounts for the Magus's courage in publishing the treatise. That such a conclusion would be wide of the mark, however, is proven by his attempts a decade later to publish another, more unambiguous indictment of the king's policies, addressed to the "Solomon of Prussia."

To the Solomon of Prussia, written in 1772, was intended as a companion piece to *Philological Ideas and Doubts about an Academic Prize-Essay.* One is not surprised to learn that no publisher would touch the French essay, which was addressed to the king directly and mixed remonstrance with flattery. That Hamann submitted the twin essays for publication in the *Allgemeine Deutsche Bibliothek* in Berlin is nothing short of astonishing. In the first place, Friedrich Nicolai, editor of the journal, was the most ideologically committed Enlightener imaginable, and in the second place the publication of the diatribe right under the royal nose would have had catastrophic consequences for both publisher and author. That Hamann submitted the essays to Nicolai for publication at all is certainly convincing evidence of the seriousness of his intention, however ingenuous it may seem, to reach the ears of the king.

The title of the essay, *To the Solomon of Prussia,* is of metaschematic significance, deriving as it does from Voltaire's ode to the young Frederick upon ascending the throne: "Solomon of the North brings the light." By holding up Solomon to Frederick the Great as a royal model Hamann is simply seizing the initiative unintentionally offered him by his religious and philosophical adversary. There are two mottoes in French on the title page of *To the Solomon of Prussia* consisting of lines from the king's ode to his master chef: "The exquisite food entices the Prussians; they have become Epicureans. . . . Illusion, delusion and hunger could perhaps turn us all into cannibals." Hamann takes these lines out of context and turns them into an indictment of the hunger which is allowed to prevail among the common people of Prussia.

In the text Hamann appeals to the king to rid the kingdom of the foreign free-thinkers who dominate the Berlin Academy, and to recognize the genius of his own sons of the Prussian fatherland. If such recognition is bestowed,

the blood of the great Winckelmann will be avenged, and your native subjects will henceforth not run the risk of being murdered [like Winckelmann]. . . . Herder will be Plato and president of your Academy of Sciences. Prussia will bring forth its Rabelaises and Grécourts,[13] and they will be more splendid than the apes and peacocks of Ophir [foreigners at Frederick's court], and you, Sire, will be like God on high (III, 59).

Of the general conditions prevailing in Prussia Hamann adopts the impassioned diction and pathos of an Old Testament prophet:

Because the Eternal has loved His people, Solomon has been established king over all the Prussians. But where are the temples? the altars? the priests consecrated to the religion of the Supreme Being of Prussia? The sublime taste of Your Majesty, like the spirit of the Christians, wishes no other worship that that of the spirit and of truth, no other altars than the hearts of his subjects, no other ministers than those who love and preach truth, who love and practice virtue. Where is that elect race? that holy nation? that devoted people? . . . Your age, Sire, is nothing but a day of anxiety and of reprehensibility and of blasphemy . . . (III, 57).

To the Solomon of Prussia is remarkable both as a biblical cento and as an example of metaschematism. For, if one were to subtract the biblical expressions and the metaschematized French terms, there would be little left of the entire treatise. The passage just quoted is typical, for in it Hamann has utilized no less than five biblical expressions and five from Voltaire's eulogies of Frederick II: "Supreme Being"; "taste"; "spirit"; "truth"; and "virtue." His virtuoso use of metaschematism is further demonstrated by the quotation: "The most astonishing monstrosity in society is, as a modern author says,[14] a slave who thinks freely" (III, 58). The original

French expression "qui pense librement" immediately suggests "free-thinker" in either English or German. Thus the statement has a double meaning: on the one hand, it is a contradiction to be a slave and yet think as if one were free; on the other hand, it is ironical for the coterie of free-thinking rationalists around Frederick to imagine that they have any freedom apart from the royal will.

Less important for an understanding of Hamann's relationship to Frederick II are his other publications in French, all aimed ultimately at the king, even if indirectly. The most important of them is the *Lettre perdue d'un sauvage du nord à un financier de Pe-Kim*, 1773 (Lost Letter of a Northern Savage to a Financier of Peking). The "northern savage" is Hamann; the "financier" is a Frenchman named de Lattre, a high tax official in the *Regie;* "Peking" is Berlin. Ostensibly a discussion of Guillaume Raynal's *Philosophical and Political History of European Settlements and Commerce in the Two Indies* (1772), which was vastly popular at the time, the *Lost Letter* is in actuality yet another criticism of Frederick's regime. Raynal had espoused the idea that the Christian religion had been indispensable for the development of commerce and industry in England. Hamann ironically suggests that the financier at Berlin should persuade Frederick to root out the paganism prevailing in Prussia and introduce Christianity in order to promote commerce and industry there, even if it meant enlisting Jesuit missionaries (III, 304–305).

The many quotations from Raynal in the *Lost Letter* might be considered metaschematic vis-à-vis Frederick except for one fact: the monarch, who was at first enthusiastic about Raynal's book, became suddenly and irretrievably disenchanted when he came upon a section of it in which the author took him roundly to task for having abandoned the idealism of his youth. The most remarkable thing about the *Lost Letter,* however, is that Hamann should have attempted by means of it to reach the king himself. The contact was to be made through Frederick's favorite, Quintus Icilius (Karl Gottlieb Guichard), to whom Hamann sent a copy, and who—fortunately for the Magus—refused to be a party to the matter.

Although the French writings against Frederick II provide a unique opportunity to gain an insight into Hamann's opinion of his monarch, there are numerous references to him in the German writings. Josef Nadler and Wilhelm Koepp have collected most of the "masks" which Hamann applies to the king. However, in order to understand all the nuances of the Magus's criticism of the king through three decades, it would be necessary to categorize and analyze his numerous veiled references. His favorite device in this connection is antonomasia. The Hamannian names or masks for the king derive almost entirely from biblical and classical sources. We have already considered the important biblical antonomasia "Solomon," which Hamann uses in the French writings partly ironically, partly in a straightforward manner. Biblical allusions to Frederick as ruler in the German writings are, for example: "Saul"; "Nebukadnezzar"; "Rehoboam"; "Belzazzar"; "Herodes," each name revealing a different aspect of the monarch's rule as Hamann saw it.

The most unusual appellation is "Nimrod," the founder of Babel and the prototype of the tyrannical ruler, "the prince of this world," who deals with men as the hunter deals with animals. A closer analysis of the meaning of this particular mask would reveal in an exemplary way the richness of hidden allusions in Hamann's use of antonomasia. Thus when he refers to Frederick II as "Nimrod" he has touched on three important aspects of the king's reign: his power, his absolutism, and his role as the proud founder of new communities in his domains. But classical names for Frederick also abound: "Apollo"; "Jupiter"; "the White Bull" [Zeus abducting Europa/Europe]; "Poseidon"; "Saturn"; "Midas"; "Philipp"; and "Marcus Aurelius." At another time he is "Amphion" (the legendary king of Thebes, who miraculously raised the city's walls through the music of his lute). By using this name Hamann amusingly links Frederick's flute-playing to his activities as the founder of cities.

But in addition to his kingly role, Frederick the Great felt that he was the best judge of German literature. Hence Hamann's allusion to him as "Orbil" (after Orbilius Pupillus, Horace's disciplinarian-teacher). Nowhere is Hamann's opposition to the ideas of the king more pronounced than in the area of language and literature. In his essay on the state of German literature (1780) Frederick stresses again and again the need for observing the "rules" of literary composition which are to be derived from the classics of Greece and Rome, and especially from seventeenth-century France. In order for a language to be a proper vehicle for literature, it must be characterized by clarity, polish, purity, and good taste. The German language of his day, he argues, lacks all of these things, but there is hope for the future if aspiring writers will imitate the classical models. Frederick's essay can be read as a catalogue presenting ideas on language and literature diametrically opposed to Hamann's. At the one point where they may seem to converge, in their mutual respect for the power of language, the agreement is illusory. For an examination of the metaphors which Frederick employs in praise of language reveals that he views it as a means of imposing his will upon, and manipulating, others, not as a means of expressing or attaining truth.[15] Hamann read the king's treatise on the evening of the day he had pondered the Old Testament account of the drunken, uncovered Noah. With a typically drastic metaphor he spoke in a letter to Herder of the king's essay as the "Herculean pudenda of ignorance and conceit," revealing "the true character of his greatness" (4, 254). A few days earlier he had written to the publisher J. F. Hartknoch that Frederick's essay was "a true model of French ignorance and insolence" (4, 250).

Since Prussia under Frederick William I and Frederick II was a small state with a relatively enormous army, great revenue was needed at all times. This was especially true since the army was kept in a state of constant combat-readiness. Hamann has little to say about militarism directly, but what he does say is unambiguous enough. In the *Supplement to Dangeuil* he had denigrated the profession of arms in favor of that of the merchant.[16] Some years later he compared the old "Roman bravery and magnanimity," which did not prevent the warrior from taking up the plow in times of peace, rather sarcastically with the "heroic spirit" of the martinet on the parade grounds in times of peace.[17] Prussia's power was based on the efficiency of its army and bureaucracy, the latter being chiefly the civilian arm of the former. Although Hamann was not involved with the military (except to be subject to the *Kantonreglement*, under which he might legally have been conscripted), he was very much involved, albeit in the role of minor civil servant, in that segment of bureaucracy so necessary to the smooth operation of the military machine, the tax administration. In this position he felt the full force of the Frederician fiscal policies in his private life and was able to observe its effects on the lives of the populace.

It is thus from his experience as a civil servant that he had so much to say about the "political arithmetic" prevailing in Prussia. The fact that the king had brought in foreign tax collectors to squeeze from the populace revenue which the native German tax officials had deemed impossible incensed him doubly since they were Frenchmen. He considered the *Regie*, the administration under which they operated, as simply an extension of the noxious French influence emanating from Berlin into another and most vital area of German life. Given Hamann's penchant for indulging in *Stilbruch*, it is small wonder that his abomination of the Prussian "arithmétique politique" should cause him to shift at the end of *To the Solomon of Prussia* from his lofty and passionate plea to the monarch to the level of personal complaint: he makes it known that he would gladly perish with the "Arithméticiens politiques," who had deducted five thalers from his salary, if he could thereby guarantee their destruction (II, 60)!

Hamann's attitude toward Frederick the Great, though radically and at times outrageously critical (e.g., the arbitrary imputation of homosexuality to the king, often expressed in obscene metaphors), was nevertheless complex and not without explicit acknowledgment of the monarch's greatness. Thus he wrote to Jacobi just a few days after the king's death: "What a vital warmth, what a vital fire must have glowed within him. . . . He was a man, a great man in the art of ruling his own kind. He was a faithful servant of his ego, which was his master. In spite of his good intentions to become an anti-Macchiavelli he became through destiny and misunderstanding a meta-Macchiavelli" (G, 384). This epitaph upon the king is not the first evidence that Hamann saw Frederick II as more than the monarch wished himself to be. For Frederick sought nothing if not to be the man of reason, observing *bon sens* in all the affairs of life. Yet as early as the *Philippic Gloss* Hamann recognized, as we have noted, that "Solomon of the North Wind" had performed marvels on the field of battle. Thus Hamann, like Goethe,[18] saw Frederick as a daimonic figure, impelled by forces which could not be caught in the fragile net of *bon sens*. Wilhelm Koepp probably goes too far when he says of Hamann's relationship to Frederick II that it was "the most complete and one-sided hate-love, such as is rarely encountered in intellectual history."[19] Certainly the Magus's attitude toward the king was ambivalent. Yet, while there *is* evidence of his admiration, there is little or no evidence of love or affection for this apostate "Solomon," who in the end revealed himself more clearly to be a "Nimrod," the bloody and tyrannical "Prince of this World."[20] Nevertheless, Hamann recognized how strangely and how ineluctably his life had been intertwined with that of his monarch, despite the fact that Frederick either had no knowledge of his existence or, if he did, failed to give evidence of it. Just a few weeks before the king's death and two years before his own Hamann wrote prophetically: "Perhaps our fates hang from magic threads which will be sundered at the same time" (G, 350).

CHAPTER 10

The Road to Nihilism

HAMANN was convinced that the excessive emphasis on reason which characterized his century harbored a danger which its various proponents were either unwilling or unable to recognize. His conclusion in this regard may be simply stated: a consistently rational approach to the great questions of religion and ethics, of theology and philosophy, leads inescapably to nihilism. However different the routes taken by the various systems which emerged in the eighteenth century may have been, they all lead to the same destination. This conviction is well illustrated by his incisive critique of four contemporary but disparate approaches, namely Wolffian philosophy, the neological movement within Christian theology, rationalism,[1] and the Kantian critical philosophy. Specifically, it is in his reckoning with Moses Mendelssohn, J. A. Starck, Lessing, and Kant that he comes to terms with each of those systems. But it is their common drift toward nihilism which unites them in an important way, and which forms the subject of the present chapter. Hamann's relation to each of these thinkers is highly complex, and the full story of his reckoning with Lessing and Kant remains to be told.[2]

Despite the fact that Hamann does not employ the term "nihilism" (Jacobi was to introduce it later into modern philosophy),[3] the concept is not only clearly implied in his thought but is seen to be basic to it.[4] Thus in *Konxompax* he speaks of "Nothing and Something" along with "good and evil" as the "highest, most universal generic concepts" (III, 218). Nihilism has for him two aspects. In the first place, it means a "Material Nothingness"[5]—the absence of all matter, or a physical void; in the second place, it means the "Nothingness" of man's wisdom apart from God, a state which he equates with spiritual death (cf. II, 74). Hamann is not primarily interested in demonstrating the ultimate unreality of the physical world or its finiteness, but in demonstrating the power and majesty of God. Thus in the *Philippic Gloss,* he speaks of God as "the Creator Genius, who by the energy of his *bon mots* causes the representative universe to spring forth from Nothingness and to return to Nothingness" (II, 294). In short, his view of the physical world is essentially biblical. Like the history of man, which is meaningful only when seen as characterized by a "Spiritual Something" (III, 144), the world apart from God has no meaning.

Although a far less important figure in German intellectual history than the other thinkers dealt with in this chapter, Johann August Starck (1741–1816), elicited, through his writings on church history and Freemasonry, some of Hamann's most important thoughts on religion and the mystery cults of antiquity. The son of a Lutheran pastor, Starck had studied theology and Oriental languages at Göttingen, becoming, as far as biblical exegesis is concerned, a faithful disciple of Michaelis. After various travels and teaching positions in Germany and abroad, he appeared in Königsberg in 1769, and in the same year became associate professor of Oriental languages at the university there. His rise thereafter was surprisingly rapid. In 1770 he became the second court chaplain, two years later a member of the theological faculty of the university, and by 1776 was made head court chaplain. He left Königsberg, however, the following year for a teaching post in Courland, no doubt because of the unpopularity of his views among colleagues of the theological faculty and their jealousy of his meteoric rise to power. Four years later he was called from Courland to Darmstadt, where he remained well entrenched until his death. After his death, charges of crypto-Catholicism, which had been brought against him by Friedrich Nicolai and other Berlin Enlighteners many years previously, were confirmed. It appears that Starck had been converted to Catholicism while in Paris in 1766.[6] In addition he was a member of the Freemasons, whose cause he openly and zealously espoused.

It was Starck's Latin treatise, *Pagan Influences on the Christian Religion* (1774),[7] however, which first became the target of Hamann's attacks. In it Starck argues that the early church was characterized by purity of doctrine and simplicity of rites, but that with the passage of time more and more pagan ideas and practices crept into the church. Among these was the idea of the sacraments as well as the practice of monasticism and celibacy. Some of these accretions were valuable, he argues, since they made the truths of religion more palatable to worshipers, and since they lent dignity to the service of worship; some, however, were harmful since they did not accord with sound reason. Latter-day reformers like John Calvin and George Fox were in error in wanting to extirpate all rites not in accord with New Testament practices. In contrast, he continues, both Roman Catholicism and Freemasonry understand the value of formalistic ritual. Although officially a Lutheran theologian, Starck fails to mention Luther, but the reason soon becomes obvious: Luther was not as iconoclastic as Calvin and the Dissenters, but taught that sinners are saved by faith alone, which in turn is elicited by the preaching of the Word, not by such "external reasons"[8] as the rites and ceremonies of the church. Starck clearly equated New Testament Christianity with Deism and was willing to accept any rites which, in his opinion, were supportive of that variety of natural religion. His rejection of the typological exegesis of Scripture constituted yet another stumbling block for Hamann, in whose biblical interpretation it plays, as we have noted earlier, a central role.

After hearing Starck publicly defend the propositions contained in the treatise, Hamann, who, contrary to his custom, had attended the disputation, was so incensed that he left the proceedings abruptly, and had no rest until he had publicly answered Starck in the *Hierophantic Letters* (1775). He was not only convinced that Starck was no Lutheran, but that he was in fact a crypto-Catholic, a presumption which was later revealed to be a fact. Four years later he again occupied himself with Starck (and Lessing) in *Konxompax. Fragments of an Apocryphal Sibyl concerning Apocalyptic Mysteries*,[9] and in *Aprons of Fig Leaves* (not published during his lifetime). These treatises, along with the *Essay of a Sibyl on Marriage* (1775), constitute the main sources for his ideas concerning the mysteries. Though exceedingly obscure, they contain important ideas, which, however, require a detailed commentary for their explication.

Hamann expresses doubt that "the poetic Golden Age of the early mother-church"—a conception basic to Starck's thought—ever existed (III, 148). Nevertheless, to the latter's argument that it is desirable to eliminate from the doctrines and rites of the church all later accretions to primitive Christianity, Hamann objects in the "Third Hierophantic Letter":

If one were, with Pharisaic criticism, to eliminate all the Jewish and heathen elements from Christianity, no more would be left of it than would be left of our body if it were subjected to a similar metaphysical chemistry—namely, a Material Nothing or a Spiritual Something, which for the mechanistic natural philosophy of sound reason amounts to the same thing (III, 142).

Underlying this line of thought is Hamann's principle of *Geistleiblichkeit* (Fritz Blanke), which holds that God never reveals himself apart from the "body" (Leib), namely, the physical aspects of existence. The analogy which he draws from the search of the human body for the soul or spirit to the search of the history of the church for the specifically spiritual element makes his point eminently clear.

Thus what one finds in examining the historical revelation depends on whether he approaches it through faith or reason. If approached through the former, the process of stripping away all alien elements will reveal certain "temporal historical truths, which occurred at one time, and will never return" (III, 304), facts which constitute the "Spiritual Something," namely, the core of the revelation. If approached through the latter, however, the same process can logically reveal only a "Material Nothing," for in Hamann's view abstract reason can only deal legitimately with physical relationships,[10] hence only with the "mechanism" of the universe. A few years later, in *Konxompax*, where he is discussing the relation of Deism to the mystery religions, he speaks of the "Ambiguous Something" or "Vain Something," which constitutes the core of both, but which really amounts in the end to no more than a "Pure Nothingness" or a "Specious Nothingness."[11]

In addition to the foregoing theoretical argument, Hamann also introduces a pragmatic one (here he is the disciple of Bacon and Hume) against Starck's belief that contemporary Christianity was in need of another Reformation, this time under the aegis of Deism. What, Hamann would know, are the world-historical effects of the so-called natural religion, whether in its manifestation as modern Deism or in its putative form as the mystery religions, in comparison with Christianity? Even that archenemy of Christianity, Voltaire, who liked to survey the vast panorama of world history in his writings, had to admit "that the Christian epoch infinitely exceeded all his aeons [namely, the eras discussed by Voltaire] in its most extraordinary effects, in its extent and duration" (III, 144). There is no name in all history, Hamann continues, than can compete with the "Jewish homunculus," Jesus (III, 144). The designation "homunculus" for Jesus is typical of Hamann's irony in dealing with his adversaries. Further, it was the Christian element ("leaven") in Mohammed's teachings which infused them with remarkable power: "A little leaven made Mohammed the greatest conqueror in human memory, in comparison with whom even Alexander the Great appears as a mere meteor" (III, 145). Through the "little leaven" of Christianity, the Roman Empire went into a decline. In his own century, Frederick II would have no more success in establishing natural religion in his realm through "the light of Deism" than Julian the Apostate had in reviving paganism in the Roman Empire. Further, Deism could never produce leaders like Oliver Cromwell or William III of England (III, 145).

Starck was obviously a committed Enlightener, but he was also a propagandist for the *Kulturpolitik* of Frederick II. Although the king was a Deist, he patronized the neological wing of the Lutheran Church as more compatible with his views than the orthodox, and it was to the royal patronage that Starck owed his rapid professional advancement in Königsberg. (That Hamann was later to choose Starck as his confessor is astonishing, but it certainly indicates that their theological differences did not disrupt a spiritual bond between them.) In the *Hierophantic Letters*, Hamann is not only attacking Starck's theology but at the same time the whole ideological complex of the Frederician state centering in Berlin, from which emanated the same kind of "military and literary tactics" (III, 156). This fact explains the otherwise puzzling appearance in the fifth *Letter* of a review of a work by the king's favorite, Karl Gottlieb Guichard ("Quintus Icilius"), on the military tactics of the Romans. The inclusion of this excursus has a two-fold purpose: first, to call the *Letters* to the attention of the king himself (since Guichard was, to some extent, a patron of German writers),[12] and, secondly, to point out how much Prussia owed to the "leaven" of Christianity, especially to the work of Luther,[13] and how little she owed to Deistic religion. Hamann explains that it was not the main topic of Guichard's work which interested him, but the "excellent observations" on the "genius and luck of Caesar" (III, 155). The clear implication here is that Frederick II, whom Hamann acknowledged to be a military genius, owed his successes, like Caesar, more to genius and to luck than to his vaunted reason, for genius and luck are not achievements of autonomous reason, but gifts of God.

If, as Hamann argues, Deism is inherently incapable of influencing the course of history in any significant way, there must be a great lack or void at its center. But Hamann does not go so far as to equate Deism with nihilism, for, after all, the Deists were heirs to a long and rich tradition of Christianity in the West, and did retain, in however rarefied a form, and, however inconsistently, many specifically Christian elements. What he does maintain, however, is that Deism, if thought through to its logical conclusion, would lead inevitably to a "materielles Nichts" or nihilism.

Insofar as the question of nihilism is concerned, Hamann's reckoning with Starck may be taken as paradigmatic for his later reckoning with Mendelssohn, Lessing, and Kant. We may say that, while Starck projects his "Golden Age" of rationalism as far back into the past as the early Christian church, Mendelssohn projects his even farther back, to the beginnings of Judaism. Lessing, however, projects his similar vision not into the past but into the future. Kant, on the other hand, seeks to establish his modified rationalism, as it were, in the present, from which vantage point it determines our perception of both the past and future. All of these approaches, if followed to their logical conclusion, would, according to Hamann, lead straight to nihilism. Here he anticipates in his own way Nietzsche's statement that "nihilism is the completely thought-out logic of our great values and ideals."[14] Subsequently, I shall consider how the Magus's charge against Starck's Neology applies, *mutatis mutandis*, equally well to the other thinkers mentioned.

If Hamann explicitly finds nihilistic tendencies in Starck's thought, he clearly implies that they are present in that of Mendelssohn. We have already had occasion to differentiate between the latter's aesthetics and that of Hamann (Chapter 5). It is in the political implications of Mendelssohn's philosophy, however, that specifically nihilistic tendencies emerge for Hamann. A disciple of the Leibniz-Wolffian school, Mendelssohn devoted his early writings to philosophy and literary criticism. It was only as a result of Lavater's ill-conceived attempt to convert him to Christianity by sending him a copy of Charles de Bonnet's apology for Christianity, challenging him either to refute the Calvinist philosopher's arguments or to accept the Christian faith that he turned his attention to religious questions.

Thus Lavater's challenge marked a turning point in Mendelssohn's attitude toward the relationship between Judaism and Christianity. No longer could he pursue his former course as expressed in the words: "I wanted to refute the world's derogatory opinion of the Jews by righteous living, not by pamphleteering."[15] Ironically, the chief result of the confrontation with Lavater was to cause Mendelssohn to reconsider his Jewish roots and to undertake to reconcile the ancient faith of his fathers with the Deistic theology to which he was committed. A part of his effort toward this end was the publication of *Jerusalem oder über religiöse Macht und Juden-tum*, 1783 (Jerusalem: Treatise on Ecclesiastical Authority and Judaism), and it was this work which elicited from Hamann two of his most important writings: *Golgotha and Scheblimini* (1784) and *A Flying Letter to Nobody, the Notorious* (1786).

Mendelssohn agrees with Lessing that the "historical truths" of religion cannot be valid for later periods; only the "eternal truths" of reason can make that claim.[16] Even though the ceremonial laws of the Jews "were revealed by Moses in a miraculous and supernatural way," they are essentially based on the eternal truths of reason.[17] The legislation of Moses involves "no dogmas, no truths necessary for salvation, no universal rational propositions. The Eternal reveals these to us, as to all mankind, always through nature and the thing, never through the word and the letter."[18] In asserting that Judaism is not concerned with dogma and truths necessary for salvation, Mendelssohn seeks to establish an essential difference between Christianity and Judaism. In other words, Judaism is revealed law, not revealed religion. Moreover, such "revealed" law is that which reason could, under the proper conditions, discover for itself.

In such a way, Mendelssohn causes Jewish legalism and the moralism of the Enlightenment to coincide. In other respects, he espouses the standard Deism of the day, namely, that the existence of God and the immortality of the soul can be demonstrated by reason. In viewing Judaism simply as revealed law, Mendelssohn ignores its prophetic and Messianic character, and thus separates himself from both orthodox Jews and Christians. Hamann, who disclaims any knowledge of "eternal truths," acknowledging only "constantly temporal truths" (III, 303), replies to Mendelssohn's position here:

The characteristic difference between Judaism and Christianity concerns . . . neither immediate nor mediate revelation in the sense in which this is taken by Jews and naturalists—nor eternal truths and dogmas—nor ceremonial and moral laws, but simply temporal, historical truths, which occurred at one time, and shall never return—facts, which through a confluence of causes and effects, became true at one point of time and in one place, and therefore can be conceived as true only from this point of time and space . . . (III, 304).

Thus historical facts, relative though they may be to reason alone, become absolutes for the believer. This involves a paradox. But, as we have seen, paradox is precisely the form in which the revelation is cast.

It is in Mendelssohn's theory of the relationship of church and state, however, that the nihilistic tendencies of his philosophy emerge for Hamann. In order to mark off the respective spheres of the church and state clearly from one another, Mendelssohn distinguishes between "convictions" (Gesinnungen) and "actions" (Handlungen), relegating the former to the sphere of religion and the latter to the sphere of the state.[19] Religion has to do with man's relation to God, the state with his relations to his fellow man. For Hamann such a conception bespeaks a misunderstanding of both relationships. As far as the former is concerned, there obtains an "infinite mis-relation of man to God," and therefore the church, in so far as it is an institution dealing with man's *relation* to God, is doomed to failure. In view of the vast gulf between man and God, "man would either have to partake of the divine nature or God would have to take on flesh and blood" (III, 313).

In Hamann's view, it is equally erroneous to expect the state to preside properly over man's relations to his fellow man, for as long as the breach between man and God is not healed, "a similar mis-relation of man to man" obtains (III, 313). At this point, Hamann injects an existential note. Speaking from his experience as a Prussian tax official, he recognizes that his own state turns all of its citizens into "serfs,"[20] who must pay "double fees" precisely because of the "deterioris conditionis" imposed upon them by the state (III, 313). It is illuminating to see that Hamann, who retained an interest in economics throughout his life, invokes fiscal policy as the fitting symbol of the state of human relations in the Prussia of his day. The monarch who presides over such "mis-relations" with regard to his subjects can only be described as "a dead God of the earth" in contrast to the living and "only true God of heaven" (III, 313). Lothar Schreiner says concerning this subject: "Hamann fought and suffered for justice. Here, too, he is a forerunner—along with few others. Five years before 1789 he is to be found in the opposition" (HE, VII, 144).

Mendelssohn's idea that "convictions" can be treated separately from "actions," is for Hamann an impossible dichotomy of the subjective and objective aspects of existence.

> For the true fulfillment of our duties, and for the perfection of man both actions and convictions are necessary. State and church are concerned with both. Consequently actions without convictions, and convictions without actions mean a severing of whole and living duties into two dead halves. . . . The state becomes a body without spirit and life—carrion for eagles! The church a ghost, without flesh and blood—a scarecrow for sparrows (III, 303).

Again and again in *Golgotha and Scheblimini* Hamann employs metaphors which describe Mendelssohn's version of Judaism as empty, artificial, or devoid of life. Thus his constructs are simply "empty puppet-play, his idol, the vain, botched work of human artifice" (III, 301); "Penelope's web," namely, never-ending make-work (III, 302); "the golden calf of Egyptian tradition and of human, rabbinical precepts"; "the dead body of his [Moses'] decayed legislation" (III, 306), and so forth.[21]

In a remarkably concise passage, Hamann sums up his thought as to how the rationalism of a Mendelssohn, even though unwittingly, makes common cause with the soulless aspects of the Frederician state, and leads inevitably to nihilism:

> Through contemptuous and hostile opinions, full of lies and anger, the whole mechanism of religious and political legalism is driven with an infernal, fiery zeal, which consumes itself and its own work, so that in the end nothing remains but a *caput mortuum* [dead residue] of divine and human form (III, 314).

We have seen, in the case of Starck, how Frederick II favored and promoted Deism in the state church. Mendelssohn's own doctrine that, despite the separation of church and state, the state has the duty to protect natural religion,[22] thus adds fuel to the fire which drives the machinery of the Prussian state. Its main driving force, "the infernal, fiery zeal," was, of course, the demonic energy of Frederick the Great, which Hamann both reprobated and admired (cf. Chapter 9). After Mendelssohn's death, the Magus wrote to

Jacobi that his real target in *Golgotha and Scheblimini* was not the Jewish philosopher but the "Berlin critics," and regretted that he had not assured Mendelssohn of that fact.[23]

In Hamann's view, the Mendelssohnian apostasy from genuine Judaism was made possible through the "serpent's deception of language."[24] As Nadler says of Hamann's thought here, "Abstract reason (die denkende Vernunft) is seduced again and again by language" (VI, 339). For it is the abstracting process which robs language of its power to convey spiritual or ethical truth. In succumbing to this temptation, man falls away from, or subverts, the image of God in him. For it is precisely in faithfulness to the connection between the word and truth, on the one hand, and the word and the deed, on the other, that man gives evidence of the image of God within him (III, 301). For example, it is only through the misuse of language that Mendelssohn can, in effect, equate the idea of God's covenant with Israel with the contemporary rationalistic idea of the social contract. Indeed, the validity of *all* agreements between man and man is undermined by the divorce of the word from its natural meaning: "The misuse of language and its natural testimony is therefore the greatest perjury, and makes the transgressor of this first law of reason and its legitimacy the worst misanthropist, traitor, and adversary of plain sincerity and honesty, on which our dignity and felicity rest" (III, 301). But it is the falling away from the image of God in man here which is of primary importance. God never perjures himself, for "when he speaks, it is done."[25] Thus it should be with man after his own fashion. In the *Flying Letter*, Hamann ironically sums up his opinion of Mendelssohn's treatise: " 'Samaria' would have been a far more appropriate [title] than 'Jerusalem' for the theory of Judaism which is revealed in the book, and which is decked out with extraordinary academic and linguistic wisdom" (III, 383). "Samaria" is, of course, a byword for adulterated Judaism.

In a society still dominated by the (spurious) feudal conception of nobility, Hamann stresses the nobility of the spiritual man. The prototype of the spiritual man is the Jew, "the authentic original nobleman of the whole human race" (III, 309). (Here he parallels but reinterprets Lessing's portrait of the Jew in *Nathan the Wise*.) But such nobility as the Jew possesses derives from God's covenant with Abraham, which ultimately extends, through Christ, to all mankind. Hamann contrasts the divine legacy of the Jew with that of the "European centaur-knighthood," namely, the feudal nobility.

The "titles" of such wordly nobility are "ridiculous" in comparison with the Abrahamic covenant (III, 309). Therefore, for Mendelssohn to equate that covenant with the social contract, and to attempt to reduce Judaism to Deism constitutes, in Hamann's eyes, an outright betrayal of his religious heritage.

Although Lessing was a much more important figure in the history of philosophy than either Starck or even Mendelssohn (a fact of which Hamann was quite aware[26]), and although he was clearly in the background of Hamann's polemic with the rationalists in general, no single work by Hamann was exclusively devoted to a discussion of Lessing's ideas. Nevertheless, the major outlines of his criticism are clear enough. Essentially, the Magus's criticism of Lessing is the same as that of Kant, namely, that each thinker nullifies, in his own way, the natural bond of man with experience. While Lessing attempts to separate man from his dependence on the biblical revelation, Kant is more radical: he seeks, as we shall see, to free man from experience in general.

Lessing's theological position differs from that of the typical Deist, on the one hand, and the Neologists on the other. The light of reason cannot fully disclose religious truth in the present, as maintained by the former, nor did it shine with pristine clarity in primitive Christianity, only to be obscured in the course of history, as maintained by the latter. Lessing does maintain that "accidental historical truth can never become proof of the necessary truths of reason."[27] That is to say, there are two kinds of truth, one historical, the other rational. This discontinuity of rational truth with historical truth (experience) constitutes for him "the loathsome, wide ditch across which I cannot get, however often and earnestly I have attempted the leap."[28] What distinguishes Lessing from the typical Deist is his belief that reason has not yet, so to speak, come of age, though it certainly will in the future.

As explicated in *The Education of the Human Race*, Lessing's position is that mankind, conceived of as a corporate individual, is gradually being led to become rationally autonomous: "What education is for the individual person, revelation is for the whole human race."[29] In this process there are three stages: the first was realized in the Old Testament revelation ("the first primer"); the second stage was realized in the New Testament revelation ("the second primer"); the third and final stage will be realized in the distant future, when men "will do the good, because it is the good, and not because arbitrary rewards result from it. . . . It will certainly come, the age of a *new eternal gospel,* which is promised to us even in the primer of the New Testament."[30] In the meantime, however, it is necessary to retain the teachings of the "second primer," the New Testament. At the end of the tract, Lessing abruptly introduces the idea of metempsychosis, thus reiterating for the individual the ideal he had envisioned for the whole human race, namely, progress toward "perfection" and the acquisition of "new knowledge" and "skills."[31] Sincè one life may not suffice for such progress, reincarnation, he suggests, may be the answer.

Lessing's basic metaphor for revelation is that of the answer to a mathematical problem which is given to the pupil before he has worked it out for himself. The teacher does this not only to give the pupil knowledge he cannot yet attain unaided, but to assist him in understanding the rational steps by which the knowledge is validated. Strictly speaking, God is not necessary to this process, for man, given enough time, *could* arrive at religious truth on his own.[32] It is not at all surprising that Hamann, for whom reason can never be legitimately divorced from revelation should reject out of hand Lessing's thesis in *The Education of the Human Race.* Moreover, God has been relegated to the role of a (possibly dispensable) German schoolmaster.

Despite Lessing's bow to the importance of the historical process in this work, Hamann sees no difference between its thesis and that of the "fashionable philosophy" of the day (4, 192). Other rationalists had conceived of God as the Cosmic Philosopher ("summus Philosophus"), but Lessing now presents Him as the Cosmic Schoolmaster ("summus Paedagogus"). Therefore Hamann finds in *The Education of the Human Race* "nothing but the transmigration of [old] ideas into new formulas and words . . . no Reformation-spirit, no conception which might deserve a magnificat."[33] Here, as elsewhere, Hamann stresses Lessing's departure from the real spirit of Luther despite his great admiration for the reformer.[34] Lessing averred that Luther had freed men "from the yoke of tradition," but asks: "Who will save us from the yoke of the letter?"[35] Behind this question lies Lessing's rejection of a basic tenet of Hamann's language philosophy, namely, that veridical language always possesses literal and nonliteral levels. For Lessing to reduce language merely to its literal level does mean that he occupies common ground with his theological adversary, the orthodox Pastor Johann Melchior

Goeze, but not with Hamann. Thus both Lessing and Goeze are arguing over "the dead body of the letter."[36]

Lessing's view of reason would naturally relegate him, in Hamann's eyes, to the company of those who, like Starck and Mendelssohn, clearly tend, however unconsciously, to nihilism. Thus Hamann wrote to Jacobi in 1784:

Being is the sine qua non of everything. But the το ον of ancient metaphysics has unfortunately been transformed into an ideal of pure reason, whose Being and non-Being cannot be determined thereby. Original Being is truth; communicated Being is grace.[37] Non-Being, a lack, indeed even an appearance of both, at whose manifold Nothingness unity and center vanish. Thus it was with Spinoza and perhaps Lessing (5, 271).

The "manifold Nothingness" which lies, according to Hamann, at the basis of Spinoza's thought does not yet characterize Lessing's, for the step in that direction can only be taken in the future, when reason will, according to his conception, have achieved complete autonomy. This, no doubt, is the reason for the qualifying "perhaps" in Hamann's statement about Lessing.

If the thinkers dealt with so far in this chapter relegate the undisputed reign of reason either to the past or future, Hamann understands Kant, by virtue of his radical epistemology, as establishing it in the present in such a way that it governs our perception of *all* temporal divisions. In the first *Flying Letter*, Hamann states that "the present is an indivisible, simple point in which the spirit of observation [reason] is concentrated, and from which it influences the whole sphere of the general power of cognition."[38] Though this idea is expressed in a discussion of Mendelssohn's thought, Kant's critical philosophy would seem to be the prime example of what Hamann had in mind here. It is Kant's attempt to free himself entirely from experience, past, present, or future, thus to "purify" reason, that causes Hamann to criticize his thought in terms of what might be called the world-historical progress of reason into Nothingness.

The relationship between Hamann and Kant is a long and complex one in both its personal and philosophical dimensions, many of which need to be illuminated by further research.[39] It is well to remember that, despite the great gulf between their philosophies, the two thinkers have much in common: both were influenced by

Pietism and the Enlightenment; both reject classical metaphysics as well as the theological dogmatism often bound up with it; both seek to establish the outer limits of reason; both are concerned with ethics and aesthetics; both are critical of the Enlightenment as a historical movement; both are critics of Frederick the Great as the chief proponent of the Enlightenment in Prussia. To be sure, their position on these matters is usually diametrically opposed, but the common ground is nevertheless obvious. In the sequel, however, we shall note only briefly Hamann's reckoning with Kant's critical philosophy as it relates to the theme of this chapter. For Hamann, while recognizing the fundamental difference between the Kantian philosophy and that of the other thinkers we have considered, felt that, in the final analysis, Kant was still infected with the same error.

Kant published his *Critique of Pure Reason* in 1781. Hamann had eagerly awaited its appearance, and with good reason. He had long since invoked Hume against Kant, and had only recently enjoyed Kant's commendation of his translation of Hume's *Dialogues concerning Natural Religion*. Being aware that it was precisely Hume's influence which had caused Kant's thought to take a new direction, Hamann could hope that he would find Kant's *magnum opus* (for which he had even mediated a publisher!) to be more to his liking than the author's previous writings. But in that hope he was to be quite disappointed.

Hamann's response to the work found expression in a review and in the brief but important *Metacritique of the Purism of Reason*. The former was written in 1781 and the latter two years later, but neither was published during his lifetime. The reasons for this seem to have been purely personal. The *Metacritique* was, however, soon shared in manuscript form with Herder and Jacobi. If Kant's *Critique* may be described as an investigation of reason in the light of reason, Hamann's brief *Metacritique* may be described as a prolegomenon to an investigation of reason in the light of language. It provides us with what might be called, in Spenglerian terms, a morphology of the history of the rational method in philosophy. Hamann undertakes to set the Kantian effort to delimit the province of reason in its world-historical framework. Accordingly, he sees it as the second great stage in the evolution—or devolution—of reason. The first stage was attained in the Enlightenment, when reason was freed from dependence on social experience, namely, tradition:

"The first purification of philosophy consisted in the partly misunderstood, partly unsuccessful attempt to make reason independent of all custom and tradition and all faith in them" (III, 284). Here Hamann has reference to the attempts of the pre-Kantian rationalists to free reason of all heteronomous influences—the authoritative church, the authoritative book or creed, and the authoritative political system. Formerly reason was in the service of tradition; now it attacked and disposed of tradition. Lessing, though he provisionally retained the biblical revelation, must, as we have seen, be included here. The second stage in the "purification" of reason was reached in the work of Kant. For it was he who attempted to divorce reason from the one thing the Enlighteners had left in company with it, namely, individual experience. "The second purification," Hamann continues, "is even more transcendental and aims at freedom from experience and its everyday induction" (III, 284). This constitutes Kant's contribution, his "purism." But even at this stage there still remains an empirical element—language. For the visible and audible signs of language belong to experience. Hence, to reach his goal Kant would have to eliminate language: "The third, highest and, as it were, empirical purism concerns therefore language, the first and last organon and criterion of reason, without any other credentials than tradition and usage" (III, 284). But the philosopher is still dependent on language, as rarefied and attenuated as his abstract terminology may be. As a result, the third purism must suffer shipwreck. But the advantage of this *reductio ad absurdum* is that it reveals the fundamental error in the whole attempt at purification.

Thus the progress of reason on its journey of purification is not a progress into life, but an egress from life, from the sense experience represented by language, upon which our humanity is founded. Hamann could scarcely have rendered more graphic his belief that Kant had set out on the road to nihilism—indeed had outdistanced his predecessors on that journey—than with his outlining the development of reason by historical stages.

Hamann sees Kant's epistemological procedure as essentially parallel to Starck's historical method, which, as we have seen, he held to be explicitly nihilistic. In fact, it is significant that Kant strongly defended Starck's historical method as well as his appointment to the theological faculty of the university in a letter to Hamann (3, 86). Strong overtones of Hamann's indictment of

Starck's tendency to nihilism may be heard in the following words of the *Metacritique* directed at Kant:

> Metaphysics misuses all the word-signs and figures of speech of our empirical knowledge so that they become nothing but hieroglyphs and types of ideal relations, and works over by means of this learned mischief the straightforwardness of language into a meaningless, ruttish, unstable, indefinite something = ×, so that nothing remains but the soughing of the wind, a magic phantasmagoria . . . the talisman and rosary of a transcendental, superstitious belief in *entia rationis,* their empty bags and waste places (III, 285).

In other words, what Starck had done to the historical revelation Kant is doing to language, namely, separating form and content to such an extent that "nothing remains" but illusion or emptiness. As early as his "Socratic year" Hamann had warned Kant, in a striking allegory, of the nihilistic tendency of all thoroughgoing rationalism. In the famous letter of July 27, 1759, he wrote: "Truth wanted to avoid being violated by highwaymen. She wore garment upon garment, so that they would despair of finding her body. How terrified were they when they had their way, and beheld that dreadful spectre, the truth" (1, 381; cf. 4, 403). Thus, in the process of stripping away all experience, the "truth" at which the rationalists ultimately arrive is the "dreadful spectre" of Nothingness.

A passage in the *Aesthetica in nuce,* which we have already had occasion to notice, throws further light on Hamann's conception of nihilism. For there he states that God's being embraces the opposites of "infinite calm, causing God to resemble Nothingness" and "infinite energy, filling all in all" (II, 204). Since God's working in the world, His omnipresent energy or power, cannot be perceived solely by reason (II, 65, 108), it is obvious why the thoroughly consistent rationalist would "deny His existence" (II, 204). Thus Hamann provides a speculative theological basis for the genesis of the idea of religious nihilism. It is important to note, however, that the divine attribute of "infinite calm" is held only to *resemble* Nothingness, and therefore it is not to be equated with a Void. To do so is to be deceived by the illusion arising from a false perspective.

If Hamann's verdict on his rationalistic adversaries, including Kant, seems too harsh, it must be borne in mind that he saw in them the (genuine) threat to a religious faith such as his, which was grounded in the conception that the transcendent God had broken into human history at certain times and places, and indeed had broken into his own life at a critical juncture, giving it an entirely new direction. For Hamann, man is not at home in the world, however much a child of nature he is. Further, he sees in existential "dread" or "anxiety" convincing evidence of the existence of a world which transcends created nature:

This anxiety *(Angst)* in the world is, however, the only proof of our heterogeneity. For if nothing were lacking, we would be no better than the heathen and transcendental philosophers [who deny transcendence], who know nothing of God and become foolishly enamored of our dear Mother Nature. We would feel no homesickness. This impertinent unrest, this holy hypochondria is perhaps the fire with which we sacrificial animals must be salted and preserved from the decay of the present age (4, 301–302).

Hamann was aware that none of the thinkers dealt with in this chapter intended to open the door to a nihilistic philosophy, but rather to do the opposite. Nevertheless, he felt that they had all set out on a path which would most surely lead in that direction, and that therefore it was incumbent upon him to draw the logical conclusion from their efforts. We may observe that he never dealt with the possibility that an excessive emphasis on either faith or feeling might lead in the same direction. Yet well he might have, for a basic tenet of his thought is that "faith has need of reason just as much as reason needs faith" (G, 504), and again, "the spirit of observation [reason] and prophecy [faith] are expressions of a single, positive power, which cannot be divided . . . in fact they presuppose each other" (III, 396). But the grounds for Hamann's unrelenting attacks on excessive rationalism are essentially historical. That many of the greatest minds of the age failed to see the malaise of "his tragi-comic century" (II, 52), or even hailed it, in the words of Kant, as an "age of enlightenment," eagerly moving toward even greater enlightenment in the future,[40] was the source of what may be called his loyal opposition to it.

CHAPTER 11

Conclusion

T HERE can be no doubt but that, from today's perspective, Hamann emerges as one of the key figures of German cultural history in the eighteenth century. This confirms, of course, the judgment of his most perceptive contemporaries. The question remains, however, whether he belongs to a past century, and therefore has nothing of consequence to say concerning the existence of man in the modern world. It should be obvious from our brief survey of his thought that he addresses himself to major concerns of contemporary man in a unique and challenging way. In his recent, important work, *After Babel* (1975), George Steiner says of Hamann: ". . . the originality and foresight of his conjectures on language are, particularly today, uncanny." This statement can, *mutatis mutandis*, be extended to other important areas of his philosophy and theology on which we have touched in this introductory study.

It is true that the so-called "Hamann renaissance," of which some scholars enthusiastically spoke in the 1950s and 1960s, has not materialized, at least not in the form, and to the extent, anticipated. But it is now clear that such an expectation was based on the false analogy with the Kierkegaard renaissance which we have witnessed in the twentieth century. No matter how dependent on Hamann's thought the Danish philosopher may have been, the former's relation to his readers is quite different from that of the latter. Walter Lowrie, the eminent Kierkegaard scholar and translator who became in his later years a great admirer of Hamann, wrote about his reading of the Magus: "I was prepared to delve, but had not expected to find the digging so hard." The truth is that Kierkegaard's "indirect communication" is, in comparison with Hamann's, crystal clarity itself. This fact accounts for Kierkegaard's appeal, not only to theologians and philosophers, but to a large, cultivated reading public as well. But Hamann has always been at best a theologian's theologian and a philosopher's philosopher. Whether his appeal will ever extend beyond such circles to the general, cultivated public is an open question.

The appeal to a wider audience will depend largely on the work of numerous scholars. (An encouraging augury for the future was the First International Hamann-Colloquium, which took place June 6–10, 1976, in Lüneburg, Germany, where most of the leading Hamann researchers from various countries were foregathered.)[1] As Karlfried Gründer has aptly said, "Hamann can scarcely be read without a commentary." This does not mean that his aphorisms will not, in any case, continue to be read and treasured as in the past, especially by those who are spiritually and intellectually attuned to him. But a proper reading of Hamann means more than that. The paradox is that Hamann, for all his animadversions against system, does in fact possess his own system, if that term be defined as a sense of order. We have looked in some detail at the kind of order which he described in nature, in history, both sacred and profane, and which became the ideal for his own writing. It was the weakness of some of his most enthusiastic proponents in recent years that they continued to understand his style, hence his thought, as simply "tumultuous, obscure and perverse" (Ronald Gregor Smith) instead of recognizing its inner coherence and consistency. Goethe, for all his underscoring of Hamann's obscurity, knew better. For what sort of a "codex" could Hamann ever become for his people, if there were no underlying order in his works?

Perhaps the most important development in the contemporary interpretation of Hamann is a demonstration of the falsity of the cliché concerning his "irrationalism." In the *Vorschule der Asthetik*, Jean Paul wrote that "the great Hamann is a deep sky full of telescopic stars with many a nebula which no eye will resolve." Nevertheless, thanks to modern scholarship, many of the "telescopic stars" and "nebulae" of the Hamannian universe of discourse have been brought closer and into clearer focus. Whether this development will continue depends entirely on the dedication of those scholars who study the "deep sky" of Hamann's universe of discourse.

Key to Abbreviations

R   *Hamann's Schriften,* ed. Friedrich Roth, 7 vols., Berlin: Reimer, 1821–25; vol. 8, ed. G. A. Wiener (appendix and concordance), ibid., 1842–43.

I–VI   *Johann Georg Hamann. Sämtliche Werke,* ed. Josef Nadler, Historical-Critical Edition, 6 vols., Vienna: Herder, 1949–57.

G   C. H. Gildemeister, *Hamann's Briefwechsel mit Friedrich Heinrich Jacobi,* vol. 5 of *Johann Georg Hamann's, des Magus in Norden, Leben und Schriften,* Gotha: Perthes, 1868.

1–6   *Johann Georg Hamann. Briefwechsel,* ed. Walther Ziesemer and Arthur Henkel, 6 vols., Wiesbaden: Insel, 1955–75.

NB   *Johann Georg Hamann. Der Zeuge des Corpus Mysticum,* Salzburg: Müller, 1949.

HE   *Johann Georg Hamanns Hauptschriften erklärt,* ed. Fritz Blanke and Karlfried Gründer, vols. 1, 2, 4, 5, 7, Gütersloh: Bertelsmann, 1956–63.

U   Rudolf Unger, *Hamann und die Aufklärung,* 2 vols., Jena: Diederichs, 1911.

Notes and References

Chapter One

1. In the account of Hamann's life I have followed chiefly: Josef Nadler, *J. G. Hamann. Der Zeuge des Corpus Mysticum* (Salzburg, 1949). Though Nadler's interpretation of Hamann's theology and philosophy is questionable, the wealth of (generally) reliable biographical detail makes this volume invaluable.

2. "Denkmal." See Johann Georg Hamann, *Sämtliche Werke*, Historical-critical edition, ed. Josef Nadler, III (Vienna, 1950), pp. 233–38.

3. *J. G. Hamanns Bekehrung. Ein Versuch, sie zu verstehen* (Zurich, 1969, 71 ff. See Bernhard Gajek, *Sprache beim jungen Hamann* (Bern, 1967) for the impact of the conversion on Hamann's language.

4. *Philosophischer Beweis von der Wahrheit der christlichen Religion.* 4th ed. (1747).

5. *Dichtung und Wahrheit*, Dritter Teil, Zwölftes Buch.

6. IV, 225–42.

7. Alexander Mihailovich Golitsyn (1718–83), not Dmitri Alexevich Gallitzin (Golitsyn), as stated in *J. G. Hamann, Briefwechsel*, ed. Walter Ziesemer and Arthur Henkel, V (Wiesbaden, 1965), p. 506. Hereafter volumes of this edition: I (1955); II (1956); III (1957); IV (1959); VI (1975) will be referred to parenthetically in the text and in the notes only with an arabic number, followed by the page number.

8. See H. A. Salmony, *J. G. Hamanns metakritische Philosophie* (Zollikon, 1958), pp. 75–76, 78 ff., who maintains that Hamann had a homosexual experience in London. His argument is countered by Wilhelm Koepp, "Hamanns Londoner Senelaffäre, Januar 1758," *Zeitschrift für Theologie und Kirche*, 57 (1960), 92–108; 58 (1961), 68–85.

9. Sievers, *Hamanns Bekehrung*, p. 149.

10. Selections were available in volume I of *J. G. Hamann's Schriften*, ed. Friedrich Roth and G. A. Wiener (Berlin, 1821–43). Roth edited vols. I–VII, which had appeared by 1825; Wiener edited vol. VIII with its valuable supplement and concordance to the works, appearing in 1843.

11. In the sixteenth *Literaturbrief*. For a discussion of Hamann's re-

lationship to von Moser see Rudolf Unger, *Hamann und die* Aufklärung, I (Jena, 1911), 418 ff. For a valuable study of the Magus epithet, see Wilhelm Koepp, *Der Magier unter Masken. Versuch eines neuen Hamannbildes* (Göttingen, 1965), 84–114. Variant forms of the epithet are: "Magus im Norden"; "Magus in Norden"; "Magus aus Norden"; "Magus des Nordens."

12. Letter to his father January 9/ 20, 1758 (1, 288; cf. NB, 88–90).

13. In 1851 Hamann's remains were transferred to the Catholic cemetery in Münster. No objection was raised by the Catholic clergy to his interment in consecrated ground there. See my *Hamann's Socratic Memorabilia*, p. 36, n. 46.

14. See Sven-Aage Jørgenson's excellent commentary, *J. G. Hamann. Fünf Hirtenbriefe das Schuldrama betreffend. Einführung und Kommentar* (Copenhagen, 1962).

15. The term "natural language" is used in this work, as in my *Unity and Language: A study in the Philosophy of Hamann* (Chapel Hill, 1952; rpt. New York, 1966), as the equivalent of Hamann's expression "die Sprache der Natur" (II, 211). In the earlier study I should have pointed out as a caveat that Hamann could, on the analogy of "natural religion," use the term "natürliche Sprache" as denoting the opposite of my term "natural language" (cf. 4, 183). However, in an important context *(Metakritik)* he uses the term "Natursprache" in the precise sense of my "natural language" (III, 287). See Georg Baudler, *Im Worte Sehen: Das Sprachdenken J. G. Hamanns* (Bonn, 1970), pp. 31 ff., 99, 193, 197, for a judicious discussion of the problems involved in the terminology here.

16. Available in III, 245–74.

17. See Nora Imendörffer, *Hamann und seine Bücherei* (Königsberg and Berlin, 1938).

Chapter Two

1. *The Autobiography of Goethe*, trans. John Oxenford, 2 vols. in one, vol. 2 (New York, 1969), p. 136.

2. *J. G. Hamann. Briefwechsel*, ed. Walther Ziesemer and Arthur Henkel, III (Wiesbaden, 1957), p. 103.

3. *J. G. Hamann's, des Magus im Norden, Leben und Schriften*, ed. C[arl] H[ermann] Gildemeister, 5 (Gotha, 1868), p. 137. This edition appeared in six vols. from 1857–73. Hereafter vol. 5, containing the correspondence with Friedrich Heinrich Jacobi, will be referred to parenthetically in the text and notes with the letter "G" followed by the page number. See Renate Knoll, *Johann Georg Hamann and Friedrich Heinrich Jacobi* (Heidelberg, 1963), for a study of this important relationship.

4. *Metacritique of Pure Reason* (III, 286; cf. 278, 300).

5. In his long and significant review of Hamann's collected works Hegel indicated that "die denkende Vernunft" was completely uncongenial to Hamann. G. W. F. Hegel, *Sämtliche Werke*, ed. J. Hoffmeister, New Critical Edition, XI (Hamburg, 1956), p. 226.

6. *Hamann und die Aufklärung* (Jena, 1911), I, pp. 559–64.

7. NB, pp. 236–45, 253 et passim.

8. *J. G. Hammans metakritische Philosophie*, passim.

9. See esp. "Versuch einer Sibylle über die Ehe," ed. with commentary by E. Jansen Schoonhoven and "Schürze von Feigenblättern," ed. with commentary by Martin Seils in *J. G. Hammans Hauptschriften erklärt*, ed. Fritz Blanke and Karlfried Gründer, V (Gütersloh, 1962), pp. 127–63 and 263–372.

10. II, 62. Cf. Hermann Schlüter, *Das Pygmalion-Symbol bei Rousseau, Hamann, Schiller: Drei Studien zur Geistesgeschichte der Goethezeit* (Zurich, 1968), pp. 45–71.

11. *God and Man in the Thought of Hamann* (Philadelphia, 1966), p. 14.

12. See my *Unity and Language*, pp. 36–40.

13. "Winckelmann," in *The Renaissance* (London, 1967), p. 229.

Chapter Three

1. See Benno Böhm, *Sokrates im achtzehnten Jahrhundert* (Leipzig, 1929).

2. The principal work was *Das Leben Socratis nebst Xenophons Beschreibung der Denkwürdigkeiten Socratis. Aus dem Frantzöischen des Herrn* [M.] *Charpentier von Christian Thomas* [Thomasius] übersetzt. 2nd ed. (Halle, 1720), largely an unimaginative paraphrasing of Xenophon. Also utilized: John Gilbert Cooper, *The Life of Socrates* (London, 1749) and Christoph Heumann, *Acta Philosophorum*, 3 Vols. (Halle, 1715–23). Hamann read the Greek sources later but, except for a few errors of fact, he felt confirmed in what he had written (cf. 2, 117).

3. Cf. II, 62, 67, 68, 69.

4. *Sein und Zeit*, 8th unrev. ed. (Tübingen, 1957), pp. 126–27.

5. *Blätter und Steine* (Hamburg, 1942), Aphorism 87. Hamann's own explicit metaphor is "subterranean" ("unterirdisch," G, 497).

6. II, 62. The works referred to are: Thomas Stanley, *History of Philosophy*, 3 Vols. (London, 1655–62), and Johann Jacob Brucker, *Historia critica Philosophiae*, 4 Vols. (Leipzig, 1742–44).

7. A. F. B. Deslandes, *Histoire critique de la philosophie*, 3 Vols. (Amsterdam, 1737).

8. Charles Pinot Duclos, *Mémoires pour servir à l'histoire des moeurs du dixhuitième siècle* (Berlin, 1751).

9. Acts 14:17.

10. The earthquake at Lisbon, 1755, caused Voltaire to turn from an optimistic to a pessimistic outlook.

11. A reference to the death of Klopstock's wife, Meta, 1758.

12. Hamann can equate the "wind" of the daimon with *spirit (Geist)* since the word *pneuma* in the Greek New Testament has both meanings.

13. *Søren Kierkegaard's Journals and Papers*, ed. and trans. Howard V. Hong and Edna H. Hong, II, F–K (Bloomington and London, 1970), p. 252.

14. 1, 372. See also Jørgensen, *Sokratische Denkwürdigkeiten. Aesthetica in nuce. Mit einem Kommentar* (Stuttgart, 1968), p. 66, n. on lines 8–12. Hereafter this work is referred to simply as *Kommentar*.

15. Letter to Friedrich Nicolai, August 25, 1769. See *Sämtliche Schriften*, 3rd ed. Karl Lachmann and Franz Muncker (Leipzig, 1904), rpt. (Berlin: de Gruyter, 1968), vol. 17, p. 298.

16. One Robert François Damiens attempted to assassinate Louis XV in 1757, and as a result was tortured for months before his execution by quartering. Hamann calls him "parricide" ("Vatermörder") because he attempted to murder his sovereign.

17. See *Hamann's Socratic Memorabilia*, pp. 8–13.

18. Johann Wolfgang von Goethe, *Werke*, Weimar Edition, Section 4, vol. 2 (Weimar, 1887), pp. 11–13.

19. See my "Socrates in *Hamann's Socratic Memorabilia* and Nietzsche's *The Birth of Tragedy*," ed. J. C. O'Flaherty et al. *Studies in Nietzsche and the Classical Tradition* (Chapel Hill, 1976), pp. 134–43.

20. See *Hamann's Socratic Memorabilia*, esp. pp. 76–78.

21. Philip Merlan says: "Only the interpretation of Hamann and Kierkegaard, both of whom were possessed by an eminent sense of the demonic, does full justice to the demonic element in the Platonic (and . . . even in the Xenophontic) Socrates," "Form and Content in Plato's Philosophy," *Journal of the History of Ideas*, 8, 1947), 417, n. 33.

22. *Søren Kierkegaard's Journals and Papers*, p. 204.

23. II, 97. Hamann quotes Isaiah 53:3.

Chapter Four

1. J. G. Hamann. *Sokratische Denkwürdigkeiten. Aesthetica in nuce.* Edited with commentary by Sven-Aage Jørgensen (Stuttgart, 1968), p. 76. Hereafter this work will be referred to as *Kommentar*, followed by page number. Also indispensable is the commentary contained in Hans-Martin Lumpp, *Philologia crucis. Zu J. G. Hamanns Auffassung von der Dichtkunst* (Tübingen, 1970). Marie-Theres Küsters, *Inhaltsanalyse von J. G. Hamanns "Aesthetica in nuce"* (Bottrop, 1936), though brief and colored by Neothomism, contains helpful interpretations.

2. Job, 32:19–22.

3. "Iam satis terris niuis atque dirae"

4. Judges 5:10 (Hamann's note).

5. Hamann cites Plato's *Cratylus*, 396d–397 and 407d in a footnote.

6. Michaelis objected to the imagery and parallelism in Hebrew poetry, both essential features of the genre.

7. Psalm 73:21–22 (Hamann's note).

8. Cf. II, 394 where Hamann refers to the Bible as God's "Memoires pour servir à l'histoire du ciel & de la terre . . ."

9. Hamann refers to Rev. 16:15 ("Behold, I come as a thief. Blessed is he that watcheth . . .).

10. II, 213; cf. 210.

11. Cited by Jørgensen, *Kommentar*, 96.

12. Cf. Job 2:13–3:1 ff.

13. E. R. Curtius has shown that the topos "Buch der Natur" did not originate in the Renaissance but was already current in the Middle Ages. *Europäische Literatur und Lateinisches Mittelalter* (Bern and Munich, 1967), pp. 323 ff. Curtius further conjectures that the idea of "Buch der Geschichte" stems from classical antiquity. Ibid., p. 314.

14. Cf. Psalm 19:2–4.

15. "Kyriological" means here simply "literal." Hamann borrows the term from Johann Georg Wachter, *Naturae & Scripturae Concordia* (1752). See Jørgensen, *Kommentar*, 88.

16. "Die eine Metapher ist aus des Grafen von Roscommon Essay on translated verse und Howel's Lettres [*sic*]; beyde haben dies Gleichnis aus dem Saavedra [*Don Quixote*] entlehnt, wo ich nicht irre; die andere aus einem der vorzüglichsten Wochenblätter (The Adventurer) entlehnt . . ." (Hamann's note).

17. Horace, *Satires*, I,4, 62.

18. The gnostic term "aeon" suggests heresy, and therefore indicts the age as an apostate one.

19. II, 208; cf. esp. 97, 293.

20. Jørgensen, *Kommentar*, 92.

21. In the *Lettre néologique et provincial* Hamann speaks of the Koran as "the rhapsodies" of Mohammed (II, 281). Cf. my "East and West in the Thought of Hamann," *The Germanic Review*, 43, 2 (1968), esp. 92–93.

22. Cf. James 1:23 ff.

23. Here Hamann refers to the flower.

24. Bernard le Bovier de Fontenelle (1657–1737) considered the myths irrational, but believed they could be so used as to convey rational truths.

25. III, 59.

26. Jeremiah 2:13.

27. II, 208; cf. III, 387.

28. U, I, 262.

29. II, 201.

30. II, 200–201; cf. Acts 10:9 ff.

Chapter Five

1. II, 139; cf. 198; III, 72.

2. Friedrich Nietzsche, *Werke*, ed. Karl Schlechta, I (Munich, 1966), p. 50.

3. See *Unity and Language*, pp. 47 ff.

4. See *Hamann's Socratic Memorabilia*, pp. 51–52, 88–91, 187–88.

5. Ibid., pp. 207–208. Karlfried Gründer's *Figur und Geschichte*, Symposion; Philosophische Schriftenreihe (Freiburg/Munich, 1958) is basic here.

6. *Der Magier unter Masken,* cited above.

7. D[orothy] M. E[mmet], "Analogy," Encyclopaedia Britannica, 1969 edition, I, 483.

8. *Science and Metaphysics: Variations on Kantian Themes* (London, 1968), p. 18.

9. *Hamann's Socratic Memorabilia,* pp. 3–5, et passim.

10. 4, 287; cf. 3, 107; R, VII, 414. See Erwin Metzke, *J. G. Hamanns Stellung in der Philosophie des 18. Jahrhunderts* (Halle/Saale; 1934), esp. pp. 170–74; further, his *Coincidentia Oppositorum,* ed. Karlfried Gründer (Witten, 1961), pp. 264–93.

11. Quoted by Unger, U, I, 243.

12. *Confessions,* trans. and annotated by J. C. Pilkington (New York, 1943), p. 332.

13. *The Emergence of German as a Literary Language* (Cambridge, Eng., 1959), p. 447.

14. *Die Zerstörung der Vernunft, Werke,* IX (Neuwied, 1962), pp. 100, 111, 114.

15. The terminology of this passage derives from Francis Bacon, who speaks in *De argumentis scientiarum,* Bk. 53, Ch. 1, of three kinds of light rays: direct, refracted, and reflected, corresponding to man's knowledge of God, nature, and man.

Chapter Six

1. *J. G. Hamanns metakritische Philosophie,* pp. 15–16. Space forbids listing all the helpful studies of Hamann's style, but the following are basic: U, I, 482–575; Josef Nadler, *Die Hamannausgabe.* Schriften der Königsberger Gelehrten Gesellschaft, VII, 6 (Halle/Saale, 1930), esp. pp. 18 ff.; NB, 462–65; see also Elfriede Büchsel, "Untersuchungen zur Struktur von Hamanns Schriften auf dem Hintergrunde der Bibel" (unpublished diss., Göttingen, 1953); Arthur Henkel, *In telonio sedens. J. G. Hamann in den Jahren 1778–1782.* Sonderdruck aus dem *Insel Almanach auf das Jahr 1959* (Frankfurt am Main, 1959); Eric Blackall, *The Emergence of German as a Literary Language* (Cambridge, Eng., 1959), pp. 426–50; Ingemarie Manegold, *J. G. Hamanns Schrift "Konxompax."* Heidelberger Forschungen 8 (Heidelberg, 1963), pp. 62 ff. et passim; my *Hamann's Socratic Memorabilia,* pp. 6, 65 ff.; and Sven-Aage Jørgensen, "Zu Hamanns Stil," *Germanisch-Romanische Monatsschrift,* Neue Folge 16 (1966), 374-87.

2. *The Autobiography of Goethe,* trans. John Oxenford, vol. 2, p. 137.

3. *Sämtliche Werke,* ed. J. Hoffmeister, New Critical Edition, XI (Hamburg, 1956), p. 226.

4. *Concluding Unscientific Postscript,* trans. David F. Swenson (Princeton, 1944), p. 224.

5. Cf. esp. *Golgatha und Scheblimini* and *Metakritik über den Purismum der Vernunft;* see *Hamann's Socratic Memorabilia,* pp. 75–77.

6. II, 209; 177; cf. 2, 84.

7. The Nadler edition of the works has been utilized for the study of the title pages.

8. See Blackall, *The Emergence of German as a Literary Language*, pp. 426–50 et passim.

9. *In telonio sedens*, p. 11.

10. Jørgensen, "Zu Hamanns Stil," 377.

11. See *A History of Western Philosophy* (New York, 1959), pp. 830–31.

12. Rudolf Schwarzenbach, "Hamanns Prosa," *Reformation*, Heft 11/12 (1961), 644.

13. *Søren Kierkegaard's Journals and Papers*, ed. and trans. Howard V. Hong, II, F-K (Bloomington and London, 1970), p. 252.

14. 4, 202. In a letter to Jacobi he made the drastic observation January 5, 1786: "My accursed sausage-style, which is a result of constipation and is the opposite of Laveter's diarrhea arouses nausea in me and makes me shudder" ("Mein verfluchter Wurststyl, der von Verstopfung herkömmt und von L [avaters] Durschfall ein Gegensatz ist, macht mir Ekel und Grauen" (G, 186; cf. 1, 23; III, 328).

15. G, 495. Cf. Letter to Herder March 25, 1780 (5, 175).

16. I am gratified to note that E. Büchsel seems to have corroborated, in her analysis of a particular work, the generalization I have made about Hamann's idea of order. She has suggested that the structure of *Clouds (Wolken)* may best be understood by considering the epilogue (where Hamann bears witness to his faith in Christ) as the "perspectivistic vanishing-point" which gives the work its unity. In so doing she makes a very enlightening comparison between Hamann's method and that of Paul Klee in one of his sketches. See "Untersuchungen zur Struktur von Hamanns Schriften auf dem Hintergrunde der Bibel," pp. 141–43.

17. *Sämtliche Werke*, XI, p. 226.

18. *Hamann* (Stuttgart, 1973), p. 297.

Chapter Seven

1. *A History of Western Philosophy*, p. 595.

2. See Sten G. Flygt, *The Notorious Dr. Bahrdt* (Nashville, 1963), pp. 71–81, for a succinct account of von Moser's *Der Herr und der Diener*.

3. By using this epithet for Hamann, von Moser was ascribing deep religious faith to him. Like the Magi of the New Testament, von Moser averred, Hamann had seen the Star of Bethlehem. Although Hamann accepts it in this sense, he also allows at times the connotations "priest" and "magician" to shine through. Yet the major emphasis is always Christian. See Koepp, *Der Magier unter Masken*, pp. 84–114, for a thorough discussion of the subject. Cf. my *East and West in the Thought of Hamann*, 86–114, for a thorough discussion of the subject. Cf. my *East and West in the Thought of Hamann*, 86–89.

4. Martin Luther (2, 10).

5. *Beurtheilung der Mittel, welche man anwendet, die ausgestorbene Hebräische Sprache zu verstehen.* See Hoffmann, J. G. *Hamanns Philologie* (Stuttgart, 1972), pp. 163 ff.

6. II Corinthians 4:7.

7. II Kings 9:30–37.

8. III, 91; cf. Luke 16:10.

9. III, 97; cf. ibid., 142.

10. Friedrich Melchior Grimm attacked the French opera in a farcical work, *Le Petit Prophéte de Böhmischbreda* (1753), written in the style of the Jewish chronicles.

11. For a discussion of *Zwey Scherflein*, see Rudolf Unger, *Hamanns Sprachtheorie im Zusammenhang seines Denkens* (Munich, 1905), pp. 200–207.

12. II, 72. Cf. Baudler, *Im Worte Sehen*, pp. 218–19; further, Simon, J. G. Hamann. *Schriften zur Sprache*, p. 57.

Chapter Eight

1. *Abhandlung über den Ursprung der Sprache.* References in the present chapter are to the first part of the second edition of the work (1789), reprinted in J. G. Herder, *Sämtliche Werke*, ed. Bernhard Suphan, V (Hildesheim, 1967), pp. 4–90, and hereafter referred to simply as "Suphan," followed by the page number.

2. For a treatment of Hamann's criticism of Herder's treatise, see Unger, *Hamanns Sprachtheorie*, pp. 155–87; Simon, *J. G. Hamann. Schriften zur Sprache*, pp. 35–56, 229–63; Baudler, *Im Worte Sehen*, pp. 127–37, 158–78 et passim; Erich Ruprecht, "Vernunft und Sprache. Zum Grundproblem der Sprachphilosophie J. G. Herders," *Bückeberger Gespräche über J. G. Herder*, ed. J. G. Maltusch (Bückeberg, 1975), 58–84; James H. Stam, *Inquiries into the Origin of Language*, Studies in Language (New York, 1976) pp. 131–64 et passim. Elfriede Büchsel's model commentary on Hamann's *Herderschriften* in HE, IV, is basic.

3. Almost exactly a century later the Linguistic Society of Paris Officially banned discussion of the origin of language within its ranks (1865). It was not theological acrimony, however, which was at the root of the ban in the nineteenth century but the predominance of positivism.

4. *Dichtung und Wahrheit*, Zweiter Teil. Zehntes Buch.

5. Suphan, 3.

6. Herder uses both the term "Sprache der Natur" and "Natursprache" for animal language. Cf. Suphan, 7.

7. Ibid., 31.

8. Ibid., 34–35.

9. Ibid., 35–36.

10. Ibid., 35.

11. Ibid., 38.

12. III, 42–43, 47.

13. Dietrich Tiedemann published *Versuch einer Erklärung des Ursprungs der Sprache* in 1772, in which he argued that language is not of divine origin because of its imperfections, thus reversing Süssmilch's thesis.

14. Suphan, 147.

15. See HE, IV, 167–71 for an elucidation of the title.

16. Suphan, 49.

17. Suphan, 27.

18. Cf. III, 39, 48.

19. III, 37. Cf. HE, IV, 214–17.

20. Cf. III, 51; cf. 139, 140. In *Au Salomon de Prusse* Hamann writes that Herder is "lost for his fatherland [Prussia], but worthy to be president of the Academy of Sciences, by which he was crowned for a treatise which is no better than this century . . ." (III, 57).

21. Cf. Suphan 28–29.

22. Ibid., 29.

23. III, 40; cf. 286.

24. III, 40; cf. Suphan, 28.

25. I Corinthians 3:9.

26. J. G. Hamann, *Schriften zur Sprache*, Theorie I, ed. Hans Blumenberg, et al. (Frankfurt a.M., 1967), p. 38.

27. III, 51; cf. ibid., 115, 118, 163, 164; II, 302; see W. M. Alexander, *J. G. Hamann, Philosophy and Faith* (The Hague, 1966), pp. 92–96, 120–22 et passim for a discussion of Hamann's idea of tolerance. Even Kant, Hamann maintained, was infected by the intolerance of the age regarding Jews. In a letter to Herder May 6, 1779, he wrote that Lessing's *Nathan der Weise* displeased Kant because he could not "tolerate a hero from this people." Hamann adds ironically: "So divinely strict is our philosophy in its prejudices with all its tolerance and impartiality!" (4, 77).

28. *Matinées Royales ou Entretiens sur l'Art de regner.*

29. III, 29. See HE, IV, for commentary.

30. *Sämtliche Werke*, ed. G. Fricke and H. G. Göpfert, V (Munich, 1959), p. 461.

31. Ibid., p. 470.

32. Ibid., p. 468.

33. Letter of September 18, 1785 (6, 68).

34. The Latin words are from an ode by Horace (BK, IV, 30). Francesco Algarotti (1712–64), a writer of the Enlightenment and a favorite of Frederick II, had these words inscribed on his gravestone. Hamann resented the fact that the monument was erected in Pisa at the king's expense. Thus we have here another thrust at the monarch.

35. III, 52–53. With the word "exegi" ("I have reared"), also from the ode cited in n. 35, Hamann is indicating that he, too, has reared his own monument with his words.

36. For a discussion of the symbolism of bread and wine in Hamann's

thought, see Max L. Baeumer, "Hamann's Mythologisierung von Sinnen und Leidenschaften," *Monatshefte*, 67 (1975), 370–86, esp. p. 383.

Chapter Nine

1. G, 199; cf. further: ". . . the Berliners are my adversaries and philistines, on whom I avenge myself." Ibid., p. 195.

2. See NB passim for the veiled references to Frederick II; also Koepp, *Der Magier unter Masken*, pp. 172–79.

3. See Rudolf Augstein, *Preußens Friedrich und die Deutschen* (Frankfurt a.M., 1968), pp. 197–98, 445. W. L. Dorn puts the matter quite succinctly: "To criticize the king's measures openly was to court disaster." See "The Prussian Bureaucracy in the Eighteenth Century," *Political Science Quarterly*, 46 (September 1931), 415.

4. Only when Hamann's superior in the *Regie* threatened him with "unpleasant measures," because of a "satire" he had written, did he cease writing his French-language diatribes. Letter to Herder October 14, 1776 (3, 256).

5. NB, 131.

6. Letter to Franz Kaspar Buchholtz, September 7, 1784 (5, 207).

7. Quoted by Helmut Fechner, *Friedrich der Große und die deutsche Literatur* (Braunschweig, 1968), p. 49.

8. For a discussion of the quality of Hamann's French, see Edith Saemann, *J. G. Hamann und die französische Literatur* (Königsberg, 1931); further, Jean Blum, *La vie et l'oeuvre de J. G. Hamann, le Mage du Nord* (Paris, 1912), esp. Chs. III, VI.

9. *Au Salomon de Prusse* has, however, been dealt with very helpfully by Elfriede Buchsel. (HE, IV, 271–85); see also Josef Simon, *J. G. Hamann. Schriften zur Sprache*, pp. 167–77, 250–52, whose notes are generally dependent on Büchsel, but who provides his own translation of the French text. Sven-Aage Jørgensen calls attention, nevertheless, to the unfortunate general neglect of the French writings, esp. the *Essais à la Mosaique*, in *J. G. Hamann*, Sammlung Metzler Band 143 (Stuttgart, 1976), p. 55.

10. Hamann to his brother February 12, 1760: "Die Critik ist eine Schulmeisterinn zu Christo; sobald der Glaube in uns entsteht, wird die Magd [reason] ausgestoßen und das Gesetz hört auf" (2, 9).

11. II, 293.

12. II, 294. Unger annotates this expression thus: "the symbolic interpretation of the Scriptures" (U, II, 680).

13. Jean Baptiste Villart de Grécourt (1683–1742) was the author of fables, epigrams, and obscene tales. Why Hamann mentions him in the same breath with Rabelais is puzzling. At another time Grécourt is used simply as a convenient example of lasciviousness (III, 201).

14. The reference here is to G. Littleton, who wrote a sequel to Montesquieu's *Lettres Persanes*. See HE, IV, 276.

15. *Friedrich der Große. De la littérature allemande,* ed. Christoph Gutknecht and Peter Kerner (Hamburg, 1969), p. 59.

16. IV, 234–35. Selections from the *Beylage zu Dangeuil* in English translation appeared in *The Prose Writers of Germany,* ed. Frederic H. Hedge (New York and London, 1856), pp. 121–27, with the title "The Merchant."

17. II, 354. Hamann's sarcasm about the spirit of the parade ground (undoubtedly he had Potsdam in mind) strikes at the very heart of Prussian militarism. For the success of Prussian arms depended chiefly on the relentless drilling of the army in times of peace.

18. Conversation with Eckermann, March 3, 1831. Cf. the conversation of March 11, 1828.

19. Koepp, *Der Magier unter Masken,* p. 172.

20. II, 208. Cf. John 12:31: "Now is the judgment of this world: now shall the prince of this world be cast out."

Chapter Ten

1. Karl Aner, *Die Theologie der Lessingzeit* (Hildesheim, 1964), makes a clear distinction among the three theological movements.

2. A detailed commentary on the *Kantschriften,* for example, has not appeared, a necessary first step toward clarification of the Hamannian criticism of Kant. See Jørgensen, *J. G. Hamann,* Sammlung Metzler Band 143, passim. For a thorough report on the state of recent research on the Hamann-Lessing relationship, see Willi Oelmüller, "Lessing und Hamann: Prolegomena zu einem künftigen Gespräch," *Collegium Philosophicum* (Basel/Stuttgart, 1965), pp. 272–73.

3. Apparently Jacobi first introduced the term "Nihilismus" into modern philosophy. See Wolfgang Struwe, "Die neuzeitliche Philosophie als Metaphysik der Subjektivität, *Symposion,* Jahrbuch für Philosophie, ed. Hedwig Conrad-Martius et al., I (Freiburg, 1948), p. 282. Jacobi specifically imputes to Kantianism an inevitable tendency to "Nihilismus." See *David Hume über den Glauben, oder Idealismus und Realismus, Werke,* ed. Ȑ. Roth and F. Köppen, II (Darmstadt, 1968), p. 19. As used in the present study, "nihilism" is a general term denoting the "Nichts" or Void which, in Hamann's view, results when reason becomes the sole criterion of knowledge and source of values. It is not to be confused with later developments of theoretical and practical nihilism such as Nietzsche's doctrines or the anarchistic ideologies of the nineteenth and twentieth centuries. It is clear, however, that it is, to some degree, anticipatory of them.

4. Dr. Renate Knoll (University of Münster) states in a letter to the author, March 2, 1978, regarding the problem of nihilism in Hamann's thought: "It seems to me important that Hamann took up the problem [of

nihilism] within the framework of his thought concerning language, and therefore did not view it merely epistemologically or purely ethically. Up till now that has not been noticed." ("Wichtig scheint mir zu sein, daß Hamann das Problem in den Horizont seines Sprachdenkens gerückt hat und es daher weder bloß erkenntnistheoretisch noch rein ethisch gesehen hat. Das ist bisher nicht beachtet worden.")

5. III, 144, cf. 218, 219.

6. Flygt, *The Notorious Dr. Bahrdt*, p. 207.

7. *De tralatitiis ex gentilismo in religionem christianam.* Also, Starck's *Hephästion* (1775), propaganda for his ideas on the church, came under Hamann's fire.

8. HE, V, 23.

9. The word "Konxompax," a term of unknown origin, was uttered by the priest who opened and closed the rites of the Eleusinian mysteries. For a critical study of the text and commentary, see Manegold, *J. G. Hamanns Schrift "Konxompax."*

10. See my *Unity and Language*, pp. 74 ff.

11. III, 218, 219.

12. Augstein, *Preußens Friedrich und die Deutschen*, p. 91.

13. III, 156; cf. Augstein, 139–40.

14. *Friedrich Nietzsche. Werke in drei Bänden*, ed. Karl Schlechta, III (Munich, 1966), p. 635.

15. Quoted in *Encyclopaedia Judaica* (Jerusalem, 1971), II, col. 1332.

16. *Jerusalem oder über religiöse Macht und Judentum* (Berlin, 1919), p. 34.

17. Ibid., p. 79.

18. Ibid., p. 69.

19. Ibid., cf. L. Schreiner's comments (HE, VII, 96–97).

20. Cf. "Heloten" (III, 313).

21. III, 308, 309, 313.

22. *Jerusalem oder über religiöse Macht und Judentum*, pp. 40–41.

23. G, 192, cf. 195.

24. III, 298. Cf. Genesis 3:1–5.

25. Cf. Psalm 33:9.

26. After Lessing's death Hamann spoke of him to Herder as "a man who thought for himself, and who was intent on striking out on new paths." Letter, March 28, 1785 (5, 403).

27. "Über den Beweis des Geistes und der Kraft," *Sämtliche Schriften*, ed. Karl Lachmann and Franz Muncker XIII (Leipzig, 1897), p. 5.

28. Ibid., p. 7.

29. *Gesammelte Werke*, ed. Wolfgang Stammler, I (Munich, 1959), par. I, p. 1010.

30. Ibid., pars. 85, 86, p. 1030.

31. Ibid., pars. 96, 94, p. 1032.

32. Ibid., par. 4, p. 1010.

33. Letter to Herder, April 12, 1780 (4, 182).

34. Cf. 4, 192; see Fritz Blanke, *Hamann-Studien* (Zurich, 1956), pp. 78–79.

35. Sämtliche Schriften, XIII, p. 102.

36. II, 2031 but cf. the query to Jacobi: "Was not the Hamburg *Oelgötze* [Pastor Goeze], for all his obtuseness, basically right?" Letter December 5, 1784 (G, 24–25).

37. Of this statement (which Goethe thought important) Arthur Henkel writes: "The sentence means that biblical revelation is communication which does not require the truth of immediacy. But it also includes communication between human beings." *In telonio sedens*, pp. 1–2.

38. III, 384. For a thorough study of this work see Reiner Wild, *"Metacr it icus bonae spei" J. G. Hamanns "Fliegender Brief": Einführung, Text und Kommentar*, Regensburger Beiträge zur deutschen Sprach- und Literaturwissenschaft, 6 (Bern, Frankfurt a.M., 1975).

39. Heinrich Weber's *Hamann und Kant. Ein Beitrag zur Geschichte der Philosophie im Zeitalter der Aufklärung* (Munich, 1904) is unsatisfactory, though it contains valuable information on the personal relationship of the two men.

40. "Beantwortung der Frage: Was ist Aufklärung?" Kant's *Gesammelte Schriften*, ed. Preuss. Akademie der Wissenschaften, 8 (Berlin and Leipzig, 1922), p. 40. It is illuminating to compare Jean Paul's indictment of the "poetic nihilists" of his time with Hamann's observations: "It follows from the lawless, capricious spirit of the present age, which would egotistically annihilate the world and the universe in order to clear a space merely for free *play* in the void, and which tears off the *bandage* of its wounds as a *bond*, that this age must speak scornfully of the imitation and study of nature." *Horn of Oberon. Jean Paul Richter's School for Aesthetics*, introd. and trans. Margaret R. Hale (Detroit: Wayne State, 1973), p. 15. Both thinkers see their ages as tending to nihilism, and therefore flawed: Hamann's is "tragicomic," Jean Paul's suffers "wounds."

Chapter Eleven

1. The proceedings of this conference are scheduled to appear in 1978, published in Frankfurt a.M. by Klostermann under the title "Johann Georg Hamann: Acta des Internationalen Hamann-Colloquiums in Lüneburg 1976."

Selected Bibliography

PRIMARY SOURCES

Hamann's Schriften, ed. Friedrich Roth, 7 vols. Berlin: Reimer, 1821–25; vol. 8, ed. G. A. Wiener (appendix and concordance), ibid., 1842–43.

Johann Georg Hamann. Sämtliche Werke, ed. Josef Nadler, Historical-Critical Edition, 6 vols. Vienna: Herder, 1949–57.

Johann Georg Hamann's, des Magus in Norden, Leben und Schriften, ed. C[arl] H[ermann] Gildemeister, 6 vols. Gotha: Perthes, 1857–63.

Johann Georg Hamann. Briefwechsel, ed. Walther Ziesemer and Arthur Henkel, 6 vols. Wiesbaden: Insel, 1955–75.

SECONDARY SOURCES

ALEXANDER, WILLIAM M. *J. G. Hamann: Philosophy and Faith.* The Hague: Nijhoff, 1966. A reliable study. Alexander argues that Hamann distinguishes between a philosophy which leads away from Christ and one which leads toward Christ. Particularly suggestive is his excursus on Hamann's idea of tolerance.

BAEUMER, MAX L. "Hamann's Mythologisierung von Sinnen und Leidenschaften," *Monatshefte,* 67 (1975), 370–86. Hamann's propensity to mythologize epistemological concepts (here: "senses and passions") is well demonstrated in the account of the relation of the Christian sacraments of bread and wine to the rites of Ceres and Bacchus in his thought.

BAUDLER, GEORG. *Im Worte Sehen. Das Sprachdenken J. G. Hamanns,* Bonn: Bouvier, 1970. A systematic exposition of Hamann's philosophy of language. Baudler's strength is that he recognizes Hamann's consistency in "seeing in the word," i.e., in drawing inferences from ordinary language, or "die Sprache der Natur," to reality.

BAYER, OSWALD. "Selbstverschuldete Vormundschaft. Hamanns Kontroverse mit Kant um wahre Aufklärung," *Der Wirklichkeitsanspruch von Theologie und Religion.* Tübingen: Mohr (Siebeck), 1976, 1–34.

BLANKE, FRITZ. *Hamann-Studien.* Zürich: Zwingli, 1956. A collection of reprinted articles, containing "J. G. Hamann als Theologe"; "Hamann und Luther"; "Hamann und Lessing"; "Gottessprache und Menschensprache bei J. G. Hamann"; "Der junge Hamann"; and "J. G. Hamann und die Fürstin Gallitzin." Blanke has the gift of simplifying Hamann's thought (often oversimplifying it). Nevertheless, all the studies are valuable.

————. *J. G. Hamann. Sokratische Denkwürdigkeiten,* vol. 2 of *J. G. Hamanns Hauptschriften erklärt,* ed. Fritz Blanke et al. Gütersloh: Mohn, 1959. Succinct but adequate commentary. Blanke tends to neglect the aesthetic and sociopolitical aspects of the text somewhat in favor of the theological, and to see the Magus too simply under the aspect of Luther.

BLUM, JEAN. *La vie et l'oeuvre de J. G. Hamann, le Mage du Nord.* Paris: Alcan, 1912. Especially valuable for observations on Hamann's French writings and his relation to Frederick II.

BÜCHSEL, ELFRIEDE. "Aufklärung und christliche Freiheit: J. G. Hamann contra Kant," *Neue Zeitschrift für systematische Theologie,* 4 (1962), 133–57. The author gives a trenchant account of the genesis of Kant's famous essay, "Beantwortung der Frage: Was ist Aufklärung?" as well as Hamann's criticism of it. An important study for an understanding of both men.

————. *Über den Ursprung der Sprache,* vol. 4 of *J. G. Hamanns Hauptschriften erklärt,* ed. Fritz Blanke et al. Gütersloh: Mohn, 1963. Contains commentaries on and text of: *Zwo Recensionen nebst einer Beylage betreffend den Ursprung der Sprache; Des Ritters von Rosencreuz letzte Willensmeynung über den göttlichen und menschlichen Ursprung der Sprache; Philologische Einfälle und Zweifel;* and *Au Salomon de Prusse* (accompanied by a translation into German). The introduction is fairly comprehensive. Büchsel's orientation to the Blanke school of interpretation causes some blind spots with regard to the underlying (systematic!) substratum of Hamann's *Sprachdenken.* But, within the framework she has adopted, Büchsel is unsurpassed as a commentator.

GAJEK, BERNHARD. "Johann Georg Hamann" *Deutsche Dichter des 18. Jahrhunderts. Ihr Leben und Werk,* ed. Benno von Wiese. Berlin: Erich Schmidt, 1977, pp. 276–99. An excellent brief introduction to Hamann's life and work reflecting the most recent scholarship. The bibliography contains "Forschungsberichte" covering the period 1956–75 plus selected monographs.

————. "Hamanns Anfänge," *Eckhart,* 29 (1960), 113–16.

————. *Sprache beim jungen Hamann.* Bern: H. Lang, 1967. The author shows that Hamann's philological procedure roots in North Italian humanism and their North European successors. Stress is laid on the influence of the literary historian Jacob Friedrich Reimmann. Gajek demonstrates that the central concerns of Hamann's philosophy and theology are already present in the London writings.

GRÜNDER, KARLFRIED. *Figur und Geschichte*. Symposion: Philosophische Schriftenreihe (Freiburg/Munich: Alber, 1958). In a study of the *Biblische Betrachtungen* Gründer stresses importance of Hamann's biblical theology for his entire philosophy. Especially illuminating is the discussion of typology. The work is a milestone in Hamann research.

―――, and LOTHAR SCHREINER. *Die Hamann-Forschung*, vol. 1 of *J. G. Hamanns Hauptschriften erklärt*, ed. Fritz Blanke et al. Gütersloh: Bertelsmann, 1956. "Geschichte der Deutungen" is by Gründer, the bibliography by Schreiner. Blanke states the aims of the series in an introduction. Gründer's coverage of Hamann scholarship from the beginning is thorough and perspicacious, but at times he seems to belie his stated opinion of a work by the amount of space allotted to it (cf. pp. 112–14).

HEDGE, FREDERIC H. "The Merchant," *Prose Writers of Germany*. New York: C. S. Francis, and London: Sampson Low, 1856, pp. 119–27. An anonymous translation of selected passages from the *Beylage zu Dangeuil*.

HEGEL, G. W. F. "Hamann's Schriften" [review of Roth ed.], *Sämtliche Werke*, ed. J. Hoffmeister, vol. 11. Hamburg: Meiner, 1956, pp. 221–94.

HENKEL, ARTHUR. *In telonio sedens. J. G. Hamann in den Jahren 1778–82*, Sonderdruck aus dem *Insel Almanach auf das Jahr 1959*. Frankfurt a.M. Reprint, slightly edited, of the introduction to Volume 4 of Hamann's letters. On the basis of a thorough knowledge of the correspondence Henkel sketches a fascinating portrait of the fifty-year-old Hamann.

―――. *Wandrers Sturmlied. Versuch, das dunkle Gedicht des jungen Goethe zu verstehen*. Frankfurt a.M.: Insel, 1962. Henkel demonstrates Hamannian influence on the poem.

HERDE, HEINZ. *J. G. Hamann. Zur Theologie der Sprache*, Abhandlungen zur Philosophie, Psychologie und Pädagogik. 62 Bonn: Bouvier, 1971. A reliable guide to Hamann's theology as rooted in his conception of language. Herde sees Hamann's use of reason as characterized by (1) "prophetic criticism," i.e., reason affirming faith, and (2) "rational criticism," i.e., reason remaining within the limits imposed by faith.

HOFFMANN, VOLKER. *J. G. Hamanns Philologie*, Studien zur Poetik und Geschichte der Literatur. 24 Stuttgart: Kohlhammer, 1972. An important work. Hoffmann emphasizes that Hamann's philology has two poles: (1) concern with minute detail and (2) basic hermeneutic principles. He maintains that Hamann's quotations and annotations are to be taken seriously. Especially illuminating is his comparison of Hamann's hermeneutics with that of Augustine, Michaelis, and Kant.

IMENDÖRFFER, NORA. *Hamann und seine Bücherei*. Königsberg and Berlin: Ost-Europa Verlag, 1938.

JØRGENSEN, SVEN-AAGE. "Hamann, Bacon, and Tradition," *Orbis Litterarum*, 16 (1961), 48–73.

―――. *J. G. Hamann. Fünf Hirtenbriefe das Schuldrama betreffend. Einführung und Kommentar*, Hist. Filos. Medd. Dan. Vid. Selsk. 39, No. 5. Copenhagen: Munksgaard, 1962. Contains much valuable material apart from the commentary.

―――. *J. G. Hamann*, Sammlung Metzler, 143. Stuttgart: Metzler, 1976. A thorough report on the present state of Hamann research. Precise and quite readable.

―――. "Zu Hamanns Stil," *Germanisch-Romanische Monatsschrift*, Neue Folge 16 (1966), 374–87. A signal contribution to the study of Hamann's style.

KNOLL, RENATE. *J. G. Hamann and Friedrich Heinrich Jacobi*. Heidelberg: Winter 1963. The author gives an account of Hegel's and Dilthey's understanding of the Hamann-Jacobi relationship, and further illuminates it on the basis of new material. Especially noteworthy is her treatment of Hamann's criticism of Jacobi's *Natur-Geist* dualism.

KOEPP, WILHELM. "Hamanns Londoner Senelaffäre, Januar 1758," *Zeitschrift für Theologie und Kirche*, 57 (1960), 92–108.

―――. "J. G. Hamanns Absage an den Existentialismus," *Wissenschaftliche Zeitschrift der Universität Rostock*, 5 (1955–56), 109–16.

―――. *Der Magier unter Masken: Versuch eines neuen Hamannbildes*. Göttingen: Vandenhoeck and Ruprecht, 1965. Koepp lists the literary "masks" (read "epithets") which Hamann adopted for himself and others. The result is a new perspective on Hamann's thought-world. Though apparently thoroughly researched, the book lacks a scholarly apparatus.

KÜSTERS, MARIE-THERES. *Inhaltsanalyse von J. G. Hamanns "Aesthetica in nuce."* Bottrop: Ostberg, 1936.

LEIBRECHT, WALTER. *God and Man in the Thought of Hamann*, trans. J. H. Stam and M. H. Bertram. Philadelphia: Fortress Press, 1966. A translation of the author's doctoral dissertation. He maintains that Hamann escapes the subjectivism of Kierkegaard and the objectivism of Hegel. Though Leibrecht neglects somewhat the importance of Hamann's *Sprachdenken*, the study is an invaluable guide to his theology. The introductory essay on Hamann's contemporary significance (available only in the English version) adds to the value of the work.

LOWRIE, WALTER. *J. G. Hamann: An Existentialist*. Princeton: Princeton Theological Seminary, 1950.

LUMPP, HANS-MARTIN. *Philologia crucis. Zu J. G. Hamanns Auffassung von der Dichtkunst. Mit einem Kommentar zur "Aesthetica in nuce."* Tübingen: Niemeyer, 1970. In addition to the useful commentary, the volume contains a chapter on Hamann's concept of genius and another on his observations on literature and aesthetics.

MANEGOLD, INGEMARIE. *J. G. Hamanns Schrift "Konxompax,"* Heidel-

berger Forschungen 8. Heidelberg: Winter 1963. Manegold provides
the necessary criticism and correction of Nadler's text of this obscure
but important work. Her commentary utilizes historical and biographical material.

MERLAN, PHILIP. "From Hume to Hamann," *The Personalist*, 33 (1951),
11–18.

―――. "Kant, Hamann-Jacobi and Schelling on Hume," *Rivista Critica di
Storia della Filosofia*, 4 (1967), 481–94.

―――. "Parva Hamanniana: Hamann as Spokesman of the Middle Class,"
Journal of the History of Ideas, 9 (1948), 380–84. Merlan analyses the
Beylage zu Dangeuil and shows that Hamann was, prior to his conversion, a typical exponent of middle-class ideals, which were identical
with those which produced the French Revolution.

METZKE, ERWIN. *J. G. Hamanns Stellung in der Philosophie des 18. Jahrhunderts*, Schriften der Königsberger Gelehrten Gesellschaft, 10, no.
3. Halle/ Saale: Niemeyer, 1934. The most comprehensive and important study of Hamann's philosophy which has so far appeared, a turn-
ing-point in research on the Magus.

MINOR, JACOB. *J. G. Hamann in seiner Bedeutung für die Sturm- und
Drangperiode*. Frankfurt a.M.: Rütten & Loening, 1881.

NADLER, JOSEF. *Die Hamannausgabe*. Schriften der Königsberger
Gelehrten Gesellschaft Halle/ Saale: Niemeyer, 1930. A detailed account of the *Nachlaß*, its history, and editions of the 19th century.
Nadler justifies his redactional procedure for the planned edition. Rpt.
(1978) in "Regensburger Beiträge zur deutschen Sprach- und
Literaturwissenschaft, Reihe B: Untersuchungen, Band 12," with a
report on recent research by B. Gajek plus a checklist for the photo-
copies of the *Nachlaß* at the university library in Münster, compiled by
Sabine Kinder. An indispensable resource for the researcher.

―――. *J. G. Hamann. Der Zeuge des Corpus Mysticum*. Salzburg: Müller,
1949. Nadler has utilized a wealth of detail about Hamann's life and
writings in this biography, but his thesis concerning Hamann's mysti-
cism and idea of sexuality is highly questionable. The paraphrasing of
Hamann's works is generally helpful. Despite shortcomings and man-
neristic style the book is indispensable.

NADLER, KÄTE. "Hamann und Hegel. Zum Verhältnis von Dialektik und
Existentialität," *Logos*, 20 (1931) 259–85.

NEBEL, GERHARD. *Hamann*. Stuttgart: Klett, 1973. Not primarily a scholarly work but a worthwhile collection of essays on many of the important facets of Hamann's thought, particularly as they relate to modern
trends in philosophy and literature.

OELMÜLLER, WILLI. "Lessing und Hamann. Prolegomena zu einem
künftigem Gespräch," *Collegium Philosophicum*. Basel/Stuttgart:
Schwabe (1965), pp. 272–302.

O'FLAHERTY, JAMES C. "The Concept of Knowledge in Hamann's 'Sokratische Denkwürdigkeiten' and Nietzsche's 'Die Geburt der Tragödie," Monatshefte, 64 (1972), 334–48.

————. "East and West in the Thought of Hamann," Germanic Review, 43 (1968), 83–99. The study demonstrates that Hamann's wide-ranging interest in and congeniality with Oriental literature has epistemological roots.

————. Hamann's Socratic Memorabilia. Translation and Commentary. Baltimore: The Johns Hopkins Press, 1967. Contains: (1) the original text and translation on facing pages; (2) an account of Hamann's life and work; (3) an account of the genesis of the essay; and (4) a monograph on "Socratic form."

————. Unity and Language: A Study in the Philosophy of Hamann. Univ. of No. Carolina Studies in the Germanic Langs. and Lits., no. 6. Chapel Hill: University of North Carolina Press, 1952; rpt. New York: AMS Press, 1966. Originally a doctoral dissertation, this study defends the thesis that Hamann's thought concerning language both anticipates and goes beyond developments in modern positivistic language philosophy. Hamann's notion that abstractions are "lauter Verhältnisse" is held to be an important clue to an understanding of his total philosophy.

ROCHELT, HANS. "Das Creditiv der Sprache. Von der Philologie J. G. Hamanns und Ludwig Wittgensteins," Literatur und Kritik, 33 (1969), 169–76.

RODEMANN, WILHELM. Hamann und Kierkegaard. Gütersloh: Bertelsmann, 1922. Of limited usefulness. Needs to be amplified and brought up to date.

SAEMANN, EDITH. J. G. Hamann und die französische Literatur. Königsberg: Schultz, 1931. Outdated, but still useful.

SALMONY, H. A. J. G. Hamanns metakritische Philosophie. Zollikon: Evangelischer Verlag, 1958. Aside from Salmony's (generally disputed) imputation of homosexual experiences to the young Hamann and an interest in the orgiastic practices of the Barbelo-gnostics, the work is one of the best-written introductions to the ideas of Hamann's "Christian philosophy." Even his (debatable) theses serve as a corrective to the perennial tendency of some to canonize the Magus.

SCHMITZ, F[RIEDRICH] J[OSEF]. The Problem of Individualism and the Crises in the Lives of Lessing and Hamann. Berkeley and Los Angeles: University of California Press, 1944.

SCHOONHOVEN, E. JANSEN, and MARTIN SEILS. J. G. Hamann. Mysterienschriften, Vol. 5 of J. G. Hamanns Hauptschriften erklärt, ed. Fritz Blanke et al. Gütersloh: Mohn, 1962. Contains commentaries and text of: Hierophantische Briefe: Versuch einer Sibylle über die Ehe; Konxompax; and Schürze von Feigenblättern (the last named in a text-critical edition which supersedes Nadler's). The difficulty of determining Hamann's views of (1) the mystery religions and their relationship to the natural religion of the Enlightenment and (2) human sexuality is squarely faced. Well-supported arguments for the authors' conclusions are provided.

SCHREINER, HELMUTH. *Die Menschwerdung Gottes in der Theologie J. G. Hamanns.* Tübingen: Katzmann, 1950. Brief but significant treatment of the subject.

SCHREINER, LOTHAR. *J. G. Hamann. Golgatha und Scheblimini*, vol. 7 of *J. G. Hamanns Hauptschriften erklärt*, ed. Fritz Blanke et al. Gütersloh: Bertelsmann, 1956. The least satisfactory of the commentaries in its series. Helpful and reliable as far as it goes, but the author neglects somewhat the biographical and sociopolitical aspects of this important work (Hegel thought it Hamann's *most* important).

SCHWARZENBACH, RUDOLF. "Hamanns Prosa," *Reformation*, 11–12 (1961), 640–52.

SEILS, MARTIN. *Theologische Aspekte zur gegenwärtigen Hamann-Deutung.* Göttingen: Vandenhoeck & Ruprecht, 1957.

SIEVERS, HARRY. *J. G. Hamanns Bekehrung. Ein Versuch, sie zu verstehen.* Zürich: Zwingli, 1969. The best study to date of Hamann's London conversion experience.

SIMON, JOSEF. *J. G. Hamann. Schriften zur Sprache*, Theorie I, ed. Hans Blumenberg et al. Frankfurt a.M.: Suhrkamp, 1967. A valuable anthology of the Hamannian writings which deal specifically with the problem of language. The introductory essay is especially instructive.

SMITH, RONALD GREGOR. "The Hamann Renaissance," *The Christian Century*, 77, no. 26 (1960), 768–69.

_____. *J. G. Hamann 1730–1788: A Study in Christian Existence.* New York: Harper and Brothers, 1960. Contains an account of Hamann's life and a judicious selection from the works and letters. The translations are generally good. A weakness of Smith's criticism is his adherence to the view that Hamann was an irrationalist and that his style is simply disorderly.

_____. "J. G. Hamann and the Princess Gallitzin. An Ecumenical Encounter," *Philomathes. Studies and Essays in Memory of Philip Merlan*, ed. R. B. Palmer and R. Hamerton-Kelly. The Hague: Nijhoff, 1971, 330–40.

STOCKUM, T. C. VAN. "Goethe und Hamann: Prolegomena zu einer Monographie," *Neophilologus*, 4 (1954), 300–308. The author modestly refers to his study as "dienende Kärrnerarbeit." He has collected the direct and indirect references to Hamann in Goethe's works and letters, but refrains from generalization. Researchers can be grateful for van Stockum's labor.

STRÄSSLE, URS. *Geschichte, geschichtliches Verstehen und Geschichtsschreibung im Verständnis J. G. Hamanns.* Bern: H. Lang, 1970.

SUCHY, VIKTOR. "J. G. Hamann. Kirchenvater, 'Mystischer Zeuge' oder

Heresiarch? Hunderfünfzig Jahre Hamann-Deutung und-Forschung,"
Jahrbuch des Wiener Goethe-Vereins, 69 (1965), 47–102, 70 (1966),
5–36, 71 (1967), 35–69.

SUDHOF, SIEGFRIED. *Von der Aufklärung zur Romantik. Die Geschichte
des "Kreises von Münster."* Berlin: Erich Schmidt, 1973. In this volume Hamann's visit to Westphalia is set against the full background of
the so-called "Münster Circle." Sudhof is thoroughly acquainted with
the copious source material involved.

SWAIN, CHARLES W. "Hamann and the Philosophy of David Hume," *Journal of the History of Philosophy,* 5 (1967), 343–52.

UNGER, RUDOLF. *Hamanns Sprachtheorie im Zusammenhang seines Denkens.* Munich: Beck, 1905. Despite Unger's basic misunderstanding of
the nature of Hamann's "language theory" (he holds it to be Platonic
and "scientifically completely unsatisfactory"), the book is valuable for
such excursuses as those on the origin of language, the relation of
language to poetry, and the nature of Hamann's aesthetics.

––––––. *Hamann und die Aufklärung,* 2 vols. Jena: Diederichs, 1911. This
comprehensive work orients Hamann to the main currents of thought
since the Renaissance. Although based chiefly on the Roth-Wiener
edition and although Unger psychologizes Hamann's thought throughout, the work remains indispensable for the researcher because of the
wealth of material offered.

WEBER, HEINRICH. *Hamann und Kant. Ein Beitrag zur Geschichte der
Philosophie im Zeitalter der Aufklärung.* München: Beck, 1904. Weber's
monograph is philosophically unsatisfying, but contains helpful information on the relationship of the two men.

WILD, REINER. *"Metacriticus bonae spei" J. G. Hamanns "Fliegender
Brief": Einführung, Text und Kommentar,* Regensburger Beiträge zur
deutschen Sprach- und Literaturwissenschaft, 6, ed. Bernhard Gajek.
Bern: H. Lang, and Frankfurt a.M.: P. Lang, 1975. The author provides, along with a commentary, a philologically clarified edition of
both versions of the *Fliegender Brief.* The introduction relates
Hamann's thought concerning language interestingly to some contemporary developments. The work is a basic resource for Hamann
studies.

Index

Note: References to God, Scripture (Bible), reason, and nature occur too frequently to be included in the Index.